T0326453

Research Perspectives on Social Media Influencers and Brand Communication

Research Perspectives on Social Media Influencers and Brand Communication

Edited by
Brandi Watkins

LEXINGTON BOOKS
Lanham • Boulder • New York • London

Published by Lexington Books
An imprint of The Rowman & Littlefield Publishing Group, Inc.
4501 Forbes Boulevard, Suite 200, Lanham, Maryland 20706
www.rowman.com

6 Tinworth Street, London SE11 5AL, United Kingdom

British Library Cataloguing in Publication Information Available

Library of Congress Cataloging-in-Publication Data Available

ISBN 978-1-7936-1361-5 (cloth)
ISBN 978-1-7936-1362-2 (electronic)

This book is dedicated to my Mom.
You inspire me every day.

Contents

List of Figures and Tables

FIGURES

TABLES

Acknowledgments

I would like to thank the staff at Lexington Books, especially Nicolette Amstutz and Jessica Tepper, for their help with making this project become a reality. Thank you to all the authors who contributed thoughtful and interesting chapters. Editing chapters and seeing firsthand the creativity and variety of approaches to examining the phenomenon of social media influencers was an absolute joy. Last, but certainly not least, I would like to thank my family and friends for their constant support and encouragement.

Introduction

Brandi Watkins

At the start of each semester, I ask students in my social media class what their goal is for the class. Each time I ask there is usually at least one or two students who mention having a business or hobby they want to promote or would like to know how to build their brand on social media. As we get into the semester and take a closer look at social media as a strategic communication tool, the topic that students almost always find the most interesting is when we talk about social media influencers (SMIs). In reflection paper assignments, there will almost always be about a dozen or so that start off with some iteration of "before this class I thought I knew a lot about social media influencers" then go on to discuss some of their favorite SMIs on social media platforms such as YouTube, Instagram, and more recently TikTok.

The fascination with SMIs is not limited to the younger generations. I find myself spending an embarrassing amount of time scrolling through perfectly curated accounts on Instagram featuring beautifully decorated houses, immaculate patios and outdoor living spaces, and dreamy recipes guaranteed to make me look like a Food Network caliber chef. Most likely, this content that I spend hours devouring has been carefully and strategically planned by a SMI. And I'm not the only one, scroll through the comments of an SMI and you will see posts from social media users of all ages engaging and commenting with the SMI's content. Moreover, SMIs have garnered mainstream media attention through high-profile brand partnerships and equally high-profile scandals (see Fyre Festival).

The SMI is a particular type of social media user who leveraged their social media accounts to create a following and to position themselves as a tastemaker or leader in public opinion within their chosen specialty. User-generated content like that created by SMI has been found to be more popular and effective than traditional media (Sokolova & Kefi, 2019). SMIs are social media users who have amassed a following and leverages that following into a lucrative brand for themselves. Freberg et al. (2011) defined SMI as "a new type of third-party endorser who shape audience attitudes through blogs, tweets, and use of other social media" (p. 90). Abindin (2017) elaborated on this definition where SMI are described as "a contemporary incarnation of Internet celebrity for whom microcelebrity is not merely a hobby or a supplementary income but an established career with its own ecology and economy" (p. 1).

For the SMI, their social media account gives them a platform and access to millions of followers where they share content related to lifestyle, health and beauty, fashion, health and fitness, home decorating, crafting, and pet care, among others. Abindin and Ots (2015) describe the work of SMI as the following:

> Influencers are one form of microcelebrities who document their everyday lives from the trivial and mundane, to exciting snippets of the exclusive opportunities in their line of work. Influencers are the shapers of public opinion who persuade their audience through the conscientious calibration of personae on social media, as supported by "physical" space interactions with their followers in the flesh to sustain their accessibility, believability, emulatability, and intimacy—in other words, their "relatability." (p. 3)

Successful SMIs are adept at blending "real life" with branded content in a way that is not intrusive for followers, thus making SMI instrumental tastemakers who communicate information about trends to their followers (Audrezet et al., 2018). As such, SMIs are considered more attractive to followers because their social media content is deemed more relatable and authentic (Audrezet et al., 2018). SMIs use their social media content to develop long-lasting relationships with followers (Hwang & Zhang, 2018).

SOCIAL MEDIA AND BRAND COMMUNICATION

Nearly two decades of research on social media as a strategic communication tool has revealed a myriad of ways that social media and the unique characteristics of the Internet have changed brand communication for both brands and consumers. Kohli et al. (2015) noted that social media has created a "seismic shift in consumers' behavior" (p. 37) where consumers are more involved with brand communication (Bitter et al., 2014). Social media was originally a place to connect with family and friends online. In essence, social media is about relationships and was originally touted as the place where you can keep up with family and friends instantly and despite geographic boundaries.

Once social media platforms opened up to brands, the most successful brands were the ones that recognized that social media is still about relationships. Successful brands on social media created content that was entertaining or useful to followers, responded promptly to follower inquiries, and generally engaged with followers as if they were friends. This same principle holds true for successful SMIs—they recognize the value of the relationship they have with their followers.

The popularity and reach of SMI have not gone unnoticed by brands, which has led to an uptick in influencer marketing. Influencer marketing is "promoting brands through the use of specific key individuals who exert influence over potential buyers" (Audrezet et al., 2018, para. 3). Influencer marketing includes collaborations between brands and SMI to integrate product promotion into their social media content. Influencer marketing is designed to win over customer trust (Conick, 2018) through the relationship between followers and SMIs. SMI complement traditional brand communication efforts (Audrezet et al., 2018) because of their reach and status as tastemaker and opinion leader (Archer & Harrigan, 2016).

Marketers consider influencer marketing strategies to be effective. SMIs are effective brand communicators because followers find their content to be relatable, noncommercial, and from ordinary people like themselves (Audrezet et al., 2018). Moreover, some followers believe content created by SMI to be "one of the last few forms of real, authentic communication" (Scott, 2015, p. 295; as cited in Audrezet et al., 2018). As such, SMI can be a powerful persuasive force (Martensen et al., 2018), which explains their appeal to marketers and brand communicators.

BOOK OVERVIEW

The goal of this book is to provide readers with an overview of the current research into SMI as brand communicators and their integration into brand communication strategies. Research on SMI and brand communication is still in its early stages. Scholars and practitioners have expressed interest in this area, but to date, there has been limited access to information that organizes and provides direction for studying and incorporating SMI into brand communication strategies. As such, the chapters presented in this book represent an overview of the current research looking a SMI and their impact on brand communication.

The chapters selected for inclusion in this volume represent a unique theoretical and methodological approach to examining the emergence of the SMI as a brand communicator. Contributors examine how SMIs were integrated into brand communication strategies in a variety of contexts as well as discuss the challenges and opportunities afforded to brands by SMIs. Many of the chapters provide the foundational knowledge necessary for understanding the impact of SMIs (chapters 1–4), while other chapters examine SMI in specific brand contexts (chapters 5–7). The book concludes by investigating the ethical and legal considerations related to SMI and brand communication (chapters 8–9).

REFERENCES

Abindin, C. (2017). #familygoals: Family, influencers, calibrated amateurism, and justifying young digital labor. *Social Media + Society*, *3*(2), 1–15. https://doi.org/10.1177/2056305117707191

Abindin, C., & Ots, M. (2015, August). The influencer's dilemma: The shaping of new brand professions between credibility and commerce. In *AEJMC 2015: Annual conference*. San Francisco, CA: Association for Education in Journalism and Mass Communication.

Archer, C., & Harrigan, P. (2016). Show me the money: How bloggers as stakeholders are challenging theories of relationship building in public relations. *Media International Australia*, *160*(1), 67–77. https://doi.org/10.1177/1329878X16651139

Audrezet, A., de Kerviler, G., & Guidry Moulard, J. (2018). Authenticity under threat: When social media influencers needs to go beyond self-presentation. *Journal of Business Research*. http://doi.org/10.1016/j.busres.2018.07.008

Bitter, S., Grabner-Kräuter, S., & Breitenecker, R. J. (2014). Customer-engagement behavior in online social networks—The Facebook perspective. *International Journal Networking and Virtual Organisations*, *14*(1/2), 197–220.

Conick, H. (2018). How to win friends and influence millions: The rules of influencer marketing. https://www.ama.org/marketing-news/how-to-win-friends-and-influence-millions-the-rules-of-infleuncer-marketing/

Freberg, K., Graham, K., McGaughey, K., & Freberg, L. A. (2011). Who are social media influencers? A study of public perceptions of personality. *Public Relations Review*, *37*, 90–92. https://doi.org/10.1016/pubrev.2010.11.001

Hwang, K., & Zhang, Q. (2018). Influence of parasocial relationship between digital celebrities and their followers on followers' purchase and electronic word-of-mouth intentions, and persuasion knowledge. *Computers in Human Behavior*, *87*, 155–173. https://doi.org/10.1016/j.chb.2018.05.029

Kohli, C., Sur, R., & Kapoor, A. (2015). Will social media kill branding? *Business Horizons*, *58*, 35–44. http://dx.doi.org/10.1016/j.bushor.2014.08.004

Martensen, A., Brockenhuus-Schack, S., & Zahid, A. L. (2018). How citizen influencers persuade their followers. *Journal of Fashion Marketing and Management*, *22*(3), 335–353. https://doi.org/10.1108/JFMM-09-2017-0095

Sokolova, K., & Kefi, H. (2019). Instagram and YouTube bloggers promote it, why should I buy? How credibility and parasocial interaction influencer purchase intentions. *Journal of Retailing and Consumer Services*, *53*, 1–9. https://doi.org/10.1016/j.jretconser.2019.01.001

Chapter 1

The History of Social Media Influencers

Kelli S. Burns

Consumers have long been influenced by others, whether a salesperson pitching a product, a friend providing a word-of-mouth recommendation, or a celebrity endorser touting a product's benefits in an advertisement. Today, much influence comes from social media influencers (SMIs), a group that includes celebrities and regular people who have built large followings on social media. Research has shown that consumers find YouTube stars more influential when making purchase decisions than traditional celebrities (Arnold, 2017) and that many younger consumers are just as likely to trust an online recommendation than a personal recommendation (Bloem, 2019), which further increases the appeal for marketers to use this tactic.

This chapter will review the rise of SMIs and influencer marketing practices from the early days of social media to the present. The evolution of business models of the various platforms will be discussed as well as government regulations that have developed throughout the years to address issues with influencer marketing. Finally, this chapter will discuss changes on the horizon and make predictions for the future of influencer marketing.

EARLY INFLUENCERS ON BLOGS, TWITTER, AND YOUTUBE

Blogs

With the rise of the Internet in the mid- to late 1990s and then blogs in the early to mid-2000s, regular people had opportunities to build large followings by posting interesting content and engaging with followers. Some of the early noncelebrity influencers included "mommy bloggers" like Heather

Armstrong who launched dooce.com in 2001. Armstrong was able to support her family from her blog income, which peaked in 2009 with 8.5 million monthly readers and $40,000 a month in banner ad revenues. The same year, she was dubbed by *Forbes* as one of the thirty most influential women in media, and in 2011, *The New York Times* bestowed on her the title of "queen of the mommy bloggers" (Lieber, 2019).

Others built large followings by blogging about celebrity news, an industry which had become more democratized with online distribution tools. By mingling and reporting on celebrities, the most-followed celebrity bloggers became influencers in their own right. Possibly the most well-known influencer in the early days of celebrity blogging was Mario Armando Lavandeira Jr., also known as Perez Hilton. Lavandeira's blog catapulted him to *Time* magazine's list of the 100 Most Influential People and the number one Web celebrity spot in *Fortune* magazine (ABC Radio Networks, 2008).

Fashionistas were also early adopters of the blogging platform. Bryan Grey Yambao, who started blogging at BryanBoy.com in 2004 from his parents' home in the Philippines, first attracted global attention with a video post titled "Leave Marc Jacobs Alone," which was noticed by Marc Jacobs (Business of Fashion, n.d.). The attention resulted in a Marc Jacobs bag named after Yambao and front row seats at the Marc Jacobs show during New York Fashion Week (Business of Fashion, n.d.). Another early fashion blog was BagSnob.com, founded by Tina Craig and Kelly Cook in 2005. At first, they showcased and reviewed handbags on their blog, but have since added more categories to create more of a lifestyle brand. In 2014, Cartier hired Craig to host an event to launch their new bag line, representing the first time Cartier had hired a SMI as a brand ambassador (Lieber, 2014). Craig and Cook also collaborated with Home Shopping Network on a bag line called Snob Essentials.

When social media platforms such as Facebook and Twitter emerged in 2005, bloggers had an opportunity to promote themselves to a wider audience who did not have to search for them on the web; they could be discovered through followers sharing their content and then users clicking through to their sites to read the content. At the same time, because of these new platforms, people started consuming social media differently. Instead of visiting blogs, they were scrolling news feeds and consuming shorter and more diverse bits of content. In contrast to long essays found on blogs, users preferred visual content shared on social media sites (Bailey, 2018).

Twitter

When Twitter launched in 2005, not only did bloggers find their way there, but celebrities also joined the site and built large followings. Perhaps the earliest celebrity Twitter adopter was musician Tom Petty who joined in January 2008, followed by Lady Gaga in March 2008. The most-followed accounts on Twitter as of November 2019 represent many users who have been using the platform since 2009 or earlier (Brandwatch, 2019). Topping the list is President Barack Obama with more than 110 million followers who joined Twitter in March 2007, just a month after announcing his candidacy for president. Singers dominate the list, including Katy Perry (joined in February 2009 with 108 million followers), Justin Bieber (joined in March 2009 with 107 million followers), Rihanna (joined in October 2009 with 94 million followers), and Taylor Swift (joined in December 2008 with 85 million followers).

Twitter gained mainstream attention in 2009 with the friendly battle between CNN and actor Ashton Kutcher to be the first to reach one million followers, which Kutcher won in the early morning hours of April 17, 2009. The same day, Oprah Winfrey sent her first tweet, even though her account already had 73,000 followers, a number that quickly climbed to over 100,000 by later that day. The next day, CNN reported on the conflicting opinions about celebrity Twitter use saying, "Some bloggers and Twitter users have expressed concern that the once-cultish site is being overwhelmed by celebrities and media hype, while others are excited by Twitter's ever-growing reach" (CNN, 2009, para. 2).

YouTube

Prior to YouTube, early adopters of video blogging (vlogging), who did not have access to a user-friendly platform for video hosting, had few options but to host their videos on their own websites and distribute their content to viewers via RSS or e-mail (MediaKix, n.d.). Vlogs generally take the form of confessional video diaries shot with one person speaking directly to the camera. Rocketboom, launched in 2004, was an early vlog success story that was hosted on a website and offered a daily news broadcast with a comedic edge (MediaKix, n.d.).

After YouTube launched in 2005, the video-sharing platform changed the game for content creators who could then upload and distribute content on this free video-hosting platform. Vlogging continued to be a popular format, requiring little in terms of technical expertise and equipment and offering a way to build an intimate connection between creators and viewers. Capturing the attention of YouTube viewers in 2006 was account Lonelygirl15 and its teenage vlogger Bree who eventually claimed the top spot on the "most-subscribed" list on YouTube (Cresci, 2016). About three months after the first video was uploaded, however, Lonelygirl15 was outed as a hoax and the work of professional filmmakers who had hired aspiring actress Jessica Lee Rose to star in the videos.

In addition to vloggers, many of the first influencers on YouTube were young men with comedy channels, such as the character of Fred created by Lucas Cruikshank, who was also the first channel to gain one million subscribers (Variety, 2009); comedy duo Smosh, comprised of Anthony Padilla and Ian Hecox, who lip-synched their way to YouTube fame; Freddie Wong, aka freddiew, who shared comedy and video game-related content; Ryan Niga, aka Nigahiga, the first YouTuber to reach two million subscribers as of 2010 (VanDeGraph, 2016); Shane Dawson of ShaneDawsonTV; and Ray Williams Johnson, who had the first channel to reach five million subscribers (Humphrey, 2011). One of the early female YouTube influencers was Jenna Marbles, who was the most subscribed to woman on YouTube by 2014 (Gillespie, 2014).

Some of these viral video stars were able to capitalize on their online success with commercial offers. Back in 2007, Smosh's channel on YouTube was the most subscribed to channel of all time, with over 194,000 subscribers and the ninth most viewed channel of all time with over eighty-one million views. Around that time, the comedy team signed a deal to produce two videos a month for YouTube competitor LiveVideo and was also attracting other commercial offers (Tedeschi, 2007). Additionally, sales of Smosh branded apparel and advertising revenue from the site allowed these two filmmakers to attend college.

Another early YouTube success story was Brooke Brodack, known as Brookers on YouTube, who created quirky videos that garnered a large following. The first YouTube star to receive a development deal, Brodack was signed by Carson Daly under the Carson Daly Productions label to an eighteen-month contract (Martin, 2006). As part of her deal, Brodack was involved in creating website content for NBC's *It's Your Show TV*, hosted by Daly, and also made an appearance on *The Tyra Banks Show* as a judge for a video competition.

One early YouTube influencer who was able to secure a sponsorship deal was Matt Harding, aka Dancing Matt, known for traveling the world dancing in every location he visited and posting about his adventures on wherethehellismatt.com. The videos he created about his adventures made him a viral video sensation. Harding funded his first trip, but then found a sponsor in Stride gum to launch two additional videos titled "Dancing 2006" and "Dancing 2008" (Vulture, 2008).

Fashion and beauty videos have also flourished on YouTube. Influencer Michelle Phan launched her beauty channel on YouTube in 2006. Phan was the first woman to achieve one billion views on YouTube, and as a result of her passionate following, she was successful in building an empire worth almost $100 million (Sawyer & Jarvis, 2015). She launched a makeup line with L'Oréal called EM Cosmetics, wrote a beauty book, and founded a beauty product subscription service. Phan stepped away from the platform ten years after she launched her channel for personal reasons and now works as a more traditional model and spokesperson.

SMIS ON NEWER PLATFORMS, INCLUDING INSTAGRAM, VINE, AND TIKTOK

Instagram

Instagram, which launched in 2010, is the ideal platform for SMIs, offering a visual presentation of a variety of interests, such as food, fashion, beauty fitness, and travel, which can be easily found through the extensive use of hashtags. A 2017 study by #HASHOFF of 300 influencer respondents found that 99.3 percent have a presence on Instagram and 67.1 percent on Facebook with almost 92 percent of them saying that Instagram is their platform of choice (#HASHOFF, 2017). Additionally, #HASHOFF reported that among their 150,000 opt-in SMIs, those with between 10,000 and 1 million followers have engagement rates that are more than 10 percent higher than that of major influencers like Kim Kardashian and Serena Williams (#HASHOFF, 2017).

Many Instagram SMIs tend to be from a younger demographic. A study by Klear found almost three-fourths are eighteen to thirty-four years old, and of that group, 42 percent of them are eighteen to twenty-four years old (Chadha, 2018). The study also found that SMIs tend to be women, representing 84 percent of the population, which aligns with the fact that top industry partners represent fashion and accessories followed by beauty and cosmetics (Chadha, 2018).

Vine

Launched in 2013, Vine, a short-form video-sharing platform, had a short but productive life as a platform for SMIs. With videos limited to just six seconds, Vine users developed creative ways to work with the format. The videos of Twitter employee and Vine user Ian Padgham caught the attention of brands like Sony and Airbnb who hired him to make Vines for their brands, leading him to quit working for Twitter to focus on his creative business full-time (Newton, 2016). When Vine allowed people to use their phones' front-facing camera to record videos of themselves in 2013, the platform exploded with Vine stars, including Zack King and his magic tricks, Amanda Cerny and her physical comedy, and Logan Paul whose viewers watched his videos more than four billion times and received $200,000 to create a Vine for a brand (Newton, 2016).

Instagram became a major competitor for Vine when it introduced fifteen-second video clips, attracted video SMIs, and then eventually extended the video time limit to one minute (Newton, 2016). Marketers also started looking more seriously at Instagram as a better platform for their needs. Unable to compete and plagued with leadership turnover, Vine disabled the uploading of videos in 2016 and officially shut down in 2017.

TikTok

Founded first as Musical.ly in 2012, short-form video-sharing app TikTok was acquired by Beijing-based company ByteDance and launched outside of China in 2017. In 2019, *Business Insider* ranked the most-followed TikTok influencers who got their start on the platform or on its predecessor Musical.ly (Leskin, 2019). The most-followed TikTok influencer with almost thirty-five million followers as of November 2019 was Loren Gray, who was using TikTok when it was Musical.ly to promote her music. She also has a Snapchat show called "Glow Up" and received nominations from the Teen Choice Awards and People's Choice Awards for her social media presence. With almost thirty million followers, Ariel Martin, known as Baby Ariel on TikTok, also started on Musical.ly. Her TikTok fame has led to work on Nickelodeon and Disney Channel television shows. The third most-followed TikTok celeb is Kristen Hancher with twenty-three million followers, who gained attention through her lip-synching videos and is a member of Jake Paul's Team 10 Squad, an incubator of young social media talent who live together in a mansion in Los Angeles.

THE RISE OF BRAND USE OF SMIS

Prior to the rise of digital media, SMIs were almost exclusively journalists who had access to distribution channels or celebrities, such as actors, musicians, or athletes, who had large fan bases. Some campaigns also included community influencers who could generate favorable word of mouth. A review of *PR Week* articles revealed influencer marketing campaigns from the early 2000s. For example, in 2002, when it was still a mail-order DVD rental service, Netflix used a public relations strategy based on conversations with influencers (Hood, 2002). Also, in 2002, White Wave's soy milk product Silk used health-conscious celebrities and nutrition experts as part of an influencer and product placement campaign. The company selected vegetarian celebrity chef Akasha Richmond to host Silk coffee bars at events (Shortman, 2003). To promote the Coolpix camera in 2003, Nikon sponsored Gen Art's Fresh Faces in Fashion series during Fashion Week in three cities. Coolpix cameras were provided to high-profile guests at the events, such as actress Mena Suvari who was photographed by *Star* magazine with her camera (Greco, 2004). When the Darden Restaurant group launched Seasons 52 in 2003, they invited media representatives to dine at the new restaurant, including print and television food writers, and also approximately 1,000 key influencers from the business, arts, health, and fitness communities to spread word of mouth (Frank, 2003).

Blogger Relations

The rise of digital and then social media gave regular people an opportunity to become known to others and also distribute their own content to their audiences. During the early years of blogs, public relations firms started to launch blogger relations programs as a way to build relationships with key bloggers. Blogger relations programs were used to generate conversations with consumers through engagement with bloggers, garner higher rankings on search engines, and receive relatively free publicity (Hart, 2006). Microsoft, Nokia, Procter & Gamble, and General Electric were four early examples of companies that worked with bloggers to build support and awareness for a product or corporate initiative. Microsoft reached out to bloggers prior to the release of the Xbox game system (Barbaro, 2006). When Procter & Gamble recognized people were talking in blogs and chat rooms about Mr. Clean AutoDry prior to its launch, the company sent AutoDry kits to bloggers and asked for feedback (Oser, 2004). To promote its N-series smartphone, which was released in the fall of 2005, Nokia sent fifty phones to tech-savvy bloggers who frequently posted about mobile phones (Hart, 2006). Finally, General Electric met with key environmental bloggers to get feedback before investing in energy-efficient technology (Barbaro, 2006).

The entertainment industry also embraced bloggers during the early years of blogging. Movie studios often provided bloggers with deleted scenes or gossip in exchange for promotion of a movie or DVD release (Hart, 2006). When the first season of *Family Guy* was released on DVD, marketing agency M80 sent bloggers funny clips of the cast rehearsing, a tactic that was so effective that they did the same for subsequent DVD launches. Bloggers were also sent clips of new music videos when now-defunct video platform Gotuit was launched, resulting in blogs garnering more than 65 percent of total media coverage of the launch (Hart, 2006).

Influencer Marketing Tactics

Companies have evolved in using SMIs as new social media platforms have launched, more consumers have adopted social media, and the practice of influencer marketing has become more sophisticated. One SMI strategy that was successful for Old Spice was to engage with both celebrities and regular people on social media. Unlike other SMI programs that compensate influencers, this program was innovative in its approach to attract organic engagement. Launched in February 2010, the campaign for Old Spice made a splash with former football player Isaiah Mustafa and a commercial posted online during Super Bowl weekend and then shown on television afterward. The brand followed up in June 2010 with another commercial that was also posted online and run on television. To promote the campaign, Mustafa responded to questions on Twitter and Facebook with video responses posted on YouTube. Over two days, the marketing team created approximately 185 short videos and mentioned celebrities such as Alyssa Milano, Demi Moore, and Ellen DeGeneres (Newman, 2010). Although the campaign included responses to regular people who posted questions on these platforms, it was also savvy in its engagement of influencers who could spread the brand message to their followers.

In some campaigns, ambassadors play an important role through extensive engagement with the products. The Ford Fiesta Movement campaign of 2009 by Ford's head of social media Scott Monty provided the use of cars to 100 social media ambassadors for up to six months (Barry, 2009). In exchange, the ambassadors created social media content during themed monthly "missions." The company repeated the campaign with the launch of the 2014 Fiesta using 100 ambassadors for up to eight months and also some celebrities. All television, print, and digital advertising for the 2014 campaign was solely generated from the content created by SMIs (Vinjamuri, 2013).

Another tactic that has evolved during the past decade is working with more micro-SMIs instead of a few mega-SMIs. Online fashion retailer Revolve, founded in 2003, started working with bloggers in 2009. By 2012, they were hosting events for bloggers and other SMIs. By 2019, the company was working with about 3,500 Instagram SMIs who are compensated with either credit to purchase Revolve products or clothing gifts to showcase on their social media pages. Many of these SMIs would be described as micro-SMIs as they generally have 30,000 or fewer followers. The company also now hosts more than 100 SMI events, including one during Coachella, and also pays for SMIs to travel to photo-worthy destinations (White, 2019).

Another tactic is a collaboration between a brand and a SMI, where a product line or collection is developed together. In 2014, Target worked with three Pinterest influencers for a campaign. Joy Cho (Oh Joy!), Jan Halvarson (Poptalk), and Kate Arends (Wit & Delight) created lines for Target's party-planning collections and used social media platforms to promote the products (Champagne, 2014). More recently in June 2019, Lancôme announced a collaboration with fashion influencer Chiara

Ferragni, who founded the Blonde Salad blog (Chong, 2019). The collaboration, called Lancôme x Chiara Ferragni, offered a capsule collection of makeup in limited-edition packaging that uses the Lancôme branding as well as the winking eye branding from the Blonde Salad. These collaborations tap into the built-in audience of both the brand and the SMI on social media.

Social media platform takeovers are also popular with corporate marketers. When the Las Vegas Convention and Visitors Authority wanted to launch their VisitLasVegas Snapchat channel in 2016, it hired DJ Khaled who had about six million digital followers at the time to post on the new channel as well as promote the channel from his own profile (Swant, 2016). Disney and its ABC Family network also used a Snapchat takeover in January 2015 for the promotion of a new season of *Pretty Little Liars*. Snapchat influencer Michael Platco was paid to take over the ABC Family Snapchat channel and provide commentary about the show each week. The strategy was successful in adding 800,000 followers to the channel (Patel, 2015).

Finally, the most common tactic of marketers is to use product placements whereby the SMI is provided with the product and possibly extra compensation to feature the product in the content he or she produces. The SMI is also sometimes provided with products to give away to followers in a contest. For example, in 2014, Zico worked with SMIs for their #CrackLifeOpen campaign to promote its coconut water, and similarly, in 2015, Nespresso used top lifestyle and fashion bloggers with large followings on Instagram for its #ACupAbove campaign (MediaKix, n.d.).

When new platforms are launched, marketers often have to find new strategies. For example, marketers are learning how to gain the attention of TikTok's mostly Gen Z users. In 2019, Gymshark, an online gym clothing retailer in the UK, invited users to share a photo of themselves on January 1 and again on March 8 for their "66 Day Change Your Life" campaign. They also tapped six SMIs in various health and fitness categories to raise awareness (Lai, n.d.). Chipotle ran a campaign in 2019 inviting users to create and share a #GuacDance and also included YouTubers Loren Gray and Brent Rivera in the campaign. The campaign drove awareness and usage of online ordering and the mobile app by requiring placement of an order through either method. Sony Pictures used twin brother TikTok duo Max and Harvey to promote a contest to meet the twins and the AJR Brothers at a concert in London. To enter, TikTok users had to upload a video with the hashtag #100baddays, corresponding to the name of an AJR Brothers song. The similarity of these campaigns is that they use a small number of high-profile SMIs. TikTok users often post video content that involves dancing or lip-synching, and campaigns can be successful in encouraging users to create similar engaging content.

THE EVOLUTION OF PLATFORMS TO
SUPPORT INFLUENCER MARKETING

The monetization model in the early years of blogging often involved generating revenue from display advertising, such as banner and sidebar ads served to the blog through a program like Google AdSense. When visitors to the blog clicked on the ad, the blogger generally earned between a few cents to a few dollars per click. Over time, however, consumers became desensitized to the novelty of display advertising and click-through rates dropped sharply, therefore forcing the monetization strategy for many blogs to shift from display ads to sponsored content (Meyer, 2019). With sponsored content, SMIs are generally paid a flat rate for creating content or earn a commission on products sold through affiliate links on their channels (Kulkarni, 2017).

YouTube

Besides blogs, other platforms have had to adapt to satisfy the changing needs of content creators, marketers, and users. For example, to compete with other video-sharing platforms, YouTube added opportunities for creators to monetize their channels. The YouTube Partners Program, launched in 2007, offers preferred producers a share of the advertising revenues generated by their videos. By 2011, YouTube had signed more than 10,000 partners, and hundreds were making six-figure incomes a year (Jackson, 2011). The program, which was selective in the beginning, was opened to all creators in April 2012 who had successfully monetized at least one video (YouTube, 2012). The requirements to join the YouTube Partners Program as of November 2019 include having at least 1,000 subscribers and 4,000 valid public watch hours over the past twelve months (YouTube, 2019).

YouTube adjusted its algorithm in 2012, prioritizing videos with longer watch times over those with higher view counts. YouTube creators reacted by publishing videos longer than ten minutes (Alexander, 2019). YouTube then introduced subscription service YouTube Red in 2015 to provide ad-free viewing and original content to subscribers. Some of the content available utilized YouTube stars such as Lilly Singh and Felix Kjellberg, who were paired with professional filmmakers. Starting in 2016, prominent YouTubers noticed that their videos were being demonetized, a term that refers to the removal by YouTube of advertising and thus ad revenue (Alexander, 2019). The controversy sparked a bigger concern about algorithm changes and the videos selected for the suggested feed. Over the years, YouTube has also made changes to its platform that support influencer marketing, but other changes that SMIs have criticized. In August 2019, the site started showing rounded subscriber total (i.e., instead of 9,800,775, it would show ten million)

(Martineau, 2019). The exact counts were then only available to the account owner.

In 2016, YouTube acquired FameBit, a company that connects video content creators with marketers looking for SMIs to create sponsored content (Ha, 2016). The company provides a way for marketers to review proposals from prospective SMIs and track campaign metrics and also for SMIs to review opportunities, submit proposals, and easily collect payment.

Around 2014, Facebook started to court YouTube stars to its platform with little success. Some of the obstacles included not having an established ad revenue model or a news feed that was a good fit for video viewing, especially when a user wanted to view multiple videos from the same content creator or discover new creators (Shields, 2015). YouTube focuses solely on video, making it a better platform for video producers. Creators have also been mistrustful of Facebook, worrying that they would be pushed to buy paid ads to get their videos in the Facebook News Feed (Shields, 2015).

Instagram

In 2019, Instagram was the fastest growing social network and had already surpassed one billion users by mid-2018. At that time, users were posting 95 million photos and videos and sharing 400 million Instagram Stories every day (Influencer Marketing Hub, 2019). Instagram captures a large percentage of SMIs who use the site to showcase brand associations through visuals and captions (#HASHOFF, 2017) and has seen an increase in brand-sponsored posts with the hashtags #ad, #sponsored, or #spon from more than 1.3 million in 2016 to over 3.7 million in 2018, with projections for 2019 and 2020 at almost 5 million and more than 6 million posts, respectively (MediaKix, 2019). As the number of Instagram users and influencers have exploded, businesses who support influencer marketing programs have kept pace with the increased opportunities to serve this market. For example, the growth of Instagram and SMIs spurred the launch of 320 new platforms and agencies in 2018 that focused on influencer marketing. In 2015, the number was just 190, which rose to 335 in 2016, 420 in 2017, and then 740 in 2018 (Influencer Marketing Hub, 2019). The growth of Instagram and the rise of SMIs on the platform led to developments that supported influencer marketing. Some of the early changes to the app included trending hashtags in January 2011, photo tagging in May 2013, video-sharing of fifteen-second clips in June 2013 (which was later increased to one minute), advertising in the form of sponsored posts in the feed in November 2013, and new business tools that provide advertisers with basic analytics in August 2014 (Pollock, 2018).

Instagram changed its feed in 2016 from a reverse chronological feed to one where "the moments you care about" come first. The company's new algorithm prioritized timely content most likely to engage users because it was both relevant and posted by friends with closer relationships (Instagram, 2016). According to Instagram (2016), although SMIs might have been frustrated that content they posted would not immediately be at the top of feeds and possibly buried deep among many other posts, they were in a solid position to create the kind of content valued by the new algorithm. As the algorithm evolved in 2017, the qualities of a post that would be prioritized became more apparent. These factors included engagement of a post, time spent on a post, relevancy to other content the user engaged with, direct message sharing of posts, number of connections, searches for the profile, and timeliness of the post (Pollock, 2018).

Other changes from 2016 to 2018 included enhanced tools for post insights in May 2016, Stories that can stay active for twenty-four hours as of August 2016, live video streaming in November 2016, multiple photos and videos in a single post in February 2017, and searchable Stories by location and hashtag in May 2017 (Pollock, 2018). Most significantly for SMIs was a "Paid Partnership" identification launched June 2017 for select SMIs (Stewart, 2017). A Paid Partnership occurs when SMIs share a post or story on Instagram and tag the account of the sponsor of the content. Instagram then generates a message just under the SMI's username that reads "Paid partnership with [business name]" and links to the sponsor's page. The sponsor also has access to metrics about these paid sponsorship posts. In 2018, Instagram tested changing the look of profile pages, eliminating the post count and moving the follower count from right below the username to a smaller font below the bio (Instagram, 2018).

On a regular Instagram post, users cannot include a link, but Instagram Stories allows SMIs with more than 10,000 followers to add a link to the "swipe up" feature. In March 2019, Instagram also offered the option to "Checkout on Instagram," allowing brands to sell directly from the platform (Instagram, 2019). In addition to brands, the company also later released this option to its SMI partners.

Instagram launched a platform change in 2019 that allowed advertisers to promote the organic branded content posts of SMIs who work with them, representing an evolution from Paid Partnership ads (Graham, 2019). These ads, called branded content posts, widen the audience of users who can see the SMI's post to not just the SMI's audience like Paid Partnership ads, but also the brand's audience. In feeds, these posts are also tagged with "paid partnership with" labels for clear advertising disclosure. Instagram has also launched Branded Content Stories, but these are limited to select advertisers at the present time.

In 2019, Instagram started testing hiding like counts on posts for users in various countries around the world, including Australia, Japan, and Canada, instead showing a username who liked the post and a link to "others" who liked it. Statements from Instagram reveal that they wanted to reduce the stress individual users feel over garnering likes on their posts (BBC News, 2019). Business users, such as SMIs, can still access the analytics by clicking on their posts, but their followers will not be aware of the number of likes.

Snapchat

Snapchat emerged on the social media scene in 2011, and its early users were teenagers. At first, snaps were only viewable for a short period of time before they self-destructed, but the platform later added Snapchat Stories, allowing users to share a compilation of video and photo snippets for twenty-four hours. SMIs also found their way to Snapchat, but the platform has not been as proactive as Instagram in providing analytics to SMIs (Miachon, 2018). Instagram also launched its own Stories feature, which had been a Snapchat differentiator. Top SMIs started posting less often on Snapchat, and users also left Snapchat to follow SMIs on Instagram (Miachon, 2018). In 2018, Snapchat added more detailed insights for tens of thousands of users who create "Official Stories" (Wagner, 2018).

Facebook

Facebook also offers opportunities on its platform for SMIs, but it has not been embraced as a video platform like YouTube or a photography platform like Instagram by SMIs. In 2017, the company launched a Creator app and website for SMIs to produce and monitor content, which has since been replaced by Creator Studio. Added in 2018 was a monthly subscription, ranging from $4.99 to $29.99, similar to Patreon for content creators to charge fans for access to exclusive content. In 2018, Facebook also introduced its Brand Collabs Manager, a tool for SMIs to showcase their portfolios of sponsored content, interests, and audiences that is searchable by marketers (LaPorte, 2018).

Facebook also offers the video-streaming service Facebook Watch, with content from users and professionally-produced content sponsored by Facebook. In late 2018 and early 2019, the company was talking to publishers and production partners to develop ideas for shows that feature influencers with large followings to be funded by Facebook and produced by its production partners (Patel, 2019).

THE EVOLUTION OF SMI REGULATIONS

The U.S. Federal Trade Commission (FTC) requires SMIs to disclose the receipt of compensation, whether monetary or in-kind, in their social media posts. Social media regulation began in October 2009 when the FTC approved guidelines that addressed the practice of blogging about products and services. The revised *Guides Concerning the Use of Endorsements and Testimonials in Advertising* set out to explain blogger endorsement, which is speech that is considered sponsored based on the context of the relationship between the blogger and the marketer (Federal Trade Commission, 2009).

The 2009 guidelines defined endorsement according to the compensation provided (including free products), the length of the relationship, the previous receipt and likelihood of future receipt of products or services, and the value of the products or services. Statements about a product or service by a blogger who has readers of a particular demographic group that is in a marketer's target audience and has an ongoing relationship with that marketer were also likely to be considered endorsements. When an endorsement was made on a blog, the blogger was required to disclose the relationship with the marketer. The FTC guidelines motivated the Direct Marketing Association to revise its ethics guidelines in January 2010, requiring those who use testimonials or endorsements on social media to "clearly and conspicuously disclose any material connections between the endorser and marketer, which the consumer would not expect" (Davis, 2010, para. 2).

The *FTC Social Media Guidelines 2016* updated the existing guidelines to more specifically address influencer campaigns on various platforms (MediaKix, n.d.). Some of the new guidelines included that sponsorship communication must be included toward the beginning of posts and be located "above the fold" (which is either before a "more" button or above where a user would scroll on a blog post). The sponsorship communication should also be easy to read and stand out from the background, included even if the review is negative, and visible on all possible devices. The FTC also issued platform-specific guidelines at this time. For Instagram, the caption must include the hashtags #ad and/or #sponsored. The brand must also be tagged in the caption before the "more" button. For YouTube, the video must have the message "this video was sponsored by . . . " in the description before the "Read More" button, and sponsorship disclosure must also be included in the video itself in clear and easy-to-read text and on the screen long enough to be noticed. For Twitter, because of character limitations, all that is required is the hashtag #ad in the tweet.

In April 2017, the FTC sent letters to more than ninety SMIs as reminders that if they have a material connection to a marketer, this relationship must be disclosed. Later, twenty-one of those SMIs received warning letters pointing out specific posts and asking for a response as to whether they had a material connection to the brands and if so, the steps they would be taking to make required disclosures (Fair, 2017). Around the same time, the FTC also released *The FTC's Endorsement Guides: What People Are Asking* to clarify some of the requirements. The first point is that a relationship with a marketer must be clearly disclosed and SMIs should not assume that their followers are already aware of brand relationships. The second point is to not assume that the platform's disclosure tool is sufficient for ensuring that the disclosure is clear. The third point is that influencers should use clear disclosures like #sponsored or #ad and not #thanks, #collab, #sp, #spon, or #ambassador. Finally, the disclosure should not be placed after a "click more" button, and on platforms like Snapchat with no captions, the disclosure needs to be directly on the image (Fair, 2017).

The State of Influencer Marketing Survey 2019 by Linqua found in their survey of 197 marketers that only 63 percent indicated they were familiar with the most recent FTC disclosure guidelines (Linqia, 2019). The same survey conducted in 2018 found that only 87 percent of marketers require that SMIs disclose sponsored content in compliance with FTC regulations and that 71 percent were aware of the most recent guidelines (Linqia, 2018).

PREDICTIONS FOR THE FUTURE OF SMIS

Instagram and other social media platforms are now flooded with SMIs ranging from those with less than 1,000 followers to those with millions of followers. A study by Klear found the number of SMI posts on Instagram using the hashtags #ad or #sponsored nearly doubled between 2016 and 2017 to more than 1.5 million posts worldwide and that sponsored posts generated approximately 1 billion likes globally in 2017 (Chadha, 2018).

As the ranks of SMIs continue to grow, there are indications that marketers are becoming more interested in focusing on micro-influencers (between 10,000 and 50,000 followers) and nano-influencers (between 1,000 and 10,000 followers) to deliver campaign messages. A 2018 eMarketer study found that compared to top-tier SMIs, marketers see micro- and mid-tier SMIs with 50,000 to 500,000 followers as being more effective, having a better connection with the target audience, and producing more authentic content (Droesch, 2019). Spending by marketers is also expected to continue to grow, from an estimated $8 billion in 2019 to $15 billion by 2022 (Schomer, 2019). As more money is spent, marketers will want to become more sophisticated in their approaches and develop effective SMI strategies, possibly focusing on building longer-term relationships with influencers.

Despite optimistic projections about the future of SMIs, the industry will also likely face challenges. First, the saturation of SMIs in the marketplace is likely to depress payments because there are always SMIs willing to work for less money (Blum, 2019). The result is that some SMIs will be deterred from creating posts that are not as lucrative as they were before. Marketers should expect that they will get what they pay for, and if they do not pay competitive rates, the content, engagement, and return on investment will suffer.

Another concern for the industry is whether SMI fatigue has set in for social media platform users. Engagement with sponsored posts has been declining, which may indicate that user attention is spread too thin as users follow an increasing number of SMIs or that they are less interested in the content shared by SMIs (Iurillo, 2019). Other concerns are that consumers are more cognizant of content that appears inauthentic and are less likely to engage with SMIs they feel are not genuine (Iurillo, 2019). To combat this, marketers are encouraged to find SMI partners that are either actual fans of the products they are being asked to promote or are expected to be fans based on other posts.

Also plaguing the industry is fraud related to inflated follower counts. It is estimated that about 15 percent of spending on SMI campaigns, or about $1.3 billion in 2019, is lost to fraud (Cerullo, 2019). Some of the red flags for marketers are SMI accounts that have been recently opened, but have a significant following and little interaction on the posts. Marketers pay SMIs based on reach, but some of that reach may be manipulated if the SMI purchased fake followers. Unilever, a company that spends billions on marketing, announced in 2018 that they would make an effort to not work with SMIs who inflated their follower counts (Pearl, 2018). Additionally, many hotels around the world also made news starting in 2018 for limiting free stays for SMIs and improving their vetting process for SMIs (Lorenz, 2018).

Moving forward, the industry will continue to address these issues while becoming more sophisticated in selecting, collaborating with, and measuring the return on investment of SMIs. New platforms and new features of current platforms will likely launch in the future to provide marketers with different challenges and opportunities for influencer marketing. The industry could also realize greater success by moving influencers into other channels, like television shows, traditional advertising campaigns, and also event appearances. As influencer marketing budgets continue to increase, more influencers enter the scene, and more companies launch to support this industry, influencer marketing should be a mainstay marketing tactic for years to come.

REFERENCES

#HASHOFF. (2017). Influencer marketer: A #HASHOFF state of the union report. https://www.slideshare.net/FilippPaster/hashoff-instagram-dominates-influencer -marketing-report

ABC Radio Networks. (2008, April 17). ABC Radio Networks announces deal with "C" student entertainment for syndication of Perez Hilton. https://www.yumpu.co

m/en/document/read/48441884/abc-radio-networks-announces-deal-with-ac-affil
iates

Alexander, J. (2019, April 5). The golden age of YouTube is over. *The Verge.* https:/
/www.theverge.com/2019/4/5/18287318/youtube-logan-paul-pewdiepie-demoneti
zation-adpocalypse-premium-influencers-creators

Arnold, A. (2017, June 20). Why YouTube stars influence Millennials more than
traditional celebrities. *Forbes.* https://www.forbes.com/sites/under30network
/2017/06/20/why-youtube-stars-influence-millennials-more-than-traditional-cel
ebrities

Bailey, S. P. (2018, January 29). What ever happened to the mommy blog? *Chicago
Tribune.* https://www.chicagotribune.com/lifestyles/parenting/ct-mommy-blog
-disappear-20180129-story.html

Barbaro, M. (2006, March 7). Wal-Mart enlists bloggers in PR campaign. *The New
York Times.* http://www.nytimes.com/2006/03/07/technology/07blog.html

Barry, K. (2009, April 17). Ford bets the Fiesta on social networking. *Wired.* https://
www.wired.com/2009/04/how-the-fiesta/

BBC News. (2019, July 18). Instagram hides likes count in international test "to
remove pressure." https://www.bbc.com/news/world-49026935

Bloem, C. (2019, October 29). 84 percent of people trust online reviews as much as
friends: Here's how to manage what they see. *Inc.* https://www.inc.com/craig-bloe
m/84-percent-of-people-trust-online-reviews-as-much-.html

Blum, S. (2019, October 21). The fatigue hitting influencers as Instagram evolves.
https://www.bbc.com/worklife/article/20191022-the-fatigue-hitting-influencers-as
-instagram-evolves

Brandwatch. (2019, November 8). The most followed accounts on Twitter.
Brandwatch. https://www.brandwatch.com/blog/most-twitter-followers/

Business of Fashion. (n.d.). Bryan Grey Yambao. https://www.businessoffashion.
com/community/people/bryan-grey-yambao

Cerullo, M. (2019, July 25). Influencer marketing fraud will cost brands $1.3 billion
in 2019. *CBS News.* https://www.cbsnews.com/news/influencer-marketing-fraud
-costs-companies-1-3-billion/

Chadha, R. (2018, January 24). Instagram influencer marketing doubled in 2017. https
://www.emarketer.com/content/instagram-influencer-marketing-doubled-last-year

Champagne, C. (2014, February 10). Target to launch collections created by
Pinterest's top pinners. *Fast Company.* https://www.fastcompany.com/3026239/
target-to-launch-collections-created-by-pinterests-top-pinners

Chong, D. A. (2019, June 14). The Lancome × Chiara Ferragni collaboration just
dropped & yes, you need everything. *The Zoe Report.* https://www.thezoere
port.com/p/the-lancome-x-chiara-ferragni-collaboration-just-dropped-yes-you-ne
ed-everything-18005915

CNN. (2009, April 18). Oprah, Ashton Kutcher mark Twitter "turning point." http://
www.cnn.com/2009/TECH/04/17/ashton.cnn.twitter.battle/

Cresci, E. (2016, June 16). Lonelygirl15: How one mysterious vlogger changed the
internet. *The Guardian.* https://www.theguardian.com/technology/2016/jun/16/
lonelygirl15-bree-video-blog-youtube

Davis, W. (2010, January 25). DMA revises guidelines to comply with FTC "blogger" rules. *Online Media Daily*. https://www.mediapost.com/publications/article/121257/dma-revises-guidelines-to-comply-with-ftc-blogger.html

Droesch, B. (2019, July 16). How much are brands paying influencers? *eMarketer*. https://www.emarketer.com/content/how-much-are-brands-paying-influencers

Fair, L. (2017, September 7). Three FTC actions of interest to influencers. *Federal Trade Commission*. https://www.ftc.gov/news-events/blogs/business-blog/2017/09/three-ftc-actions-interest-influencers

Federal Trade Commission. (2009, October 5). FTC published final guides governing endorsements, testimonials. https://www.ftc.gov/news-events/press-releases/2009/10/ftc-publishes-final-guides-governing-endorsements-testimonials

Frank, J. N. (2003, March 3). Darden serving up launch effort for Seasons 52 chain. *PR Week*. https://www.prweek.com/article/1248975/darden-serving-launch-effort-seasons-52-chain

Gillespie, N. (2014, October 1). PewDiePie, Jenna Marbles, CaptainSparklez: The web's biggest stars. *Reason*. https://reason.com/2014/10/01/pewdiepie-captainsparklez-skydoesminecra/

Graham, M. (2019, June 4). Instagram will now let advertisers put more "influencer" ads in your feed. *CNBC*. https://www.cnbc.com/2019/06/04/instagram-will-now-let-advertisers-put-more-influencer-ads-in-your-feed.html

Greco, P. (2004, August 2). Branding initiative: Nikon shifts focus to new audience in latest Coolpix drive. *PR Week*, *19*. https://www.prweek.com/article/1245300/branding-initiative-nikon-shifts-focus-new-audience-latest-coolpix-drive

Ha, A. (2016, October 11). Google acquires FameBit to connect YouTube creators with marketers. *TechCrunch*. https://techcrunch.com/2016/10/11/google-acquires-famebit-to-connect-youtube-creators-with-brands/

Hart, K. (2006, August 5). Barging into the bloggers' circle: Web logs are fertile new territory for introducing products, welcome or not. *The Washington Post*, p. D1.

Hood, J. (2002, August 12). Corporate case study—From inception to IPO, PR has always delivered for Netflix. *PR Week*. https://www.prweek.com/article/1233867/corporate-case-study-inception-ipo-pr-always-delivered-netflix

Humphrey, M. (2011, June 28). Ray William Johnson: =3 adds up to most-subscribed on YouTube. *Forbes*. https://www.forbes.com/sites/michaelhumphrey/2011/06/28/ray-william-johnson-3-adds-up-to-most-subscribed-on-youtube

Influencer Marketing Hub. (2019, May 28). The state of influencer marketing 2019: Benchmark report [+infographic]. https://influencermarketinghub.com/influencer-marketing-2019-benchmark-report/

Instagram. (2016, March 15). See the moments you care about first. https://instagram-press.com/blog/2016/03/15/see-the-moments-you-care-about-first/

Instagram. (2018, November 21). Improving your instagram profile. https://instagram-press.com/blog/2018/11/21/improving-your-instagram-profile/

Instagram. (2019, March 19). New to Instagram shopping: Checkout. https://business.instagram.com/blog/new-to-instagram-shopping-checkout

Iurillo, O. (2019, July 11). Six dangers of influencer marketing. *Social Media Today.* https://www.socialmediatoday.com/news/6-dangers-of-influencer-marketing/558 493/

Jackson, N. (2011, August 3). Infographic: The history of video advertising on YouTube. *The Atlantic.* https://www.theatlantic.com/technology/archive/2011/08/ infographic-the-history-of-video-advertising-on-youtube/242836/

Kulkarni, C. (2017). Affiliate vs. influencer marketing: Which should your company use? *Entrepreneur.* https://www.entrepreneur.com/article/293224

Lai, S. (n.d.). Brands enter uncluttered TikTok market as influencer marketing gains traction. *Influencer Orchestration Network.* https://www.ion.co/tik-tok -influencers

LaPorte, N. (2018, March 19). With new tools, Facebook tells influencers: Trust us. Really. *Fast Company.* https://www.fastcompany.com/40545643/facebook-watch -enters-the-influencer-game

Leskin, P. (2019, November 4). These are the 32 biggest stars on TikTok, the viral video app teens can't get enough of. *Business Insider.* https://www.businessinsider .com/tiktok-most-popular-stars-gen-z-influencers-social-media-app-2019-6

Lieber, C. (2014, July 8). How two stay-at-home moms turned their bag obsession into a six-figure business. *Racked.* https://www.racked.com/2014/7/8/7588019/bag -snob-blog-tina-craig-kelly-cook-prada-hermes-birkin-chanel-cartier

Lieber, C. (2019, May 2). She was the "queen of the mommy bloggers" then her world fell apart. *Vox.* https://www.vox.com/the-highlight/2019/4/25/18512620/do oce-heather-armstrong-depression-valedictorian-of-being-dead

Linqia. (2018). The state of influencer marketing 2018. http://www.linqia.com/wp- content/uploads/2017/12/Linqia-The-State-of-Influencer-Marketing-2018.pdf

Linqia. (2019). The state of influencer marketing 2019. https://linqia.com/wp-content/ uploads/2019/04/Linqia-State-of-Influencer-Marketing-2019-Report.pdf

Lorenz, T. (2018, June 13). Instagram's wannabe-stars are driving luxury hotels crazy. *The Atlantic.* https://www.theatlantic.com/technology/archive/2018/06/insta gram-influencers-are-driving-luxury-hotels-crazy/562679/

Martin, D. (2006, June 12). Carson Daly bonkers for Brookers. *Variety.* https:// variety.com/2006/tv/markets-festivals/carson-daly-bonkers-for-brookers-120033 7852

Martineau, P. (2019, May 27). YouTube's change in subscriber counts sparks its own drama. *Wired.* https://www.wired.com/story/youtubes-change-subscriber-counts -sparks-drama/

MediaKix. (2019, March 7). Instagram influencer marketing is a 1.7 billion dollar industry. https://mediakix.com/blog/instagram-influencer-marketing-industry-size -how-big/

MediaKix. (n.d.a). Best Instagram campaigns: Brand sponsored posts. https://mediaki x.com/blog/best-instagram-campaigns-brand-sponsored-posts-1/

MediaKix. (n.d.b). How vloggers on YouTube are changing influencer marketing. https://mediakix.com/blog/vloggers-on-youtube-influencer-marketing/

MediaKix. (n.d.c). The FTC social media guidelines 2016. https://mediakix.com/blog /ftc-social-media-guidelines-2016/

Meyer, C. (2019). You don't need ads on your site to monetize your blog. Here's how bloggers make six figures. *Copyhackers.* https://copyhackers.com/2019/10/monetize-your-freelance-blog/

Miachon, N. (2018, April 27). What Snapchat teaches us about influencer marketing. https://www.forbes.com/sites/forbescommunicationscouncil/2018/04/27/what-snapchat-teaches-us-about-influencer-marketing

Newman, A. A. (2010, July 15). Old Spice argues that real men smell good. *The New York Times.* https://www.nytimes.com/2010/07/16/business/media/16adco.html

Newton, C. (2016, October 28). Why Vine died. *The Verge.* https://www.theverge.com/2016/10/28/13456208/why-vine-died-twitter-shutdown

Oser, K. (2004, September 13). More marketers test blogs to build buzz. *Advertising Age, 75*, 3.

Patel, S. (2015, December 17). Working with the Instagram and Snapchat elite isn't easy for brands. *Digiday.* https://digiday.com/marketing/working-instagram-snapchat-elite-isnt-easy-brands/

Patel, S. (2019, February 14). Facebook Watch has a new program to fund publisher shows starring influencers. *Digiday.* https://digiday.com/media/facebook-has-a-new-program-to-fund-watch-shows-made-by-publishers-and-starring-influencers/

Pearl, D. (2018, June 26). Unilever says no more fake followers and bots. Influencers cheer, and question the future. *AdWeek.* https://www.adweek.com/brand-marketing/unilever-says-no-more-fake-followers-and-bots-influencers-cheer-and-question-the-future/

Pollock, S. (2018, March 7). Instagram algorithm change history. *Power Digital Marketing.* https://powerdigitalmarketing.com/blog/instagram-algorithm-change-history

Sawyer, N., & Jarvis, R. (2015, March 19). YouTube star Michelle Phan: 7 things you didn't know about her. *ABC News.* https://abcnews.go.com/Business/youtube-star-michelle-phan-things/story?id=29753510

Schomer, A. (2019, July 15). Influencer marketing 2019: Why brands can't get enough of an $8 billion ecosystem driven by Kardashians, moms, and tweens. *Business Insider.* https://www.businessinsider.com/the-2019-influencer-marketing-report-2019-7

Shields, M. (2015, July 20). YouTube stars keep Facebook at arm's length for now. *The Wall Street Journal.* https://blogs.wsj.com/cmo/2015/07/20/youtube-stars-keep-facebook-at-arms-length-for-now/

Shortman, M. (2003, February 24). Campaigns: Soy milk heads to Hollywood to help shed yucky image. *PR Week.* https://www.prweek.com/article/1249027/campaigns-soy-milk-heads-hollywood-help-shed-yucky-image

Stewart, R. (2017, June 14). Instagram wants to "bring transparency" to influencer and brand content deals with fresh set of tools. *The Drum.* https://www.thedrum.com/news/2017/06/14/instagram-wants-bring-transparency-influencer-and-brand-content-deals-with-fresh-set

Swant, M. (2016, July 6). Here's why Las Vegas hired DJ Khaled to launch its Snapchat channel. *AdWeek.* https://www.adweek.com/digital/heres-why-las-vegas-hired-dj-khaled-launch-its-snapchat-channel-172131/

Tedeschi, B. (2007, February 26). Hot new properties: YouTube celebrities. *The New York Times*. https://www.nytimes.com/2007/02/26/technology/26ecom.html

VanDeGraph. (2016, October 21). The top Youtubers throughout history. *Medium*. https://medium.com/@vandegraph/the-top-youtubers-throughout-history-9f22ac4 bee45

Variety. (2009, April 9). The first YouTube channel to hit one million subscribers. https://variety.com/2009/digital/news/the-first-youtube-channel-to-hit-one-million -subscribers-33382/

Vinjamuri, D. (2013, February 19). Ford remixes the Fiesta Movement for 2014. *Forbes*. https://www.forbes.com/sites/davidvinjamuri/2013/02/19/ford-revives-the -fiesta-movement-to-launch-the-2014-fiesta/

Vulture. (2008, July 8). YouTube dancer Matt Harding taking the Stride gum message into the New York "Times." https://www.vulture.com/2008/07/youtube_dance r_matt_harding_ta.html

Wagner, K. (2018, February 14). Snapchat is finally giving influencers data about their posts and followers. *Vox Recode*. https://www.vox.com/2018/2/14/17010490 /snapchat-celebrities-influencer-data-insights

White, R. D. (2019, August 25). How two friends built Revolve into a fashion empire with Instagram influencers. *Los Angeles Times*. https://www.latimes.com/business/ story/2019-08-23/revolve-clothing-instagram-influencer-ecommerce

YouTube. (2012, April 12). Being a YouTube Creator just got even more rewarding. *YouTube Creator Blog*. https://youtube-creators.googleblog.com/2012/04/being-y outube-creator-just-got-even.html

YouTube. (2019, November). YouTube Partner Program overview & eligibility. *YouTube Help*. https://support.google.com/youtube/answer/72851

Chapter 2

Rising to the Top

Social Media (Macro) Influencers and the Democratized Brand Capital of Entertainment, Interaction, and Disclosure

Alexa Landsberger and Amanda R. Martinez

Facebook, YouTube, Instagram, Twitter, and Snapchat define our social media repertoire fueled by a converged media landscape. Media convergence is "a process, but not an endpoint" (Jenkins, 2004, p. 34), encompassing our social and mass media-saturated environment, including more channels of communication, greater portability, and shifts in media ownership. Jenkins (2008) argues that convergence culture empowers media audiences with opportunities to seek out the entertainment experiences they want across multiple media platforms, supported by the media industries' cooperation.

Kahle and Valette-Florence (2012) describe the core functions of social media as to "create and share, connect and socialize, consume and seek, and control and sense" (p. 237). Social media allow users to become 'produsers' and create and publish original content with potential to reach vast networks (Kádár & Könczey, 2014). Social media sites popularized the phenomenon of the "produser," social media users who are both consumers and content producers (Bruns, 2006; Jenkins, 2008), who are closely connected to audiences (or users/followers), and accept the dynamic mediated cultural economy that rewards participation (Jenkins et al., 2018). Social media produsers work against the oligopolistic structure of mainstream media production, creating opportunities for bottom-up messaging. However, social media aids fragmentation by democratizing media production. Some users have achieved fame by producing content that attracts substantial subscribership.

A type of produser is the social media influencer (SMI), who establishes credibility and authenticity in online industries and cultivates large audiences that help launch their careers (Freberg et al., 2011). SMIs are categorized into two groups—microinfluencers and macroinfluencers. Microinfluencers have 10,000 to 500,000 followers compared to macroinfluencers who have over 500,000 followers (Wissman, 2018). SMIs oftentimes evolve into brandable celebrities through their power and monetary influence online (Kádár & Könczey, 2014; Sanders et al., 2019). Opportunities for monetization explain SMIs' powerful potential recognized by external companies, which oftentimes secures financial sustenance and reinforces social media success, a typically mutually beneficial confluence. When advertisements and sponsors are shared on SMIs' profiles, they assume greater salience to followers. The overlap between company and influencer brand strategy presents a fusion to sustain followers by directly engaging them thereby cultivating brand communication (Booth & Matic, 2011). Direct engagement blurs lines between celebrity capital cultivation and genuine (para)social interaction with followers (Bilandzic et al., 2012). As followers develop their unique needs, audience segmentation increases, and SMIs strive for widely relevant content and interaction mechanisms. SMIs establish a monetized industry on social media that catapults them into the spotlight as their large followership lends celebrity credibility because they become esteemed within social media communities.

The current study describes the media techniques that SMIs use to create a brandable media presence founded on the integration of their personal image within a monetized industry. In order to examine the specific and unique behaviors of SMIs, a content analysis was conducted on some of the top Instagram and YouTube macroinfluencers' profiles. The content analysis revealed common patterns across all influencers in their social media production and the relationship building strategies used to form connections with other users. Using content from macroinfluencers revealed the strategies that are needed to maintain and continue to grow their already established celebrity capital and presence in an interactive media landscape. Importantly, we sought to understand the type of content deemed the most valuable on social media platforms through SMIs' profiles. We aimed to highlight how SMIs' presence on social media allows them to enter more traditional entertainment media markets.

LITERATURE REVIEW

Celebrification of SMIs

Reality TV and social media have, in their own way, reshaped the entertainment industry and democratized opportunities to gain celebrity status (Andrejevic, 2003). Social media has democratized how content is produced as a marketplace of exchange between consumption and production. The capitalistic and hyper consumption-based realm has generated a base for individuals to achieve social media-based celebrity capital, which entails public awareness and familiarity with past behaviors and favorability pertaining to personality and reputation (Driessens, 2013a). SMIs utilize social media to leverage the exposure required to achieve celebrity status like reality TV stars but without the large-scale production resources of a network (Andrejevic, 2003). SMIs create and use brands they construct to gain a loyal following and break into various industries such as film, TV, fashion, and comedy. Since the majority of SMIs' content is self-produced, SMIs must construct a strong brand that leads to follower attention and interaction, which is a burden and benefit of individualistic influencer realities inherently part of the overall visibility game (Cotter, 2019).

The accumulation of celebrity capital is a key process of celebrification or "[the] process by which ordinary people or public figures are transformed into celebrities" (Driessens, 2013b, p. 642). Driessens (2013b) explains that SMIs' celebrity capital relies upon recurrent social media representations. The autonomy SMIs have with social media affords individuals creative freedom over their own mediated self-presentations and post frequency. SMIs can construct their behaviors based on what they believe is favorable to followers while also consulting algorithmic metric data about popular content that grabs optimum attention (Cotter, 2019). Celebrity status exudes time sensitivity, so SMIs must post regularly to maintain their relevance and brand toward longevity.

SMIs erect their own guiding parameters that dictate the degree to which they utilize various social media functions, but they may not be completely unencumbered by economic ramifications. When advertisements and sponsors are shared on SMIs' profiles, they become more salient to consumers. Both company and influencer create brands and produce messages in hopes that the brand communication persuades followers to action (Booth & Matic, 2011). Celebrity capital can also be exchanged among industries, and as SMIs accumulate capital online, they can use this power to enter different industries (Weinswig, 2018). This pattern arises with Do-It-Yourself (DIY) SMIs, such as beauty bloggers, who often create their own cosmetic lines. SMIs gain celebrity status through their work in different industries such as film, music, fashion, and comedy.

Parasocial Relationships

Individualistic authenticity remains a key component of the SMIs' brand power. Influencers occupy a unique position of individuality that enables them to have a more direct interaction with followers, which helps establish parasocial relationships and, ultimately, build the SMIs' brand. In brand building, SMIs curate outward-facing personalities and engage the theoretical tenets of Goffman's (1978) looking glass self by seeing themselves through the lens of their follower base as a feedback loop. This reflection informs how SMIs continually refine their self-presentations to uphold, deepen, and communicate consistency through their displayed public personas.

On the audience side, parasocial relationships theory describes the cognitive approximation of real relationships with (social) media figures based on three important determinants: attractiveness/likeability, perceived realism, and perceived similarity (Giles, 2012; Schiappa et al., 2007). Bullingham and Vasconcelos (2013) invoke the importance of interpersonal social norms defined through online behaviors. These parasocial relationships, unlike face-to-face or traditional interpersonal relationships, do not necessarily require reciprocity. Relationships between other users and followers are fluid. SMIs must generate content that satisfies the consumption desires of their followers in order to maintain their celebrity status. Users can gratify influencers by symbolic interaction through "likes" and "comments." Nabi and Oliver (2009) point out that parasocial relationships develop through media experiences between media personalities (performers) and media consumers (audiences); the communicative prompts by media personalities strengthen perceived relationships. Consumers may interpret this as interpersonal communication because of sheer accessibility and engagement uniquely afforded by social media platforms. Bickart et al. (2015) explored links between sharing secrets and follower growth and assert that influencers share secrets (most commonly about mental health, relationships, and spoilers) to acquire followers' trust. SMIs use their position of power to drive attention to their content, validating followers for consuming the content, which comes full circle by enhancing attraction to these exclusive messages. Secrets make SMIs appear vulnerable to their followers which positively impacts their authenticity and promotes engagement. As interpersonal communication theories suggest (Braithwaite & Schrodt, 2014), personal disclosure helps build relationships and can somewhat flatten hierarchical relationships (as with traditional celebrity-audience dynamics).

Goffman's Framework

The current study draws inspiration from Goffman's major theoretical contributions about mediated social contact, face maintenance (positive social value based on interactions with others), and self-image presentation (Goffman, 1978, 2017). Goffman (1978) argues that individuals strive to act in ways with others that express their desired self-image by highlighting attributes and activities that confirm, cultivate, and refine said self-image. We live in a world that requires social encounters, which means face-saving to project the intended self-image entails navigating (non)verbal communication carefully to maintain congruity with others' perceptions of the self. Importantly, Goffman (1978) states, "commonly we find that upward mobility involves the presentation of proper performances" (p. 36). For SMIs, constant consideration must be paid to the social world that fuels the self-image projected to attract and sustain interactions with followers, such that an interdependence develops between a given social media situation and the wider social world of followers. Once a self-image is taken on, the individual is expected to live up to it and convey the communication required to maintain it to coincide with positive face and self-image maintenance (Goffman, 2017). Indeed, approved attributes and mutual acceptance uphold this basic structure for interactions as it is often the social relationship with others that drives SMIs to participate in encounters with followers and then be dependent upon them for supporting face. The unique character of each SMI must be constructed, refined, and pitched in a strategically combined way to build the attraction and sustain parasocial interpersonal relationships with followers. This transactional communication between SMIs and followers implies commitment; SMIs maintain their public image, and followers come to expect a routine and rhythm of engagement with SMIs.

Through a close qualitative textual analysis (Peräkylä & Ruusuvuori, 2018), we examine what SMI status entails and explain the processes underlying SMIs' social media usage that have escalated them to fame through self-produced professional entertainment content. Drawing upon Goffman's (1979) self-presentation, identity maintenance, and looking glass self-impression management framework, we posit the following research questions: (1) How do SMIs use social media to achieve fame? and (2) How do SMIs use their profiles to maintain their celebrity status?

METHOD

Data analysis included careful attention to how communication intertwines, which is defined as qualitative talk and text not limited to language (Peräkylä & Ruusuvuori, 2018), including nonverbals. Before developing the initial coding scheme, posts were first organized by type of content within each post, and we approached each post as a unique unit of data: media type, intention of post, theme, captions, likes, comments, reflection of brand, repeated behaviors, and unique practices. After this initial content organization, analysis of the specific communication within the content of each post ensued, including language usage, meaning embedded within captions, photos and framing, backdrop imagery, and video context, including themes and genre. Coding structures developed through close textual analysis resulted in themes that describe influencer output. Special attention was paid to patterns of originality or brand reflection.

Sample

SMIs included in the sample are macroinfluencers (over 500,000 followers each), cited in market research and business sites as some of the most prominent influencers, whose content often "trends" on Instagram and YouTube. The sample includes fifteen top posts per SMI starting from January 23, 2019 (N = 150). Since the cadence of posts is varied across media platforms and SMIs, we deemed it an important criterion for inclusion that the number of posts encompass enough depth to capture a representative sample range of the overall brand communication in each of the macroinfluencer's profiles; the decision to include fifteen posts also meant flexibility to highlight different production timelines for fifteen unique content pieces, spanning a few weeks to three to four months. The profiles are treated as public logs, and we recorded post sequence to explore patterns. All SMIs' profiles include photos and videos.

YouTube videos typically average around ten to fifteen minutes, and new content announcements are shared in advance as teasers, which is usually one or two times per week. On YouTube, personal brands arise in the video setup, such as vlogging style (Jenna Marbles), a structured show (Good Mythical Morning), or a combination (The Try Guys). Instagram's platform allows for mixed-media content on a singular platform, which includes photos, videos, and temporary stories. Instagram content can range from a single image to a series of images to a short video. Generally, Instagram content is posted every two to three days, though some SMIs may post multiple times in a single day. On Instagram, brands are highlighted through the type of content posted. Fashion, beauty, and fitness (Cameron Dallas, Michelle Lewin and HudaBeauty) SMIs use photos to promote their brands, while SMIs focused on entertainment (King Bach and Zach King) rely on short videos.

SMI Selection

A total of ten macro-SMIs were chosen for this study, including five Instagram SMIs (Cameron Dallas, King Bach, Huda Kattan, Zach King, and Michelle Lewin) and five YouTube SMIs (Rhett and Link from *Good Mythical Morning*, The Try Guys, Jenna Marbles, LaurDIY, and Nikkie de Jager). Internet personality, fitness, and beauty experts thematically align with Instagram's platform and morning shows, vlogs, and makeup tutorials align with the long-form content afforded by YouTube. Therefore, SMIs choose the media platform that best supports their individual brands, including depth, length, and content of messages for their followers.

Instagram SMIs

Cameron Dallas has 21.2 million Instagram followers, twenty-five posts to date, and has been active on social media since 2012. Dallas began self-branding as a model on Instagram, and many of his posts reflect self-promotion via ascertainably professional-quality photos. Now, Dallas' Instagram account is dedicated to his venture into the music industry, with his profile description promoting his single "Why Haven't I Met You."

King Bach began on Vine, posting comedic videos, and he now has 16.6 million followers and 3,977 Instagram posts. His Instagram reflects a mix of videos and images that promote a performative, comedic tone. Bach's profile description states that he is: "The internet guy who's in movies now," showing his transition from purely online to professional acting.

Zach King, like Bach and Dallas, got his start as a comedic Internet entertainer via Instagram. He has 21.1 million followers and a total of 819 posts. His profile states: "Stories can make people smile," which is thematically reflective of his content.

Huda Kattan has 28.7 million followers and 13,749 posts. Her profile defines her brand as a "MUA (makeup artist) & Blogger turned Business Woman." Kattan is known for her beauty tutorials and cosmetics line. Much of her content includes photo and video compilations of makeup tutorials and product features.

Michelle Lewin is a fitness Instagrammer. Lewin has over 13.2 million followers and 1,301 total posts. Her profile description links to her FITPLAN app presence, "Booty Perfection/Gluteos Perfectos," which directs people to pay to access her training programs. Her profile includes exercise videos and photos that flaunt her chiseled body.

YouTube SMIs

The YouTube SMIs are both single and collaborative YouTube SMIs. Collaborative channels are some of the most popular profiles on YouTube through which many SMIs gain status, a social media strategy that SMIs leverage to maintain relevance by working with algorithmic patterns close in mind (Cotter, 2019). The first channel is *Good Mythical Morning*, with Rhett and Link, who have hosted a daily comedy/talk/variety show since 2012. The show has over 1,400 episodes, and the channel has over 14.5 million subscribers. They have appeared multiple times on *The Tonight Show* and were among the first to make daily YouTube content production an episodic trend.

The Try Guys are a foursome who got their start with a channel on BuzzFeed and recently left BuzzFeed to start their own independent production company on YouTube. Their independent channel has over 4.2 million subscribers and forty-three videos since May 2018. They post videos every Wednesday and Saturday, depicting the group trying different things, with titles such as *The Try Guys Try 14 Hours of Labor Pain Simulation.*

Jenna Marbles has vlogged on YouTube since February 2010 and to date has 18.7 million subscribers. She posts new videos every Wednesday that, like The Try Guys, feature Marbles doing different tasks such as *Cutting and Coloring My Boyfriend's Hair.* Marbles has expanded her media content from three- to five-minute parodies to ten- to fifteen-minute task-oriented videos.

LaurDIY joined YouTube in 2011 and has accumulated 8.9 million subscribers. She branded herself initially as a DIY crafter, though her brand has evolved as she has gained more subscribers. Many of her videos maintain the DIY brand while other videos are vlogging or challenge style videos, such as *DIY Disney Halloween Costumes 2018: Lilo, Chip, and Vanellope.*

Nikkie de Jager, or NikkieTutorials, joined YouTube in June 2008, and began hair and makeup tutorials. She now has 11.1 million subscribers and posts new videos every Wednesday and Sunday. She gained online popularity after her video, *The Power of Makeup*, featured her with and without makeup. She posts *The Power of Makeup* videos with A-list celebrities like Kim Kardashian and Drew Barrymore.

RESULTS

The analysis yielded five major themes that capture SMIs' profiles and content production practices, including professional, promotion, personal, interactive, and frequency themes. All content created used these five themes to communicate brand value to followers. The goal of SMIs' content is to maintain relevancy in the greater social network, which is reinforced through posting frequency (Cotter, 2019). Through impression management strategies, incorporated into SMIs' interactive and promotional content, SMIs foster relationships with followers through interactions (e.g., comments and giveaways). Engagement strategies incentivize users to consume SMIs' valuable content as followers feel attached and involved with SMIs' content. Results reveal that macro-SMIs use social media platforms and brand communication to become dominant figures in a seemingly democratized network. Informational entertainment thematically demonstrates commonality among these ten macro-SMIs.

Professional content production characterizes the SMIs' primary function and distinguishes them from other SMIs. Self-disclosure and participatory opportunities for followers promote intimacy in engagement and prompt followers to feel as though they are interacting with the SMI on a genuinely interpersonal (sometimes parasocial) level. This combination of material enhances SMIs' longevity, in addition to their professional profiles, careful attention to detail, authenticity, and frequent posts keep followers engaged, updated, and entertained. Macro-SMIs reap rewards such as fame and expanded entry into traditional entertainment mass media markets while oftentimes maintaining their authenticity that catalyzed their initial ascendance.

Professional

Professional content posts enhance a SMIs' individual brand that solidifies celebrity credibility. Both Cameron Dallas and Michelle Lewin rely on their physical appearance as a driving force of their respective brands, featuring professional still images highlighting their bodies. As a model, Dallas posts photos taken by others that help maintain his brand by featuring himself as the central, unmistakably framed focus. Dallas's professional material often includes minimal captions, leaving followers with little photographic context. Captions typically include emojis with a tag to the photographer's account. Captions featuring the photographer's Instagram account deepen Dallas's credibility further because the photographers themselves are oftentimes communicating their own professional brands on their accounts, creating meaningful layers of status. Other model shots, featured on his profile, are presumably taken with a smartphone camera. Smartphone images supplement the higher-quality shots, communicating a balance of technological professionalism (implied through the professional photographer) and down-to-earth authenticity of selfies, which upholds his SMI celebrification and accessible persona simultaneously.

King Bach's professional short videos feature comedic skits that serve his overarching comedic actor brand. Each video captions the main theme, giving clear context, unlike the celebrity mystique Dallas employs. Bach's videos are captured with smartphones by collaborators who shoot different scenes. Bach's professional content includes pre- and postproduction elements. Preproduction occurs in the subject and clear storyline narrative format of the videos. Postproduction features include edited scene breaks to cohere shots. Bach's filming employs accessible lay user techniques, showcasing same scale relatability and functionality. Bach's preproduction and postproduction work distinguishes itself by illustrating the extra labor that goes into creating his discernibly professional content. It is precisely the lower production value via smartphone, however, that allows Bach to quickly post professional content.

Huda Beauty, Huda Kattan's professional account, consists of reposted professional content from other user's videos featuring various makeup looks. Captions include Kattan crediting profiles that posted the initial content, as she comments directly and features products. These videos simultaneously empower followers with tutorials to achieve the desired makeup looks and promote novel and new beauty products. Kattan's professional content promotes other social media profiles that share beauty-centric content to boost her credibility, by association and in her own right, as a beauty expert among peers. Kattan leverages her professional profile to build her status as a beauty influencer by creating a single space of beauty-related content which is streamlined and redistributed to vast audiences. Her professional content includes fewer original videos and more redistributing and elevating of other relevant content sent to her or that she has found useful on other profiles. Kattan's posting strategies affirm her position as a beauty expert, and her credibility boosts others in the beauty industry more broadly; her SMI status appears individualistic in brand with staunchly collaborative elements at play.

Rhett and Link, creators and stars of *Good Mythical Morning,* post daily videos on multiple YouTube channels. On *Good Mythical Morning,* they release game and activities-based content. Rhett and Link have their own studio, and their videos feature them as hosts, complete with proxemic communication of them seated behind a desk. Professional content usually features Rhett and Link playing unconventionally themed games like taste and household product tests. The *Will It . . . Taste Test* series hosts their most popular videos. Rhett and Link choose a food and test whether other objects can substitute it. Though unconventional and novel, the games incorporate brand-name products and provide viewers information about the products, reminiscent of infotainment. Some videos feature celebrity participants and the duo collaborates routinely with other YouTube SMIs, a common strategy among influencers.

Jenna Marbles's professional content skirts the large-scale production employed by *Good Mythical Morning* and The Try Guys. Marbles's boyfriend helps shoot her professional content at home with their own camera equipment in a style akin to vlogging. Marbles speaks directly to her followers, staring into the camera as she shares thoughts and experiences, such as experimenting with different painting styles, following her dog's antics for twenty-four hours, and composing an outfit to appear taller. Marbles's personality appears through her videos and reinforces her comedic personality. Marbles's overall video structure communicates an obviously simplistic production mode, which accentuates utmost priority on her talent and amusing activities as the primary entertainment force. Compared to other SMIs, Marbles's professional content centers on her personal life most and omits direct capitalistic impulses overall; her personality is her celebrity capital.

Nikkie De Jager posts weekly makeup challenges and full-face video tutorials that break complex makeup looks down into steps, complete with product recommendations like Huda Beauty does. De Jager's videos exude professionalism with a staged set and professional lighting as she speaks directly into a fixed camera. She usually discloses how and why she uses each product and its purpose for her facial complexion and the desired look; she makes complex celebrity makeup styles or looks inspired by popular media into challenges she achieves, empowering followers with steps to create them too. The tutorials range widely from creative, special-occasion looks to natural, pure beauty looks. Her brand communicates that there is something for everyone, rendering even the most high-profile professional and polished makeup looks feasible for followers.

Interactive

Instagram SMIs encourage interactivity through their captions, asking followers to leave impression comments, answer questions, or tag other profiles. This call-to-action technique lends to direct engagement with the SMIs material beyond the more passive liking and viewing consumption patterns. Calls to action fuse SMIs' impression and relational management smoothly. On YouTube, The Try Guys interact with fans in real time by commenting on fan-submitted content, while Keith (one of The Try Guys) points out additional calls to action to sustain momentum. Fully aware of the interactivity outcomes, The Try Guys communicate openly that these interactions boost follower engagement and content circulation. This responsive interactivity makes followers feel valued as they play a pivotal role in an SMI's celebrity status maintenance. SMIs manufacture these interactions intentionally to cultivate an (in)direct communication channel that feels (inter)personally meaningful, intimate even, when a follower gets a response.

King Bach and Zach King frequently call followers to action on Instagram related to their video themes. Both Bach and King use captions to prompt followers to comment about the posts' content, respond to a question, tag friends, or tag other accounts they think would relate and should be in communication with the SMI's posts. When a SMI's caption directly addresses followers with specific questions, the interaction seems personal, though indirect and primarily meant to increase visibility and traffic to the influencer's post. Followers engage with the content in more depth than just "likes" because calls to action prompt deeper thought about the post. Followers understand the voice behind the professional content produced by the SMI and are motivated to interact due to their familiarity with and attraction to the influencer's brand.

Kattan's interactive Huda Beauty Instagram content differs from that of her SMI peers in our sample. The Huda Beauty Instagram account is a conglomerate of other users' material redistributed onto her single platform. Huda Beauty's posts use captions to directly interact with the creators of the content she redistributes. Compared to other SMIs, Huda Beauty offers the most direct interactivity with other accounts as opposed to with followers. For example, Kattan engages those using Huda Beauty products as an affirmation of their support for her brand and successful company. By tagging and reposting, Kattan acknowledges her network and other beauty Instagram SMIs attempting to emulate her. Followers look to Kattan's profile as an online space with high traffic among other related beauty experts, products, and SMIs; having one's own content featured on her highly visible page elevates other beauty industry brands and personalities. Reposting follower content asserts her position as a beauty SMI gatekeeper and recognizes the followers engaging with her brand.

NikkieTutorial videos end with a segment entitled, "Dutch Word of the Day." In this segment, Nikkie shares a Dutch word with her followers, including translation and pronunciation. She then prompts viewers to comment a sentence on her video using the Dutch word or followers can tag or send a video of themselves using the Dutch word to NikkieTutorials. By doing this, followers act at the chance to be featured in her next video. Similarly, LaurDIY incorporates interactive material by featuring a subscriber profile of a "#PrettylittleLaur of the week." At the end of a video, Lauren shouts out to a member of the "#PrettylittleLaur fam," also known as her subscribers. Lauren hosts a link for followers to sign up to be featured in one of her videos. This opportunity for direct interaction with the SMI compels many to action.

Promotional

Promotional overlaps with professional material because of the shared goal of increased SMI brand exposure. Promotional differs from professional material because the promotion is more clearly visible within the posts' themes. Promotional posts range from collaborative content from outside sponsors to creative advertisements promoting side ventures not directly related to social media or their SMI presence, per se. Additionally, promotional content can be distributed on other social media platforms, creating a practice of intersocial media agenda-setting, and that loops back by way of an advertisement to the social media channel the SMI frequents most. This is seen through Instagram influencers linking their Instagram content with YouTube videos or other apps, like Lewin's FITPLAN app. The promotional material volume varies most among Instagram SMIs as they negotiate and grapple with an implied tension around how much to incorporate into their brands. Promotional material, unlike other forms of content featured on influencers' profiles, is the most dissimilar type of content circulated on Instagram by standard non-SMI users. In the creation and dissemination of promotional content, SMIs are keenly aware that this type of post maintains their heightened position within the network. Promotional posts acknowledge outside work and recognize that SMIs have obtained fame through their social media presence, expanding their horizons and capitalistic ventures beyond their SMI celebrity status.

Promotional material includes giveaways and featured clips from external content. Michelle Lewin posts giveaways hosted through the FITPLAN app. She releases the promotions on her Instagram account to advertise her FITPLAN services to her large follower network. Lewin attaches giveaways such as professional promotional videos using the resources of the FITPLAN app. Lewin can then redistribute these advertisements on her Instagram page to increase follower awareness. These promotional videos are meant to share the giveaway and advertise her profile on FITPLAN, which encourages crossover between platforms, because even the stipulations for entry into the giveaway include Instagram and FITPLAN account presence.

Followers must download the FITPLAN app and interact with the specific Instagram post in order to win the cash prize and subscription giveaway. Lewin uses her social media to promote her fitness ventures, adding to her credibility as fitness influencer and trainer. The images in the video showcase Lewin exercising, which explicitly show her fitness abilities and build her credibility in the fitness industry by way of her fit body and skillful workout techniques. Lewin's professional content has a higher production value when created in conjunction with FITPLAN. Due to the capital SMIs accumulate using social media, they enter other platforms and app markets, and continue creating content to suit those app parameters. Moreover, promotional content for most SMIs highlights the social capital within their network and enhances the accumulated credibility in the industry.

Zach King uses promotional material to advertise partnerships with outside companies. These posts are sponsored by external companies that provide resources to create professional content for King and promote their company. Outside companies use King's brand as an entertainer to create popularized, shareable content for his profile and to generate increased awareness of their cause. The intervention of a third-party sponsor is a clear recognition of the monetary power that SMIs hold. Companies recognize the outreach SMIs have in their content and by integrating their company with an SMI, they reach millions of users. SMIs receive monetary compensation for their partnerships with sponsors and elevated recognition as powerful players within the greater social media network. Outside recognition contributes to the accumulation of celebrity capital because they achieve validation from known sponsors thereby increasing an influencer's credibility within their industry.

SMIs add to their own celebrity capital and monetary value by selling merchandise that reflects their brand and advertising their merchandise in posts. SMIs weave reminders akin to product placement practices about their merchandise throughout the course of their professional content. On *Good Mythical Morning*, Rhett and Link use branded *GMM* mugs while at their desk. The Try Guys wear their merchandise in their videos to promote their brands and increase awareness and recognizability of their products. The Try Guys sometimes break from the video theme to explicitly promote merchandise. LaurDIY often wears her own merchandise in videos and segments time to showcase new or limited release merchandise to viewers, an opportunity that motivates followers to monitor for updates about new merchandise.

Promotional material on YouTube is often associated with interactive content. YouTube SMIs host giveaways and require followers to interact with their posts to be eligible for the giveaways. NikkieTutorials frequently incorporate giveaways in her professional videos. For example, over one week's span within a given month, Nikkie posted daily videos that had a different giveaway at the end of each video. All giveaways were connected to her brand as a beauty influencer, with prizes of makeup products or cosmetics gift cards tied to the product lines featured in her videos. To be eligible for giveaways, Nikkie requires viewers to be subscribed to her channel, and "like" and "comment" on the video that giveaways are announced in. Not only are followers engaging with content with the hopes of being recognized by Nikkie, but they have the chance to win tangible prizes. Giveaways drive attention to SMIs' content because viewers must interact with the material and monitor the profile to check whether they have won. Plus, Nikkie leverages her position in the beauty industry to share the benefits of freebies due to her commodified celebrity status. Giveaways highlight her elevated position within the media network but communicate genuine relationship maintenance with her followers by making sure they stay in the know so they can win products.

Giveaways, discount codes, and other promotions recognize influencer voices within the network as tangibly valuable and reward followers' engagement. Incentives create a reward system for followers' continued consumption of the SMI's content. Giveaways function similarly as a powerful form of secret sharing, a type of personal information disclosure and exclusivity that helps positively cultivate rewards and benefits of relationship maintenance, even if mostly existing parasocially; the potential for real interpersonal interaction greatly motivates loyal followers (Bickart et al., 2015).

Personal

Personal material, understood as outside the bounds of brand promotion and maintenance, varies across Instagram influencers including how they share personal information via social media. Personal content gives a more holistic, realistic glimpse into the lives of SMIs and conveys that they are attuned to the sort of content often posted by lay users. Personal material can include personal images clearly taken by the SMI, which is content not intended to pass as their professional material. This content is often removed from a lot of aspects of production seen in a SMI's professional material making it seem relatable to followers. Personal depictions include captions, pictures, and videos that share personal life moments that resonate with how lay users tend to post to their own social media profiles. Personal content often discloses information about the SMI that would not be revealed in their professional content. SMIs use their names as the foundations of their brands and generate professional content that becomes associated with their names. By including personal material, SMIs become more relatable to followers because personal material permits followers to peek into the real lives of SMIs.

Cameron Dallas uses Instagram to share personal material in many ways. Dallas's profile features personal posts that depict his family and dog. For example, Dallas shared a photo of himself in front of a board about to guess the sex of his sister's baby. These posts share personal moments in Dallas's life that do not promote his brand directly. Many distinctly personal posts are videos Dallas shoots himself of daily occurrences or special events in his family life. Personal posts capitalize on down-to-earth familiarity and routine practices many users enact, such as taking mirror selfies. This more mundane content stands in stark contrast to the professionally produced brand content. Personal content normalizes the influencer within the media network by connecting them to their followers and enhancing their authenticity by way of likeability and relatability. The strategic, selective practice of sharing personal content maintains follower-SMI relationships by demonstrating that SMIs are, to some extent, ordinary people, accessible celebrities who, in many ways, are just like their followers. Relationship maintenance continues the development of parasocial relationships that feel much like interpersonal relationships between influencers and followers. Undoubtedly, professional material assumes utmost importance to SMIs, however, accompanied with strategic, relatable, amusing, and mundane personal material gives followers a more holistic, realistic view of the type of genuine people the SMIs are, despite their celebrification.

YouTube SMIs, like Instagram SMIs, create entire vlogs based on personal material. These videos feature SMIs talking directly to the camera and sharing personal information. As with reality TV, contrived reality feels more authentic because the disclosure draws viewers in to be a part of the realities these otherwise inaccessible celebrity personalities experience (Andrejevic, 2003). Due to the nature of social media, even macro-SMIs are more accessible to viewers than TV personalities. The Try Guys' personal material usually features a single member of the group sharing a personal experience. In The Try Guys' video entitled, *My Secret Girlfriend,* Zach shares with his followers that he has been in a relationship for two years. The video is outside of the brand and focuses on Zach sharing information about his personal life that he has chosen to keep secret from followers. Zach confides in the camera, addressing both his girlfriend and followers to share publicly the reasons behind keeping the relationship a secret. The video is shot with a high-film quality, but, due to the nature of the content in the video, it requires less production which deviates from the professional content norms by also focusing on a single Try Guy. The Try Guys' standard content usually features the entire group and does not allow for a single voice to take center stage. As The Try Guys have grown in popularity since creating their own channel, they are taking noticeably more ownership over their content and including more personal information in their videos. Other SMIs create similar content where they break from their professional content to post self-disclosing information.

LaurDIY's personal material appears in her weekly vlogs as she shares clips from activities throughout her week, like shopping or getting a haircut. LaurDIY has also posted personal videos that disclose information about her intentionally private life but that she feels as though needs to be addressed on her public platform. For example, LaurDIY posted a video entitled "*i owe you an explanation,*" to explain why she and her partner broke up. LaurDIY shared personal details not only about her breakup but also the desire to keep certain aspects of her life private while understanding the role she has as an influencer to be a public figure, which includes accountability to her followership. The video's candid and honest tone describes her rationale for taking an intentional break from professional content to acknowledge important moments in her personal life and how they might intertwine with her social media practices. The vulnerability of acknowledging the challenges associated with navigating the fine line between celebrity and private person presents challenges to maintain as separate.

Frequency

For the most part, the content that is released by Instagram influencers requires a lower production value than YouTube content. As a result, the frequency that Instagram influencers release professional content is greater than YouTube SMIs. Three of the five Instagram SMIs follow a similar posting schedule debuting new content roughly every day or every two to three days (such as Cameron Dallas, King Bach, and Michelle Lewin). The content created by these three SMIs requires preproduction planning elements, though the preparation required to share personal or interactive material demands less-professional material. Frequency is also dependent on the type of message being posted. Having a rotation of professional, personal, and promotional content, SMIs may increase their content posting rate. Instagram influencers typically post multiple times a week in order to reinforce their presence in the stream of content that followers consume every day.

The key difference between the two platforms is the frequency of content production by influencers. Instagram focuses on shorter content at a lower production scale which is posted more frequently than YouTube SMIs. Therefore, YouTube SMIs' professional content is longer, of a higher production quality, and posted less frequently than on Instagram. Most SMIs publicize in their videos and on their channels when they post new videos, as constant self-promotion expectations abound for SMIs to stay relevant. Influencers remind viewers that they can activate alerts to get notifications when new content is posted.

YouTube professional content is thematic content averaging between twelve to fifteen minutes per video. Each influencer included in this study has a grounding theme that is central to their personal brand and present in their content production. Most professional videos have an activity, challenge, or tutorial as the grounding theme of the video. In order to create these videos, SMIs must account for pre- and post-production time. This time is used to edit and cut videos before posting. YouTube SMIs' strict posting schedules enable them to change content to vary the posting schedule to maintain continuity within a predictable schedule, but also include novel dynamic additions. For example, The Try Guys post new videos every Wednesday and Saturday but have released shorter videos on days off from their normal posting schedule, which excites followers because these short posts stray from the schedule rhythm. Like The Try Guys, LaurDIY follows a bi-weekly posting schedule though she mixes her content between vlogging and DIY videos. She records content throughout the week to be included in her vlogs. Her DIY challenge videos generally attract more views than her vlogs, but the vlogs facilitate relationship maintenance with her subscribers through more personal, interactive content that reaffirms followers' connection with influencers and maintains their status as a powerful voice.

DISCUSSION

SMIs mark a shift into a new category of celebrity by cultivating capital via entertaining social media activities thereby expanding the avenues through which such capital might be achieved. Unlike how most celebrities rise to prominence, SMIs build their brands through routine, direct, and engaging forms of communication with their followers. They establish an image, cultivate followers, grow their subscribership, and maintain their looking glass self-impression management of their SMI personas by posting a combination of professional and personal content related to their overarching brand in various industries. While reaching celebrity status typically requires a reliance on powerful industry resources within hierarchical structures beyond one's personal control to achieve public awareness, SMIs take a sort of grassroots approach in brand creation and public-facing content production. Like reality TV stars and the accompanying contrived reality, they immerse themselves in, with neatly packaged and edited stories, the authentic personality of the layperson-turned-celebrity SMI status appears self-made through market-driven brand cultivation and dedication to nurturing interactivity with followers. Interestingly, drawing upon horizontal communication and a collaborative approach to cross-posting, SMIs tag other SMIs or social media accounts thematically related to their own branding. This mutually beneficial leveraging potential creates a realm where SMIs help uphold one another once they ascend to macrostatus. Gaining attention, monetary support, and promotional brand opportunities from larger industry players that represent product lines, for example, enhances the already-thriving SMIs and their respective brands. SMIs, however, stay at the helm of their own content production, brand cultivation, and brand evolution that tows a careful, strategic line between professional and polished entertaining, informational, skills-based content and their own authentic, individual personalities. Indeed, SMIs who dedicate substantial time and energy into attaching a brand to their personal profiles help create a pool of micro- and macrolevel influencers that can boost discursive voices to the top of a greater network of users.

New norms, thanks to the widespread and frequent usage of social media, have fueled a perceived sense of direct accessibility of layusers to social media celebrity personalities. The unique strategies of mass interpersonal interaction help foster relationships and connections between SMIs and their followers, spawning greater expectations of accessibility perhaps spread among other types of celebrities in the public stage. We are witnessing an impact on traditional celebrity culture; SMI celebrity culture perhaps inadvertently pressures traditional celebrities into creating original content and building their personal brands through their social media presence. The democratization of celebrity capital essentially enables the bottom-up celebrification process to ensue by also influencing how traditional celebrities maintain their professional and personal profiles, as evidenced by their social media presence and posting habits. For example, actors Zac Efron and Will Smith have created YouTube channels where they publish original content outside of their established film careers. Another example includes the tendency for TV shows, particularly talk shows, to release segments from their shows on YouTube, making them accessible to millions of viewers who may not be subscribed to cable services. The *Carpool Karaoke* video segment periodically aired on *The Late Late Show with James Corden* is then released on the show's YouTube channel and typically receives over a million views, providing evidence of a rejuvenated second life of already produced and aired content. The massive popularity of social media as a powerful, dominant form of entertainment media has shifted the demand for ever-increasing accessible content that then permeates many other forms of entertainment media. We are witnessing a pivotal point in new media convergence history that levels out and effectively democratizes preexisting hierarchies of closely gatekept mass messages disseminated to diverse audiences.

CONCLUSION

Social media and SMIs have changed society's perception of celebrity status by reshaping traditional attributions of fame around a variety of expertise areas including entertainment branding as actors, models, and comedians, or informational experts on popular topics such as beauty or fitness. Once an SMI carves their own brand expertise, they actively serve their follower base by committing to the ongoing creation of new content routinely that reinforces their brand(s). As Jenkins (2008) describes, "in the world of media convergence, every important story gets told, every brand gets sold, and every consumer gets courted across multiple media platforms" (p. 3). SMIs rise as dominant figures in a seemingly democratized network through social media; they constitute a new generation of celebrities who gain recognition and popularity through repetition and frequency. Repeated exposure reinforces the presence of the SMI within their followers' network and garners recognition and credibility across an ever-expanding share of the social media and expanded digital landscape. The voices that achieve attention in our convergent media landscape often are those circulating and capitalizing upon social media productivity. For example, Jenna Marbles is a host on Sirius XM radio and The Try Guys had a book published this year. SMIs have restructured definitions of celebrity status and the tools and labor necessary to obtain it.

Our data reveal that SMIs' content thematically clusters into five key elements: professional, personal, interactive, promotional, and frequency. SMIs publish a multiplicity of thematic content to entice users' loyal followership, which increases their elevated exposure and leads to more followers, which builds celebrity capital. Self-disclosing and participatory content allow for standard users to engage and interact meaningfully with SMIs. This fusion promotes SMIs' longevity on social media, as they maintain profiles that house professionally entertaining material. SMIs expertly manage their profiles in ways that bring traditional notions of entertainment onto social media, which blur the boundaries of celebrification potential through self-branding and mass-market communication. SMIs, like reality television personalities, have established a new form of fame that is cultivated from a staged reality. Because they exude authentic personalities, lay users feel a more direct connection and relationship to influencers through personal disclosure, (para) social relationships, and promotions. Followers consume their content and attribute capital to them through millions of followers, views, tags, likes, and comments.

The SMI's brand connects them to industries where they can establish credibility and garner fame through elevated visibility. Creating brands and distributing content related to their brands establishes influencers as credible voices, and the information that they distribute is seen as exclusive information. Companies outside of social media recognize SMIs and target them to promote their products, which serves to further credit SMIs as public figures. Thus, SMIs achieve celebrity status through reinforced interactions with millions of followers. It is essential to recognize SMIs beyond their monetary market power and validate what their social media practices unveil about what it takes to achieve a popular voice with widespread attention from captive social media follower audiences who ultimately uphold SMIs' mainstay celebrity status. This ascent to fame on social media is useful to understanding the entertainment industry as media convergence culture continually evolves.

REFERENCES

Andrejevic, M. (2003). *Reality TV: The work of being watched*. Rowman & Littlefield Publishers.

Bickart, B., Kim, S., Pai, S., & Brunel, F. (2015). How social media influencers build a brand following by sharing secrets. In S. Fournier, M. Breazeale, & J. Avery (Eds.), *Strong brands, strong relationships* (pp. 212–224). Routledge.

Bilandzic, H., Patriarche, G., & Traudt, P. J. (Eds.). (2012). *The social use of media: Cultural and social scientific perspectives on audience research*. Intellect.

Booth, N., & Matic, J. A. (2011). Mapping and leveraging influencers in social media to shape corporate brand perceptions. *Corporate Communications: An International Journal, 16*(3), 184–191. https://doi.org/10.1108/13563281111156853.

Braithwaite, D. O., & Schrodt, P. (Eds.). (2014). *Engaging theories in interpersonal communication: Multiple perspectives*. Sage Publications.

Bruns, A. (2006). Towards produsage: Futures for user-led content production. In C. Ess, F. Sudweeks, & H. Hrachovec. (Eds.), *Proceedings of the 5th international conference on cultural attitudes towards technology and communication* (pp. 275–284). School of Information Technology.

Bullingham, L., & Vasconcelos, A. C. (2013). "The presentation of self in the online world": Goffman and the study of online identities. *Journal of Information Science, 39*(1), 101–112. https://doi.org/10.1177/0165551512470051

Cotter, K. (2019). Playing the visibility game: How digital influencers and algorithms negotiate influence on Instagram. *New Media & Society, 21*(4), 895–913. https://doi.org/10.1177/1461444818815684

Driessens, O. (2013a). Celebrity capital: Redefining celebrity using field theory. *Theory and Society, 42*(5), 543–560. https://doi.org/10.1007/s11186-013-9202-3

Driessens, O. (2013b). The celebritization of society and culture: Understanding the structural dynamics of celebrity culture. *International Journal of Cultural Studies, 16*(6), 641–657. https://doi.org/10.1177/1367877912459140

Freberg, K., Graham, K., McGaughey, K., & Freberg, L. A. (2011). Who are the social media influencers? A study of public perceptions of personality. *Public Relations Review, 37*(1), 90–92. https://doi.org/10.1016/j.pubrev.2010.11.001

Giles, D. (2012). Parasocial relationships: Current directions in theory and method. In H. Bilandzic, G. Patriarche, & P. J. Traudt (Eds.), *The social use of media: Cultural and social scientific perspectives on audience research* (pp. 161–176). Intellect.

Goffman, E. (1978). *The presentation of self in everyday life.* Harmondsworth.

Goffman, E. (2017). *Interaction ritual: Essays in face-to-face behavior.* Routledge.

Jenkins, H. (2004). The cultural logic of media convergence. *International Journal of Cultural Studies, 7*(1), 33–43. https://doi.org/10.1177/1367877904040603

Jenkins, H. (2008). *Convergence culture: Where old and new media collide.* 2006. New York University Press.

Jenkins, H., Ford, S., & Green, J. (2018). *Spreadable media: Creating value and meaning in a networked culture* (Vol. 15). New York University Press.

Kádár, M., & Könczey, Z. (2014). The content management of media convergence. *Journal of Media Research, 7*(3), 25–32. http://search.proquest.com/docview/1649753539/

Kahle, L. R., & Valette-Florence, P. (2012). *Marketplace lifestyles in an age of social media: Theory and methods.* Routledge.

Peräkylä, A., & Ruusuvuori, J. (2018). Analyzing talk and text. *Collecting and Interpreting Qualitative Materials, 3*, 351–374.

Pew Research Center. (2018). *Social media use in 2018.* https://www.pewresearch.org/internet/2018/03/01/social-media-use-in-2018/

Sanders, S., Sastry, A., & McCall, A. (2019, September 10). *It's been a minute with Sam Sanders: "The new celebrity": The rise of influencers – And how they changed advertising* [audio podcast]. Website. https://www.npr.org/2019/09/09/759127302/the-new-celebrity-the-rise-of-influencers-and-how-they-changed-advertising

Schiappa, E., Allen, M., & Gregg, P. (2007). Parasocial relationships and television: A metaanalysis of the effects. In R. Preiss, B. Gayle, N. Burrell, M. Allen, & J. Bryant (Eds.), *Mass media effects: Advances through meta-analysis* (pp. 301–314). Lawrence Erlbaum.

Weinswig, D. (2018, January 4). Deep dive: The rise of social media influencers and their brands. *CoreSight Research.* https://coresight.com/research/deep-dive-the-rise-of-social-media-influencers-and-their-brands/

Wissman, B. (November 18, 2018). Micro-influencers: The marketing force of the future? https://www.forbes.com/sites/barrettwissman/2018/03/02/micro-influencers-the-marketing-force-of-the-future/

Chapter 3

Micro-SMI

The Beginning of a Theoretical Model

Lisa Harrison

Communication fundamentals, combined with the complex structure of social media platforms (SMPs), and digital citizens' capability to increase influence through sharing, publishing, and networking has contributed to the emergence of the micro-social media influencer (micro-SMI) (Senft, 2013). This chapter establishes the context of a doctoral research project within disrupted contemporary media and communication practices, that examines the notion of SMP users as micro-SMI and proposes the beginning of a theoretical model for emergent practices of ordinary digital citizens as micro-SMI. This chapter presents a theoretical model that establishes five dimensions and attempts to define micro-SMI as it emerges from the literature and is supported by data from semi-structured interviews with twelve Australian micro-SMI. The theoretical model provides a foundational framework for to understand the dimensions of micro-SMI and as a guide for developing a successful micro-SMI presence.

LITERATURE REVIEW

Personal influence was first characterized by Elihu Katz and Paul Lazarsfeld (1964) in the seminal text "Personal Influence" as a phenomenon of human social structures and behaviors that describe individuals whose opinions are a valued part of a community and distinguishes them as more likely to encourage the community to act. SMP have become a major form of public communication in their own right (Bruns & Burgess, 2016), and as digital citizens learn to manipulate the megaphone effect of SMP for personal influence, the question of what defines micro-SMI arises. Micro-SMI is specific to SMP and is a new context for personal influence, celebrity, and entrepreneurship.

The notion of micro-SMI was first discussed by Graeme Turner (2004) in terms of celebrification and a mode of digital identity referring to these social media users as having microcelebrity. Since then several scholars have contributed to this field of knowledge such as Theresa Senft (2008), Alice Marwick (2013), and Chrystal Abidin (2015a). Senft (2008) defines micro-SMI as, "a new style of online performance that involves people 'amping up' their popularity over the web using technologies like video, blogs and SMP" (p. 25). John Bargh and Katelyn McKenna (2004) argue social media has weakened relationships because of a lack of face-to-face interaction; however, researchers such as Francis Fukuyama (2001) and Nancy Baym (2015) assume opportunity in the wake of SMP and argue that it changes the form and context of relationships. As paradigms of media, economy, and consumers converge (Jenkins, 2006), individuals have never had such easy access to information and knowledge or opportunity to engender influence. Described as the knowledge and attention economy by danah boyd and Alice Marwick (2011), personalized sharing of content breeds networked social information and knowledge, providing opportunities for influence to varying degrees (Kwon et al., 2014).

SMP activity is an important expression of identity and, therefore, of a personal and/or professional brand (Boyd, 2007). Central to the success of micro-SMI is how individuals manage their online brand and cultivate social capital through intimate relationships with their followers (Marwick, 2013). Researchers agree that there has been a tremendous growth in micro-SMI as a career path, and this new luminary has diverse challenges to navigate (Abidin, 2015a; Baym, 2015; Marwick & Boyd, 2011; Senft, 2013). Brooke Duffy (2016) argues that micro-SMI are aspirational laborers seeking to "mark themselves as creative producers and who will one day be compensated for their talents" (p. 446). As a micro-SMI accumulates social and economic capital, their commercial opportunities increase, creating external demands and tensions between credibility and commercial success. The emerging profession of micro-SMI is ambiguous because of contemporary challenges and pressures from followers and commercial norms.

Micro-SMI, while engaging in the public domain of SMP, are open to digital scrutiny and can be forced into open debate, which can lead to harassment or trolling (Barnes, 2018; Phillips, 2015; van Laer, 2014). Whitney Phillips (2015) study of trolls found that "trolls believe nothing should be taken seriously, and regard public displays of sentimentality, political conviction, and/ or ideological rigidity a call to trolling arms" (p. 25). Trolling, as a behavior, is the product of multiple factors, and all participants know that being more public increases the possibility of being trolled. Ironically, trolls rely on anonymity and Phillips (2015) argues successful trolling often depends on the target's lack of anonymity. James Donald et al. (2019) suggest that educational, professional, and family interventions are important to foster healthy use of SMP.

METHODOLOGY

This study used literature, informed grounded theory, twelve in-depth semi-structured interviews with Australian micro-SMIs, and reflective practice of my professional industry experience to develop a proposed model to define micro-SMI. The theoretical model presents a working set of characteristics, strategies, and indicators based on findings from current scholarship on influence. The model uses five dimensions: personal attributes, content attributes, outcomes generated, behavior and strategies, and network characteristics.

The recruitment process started with a data mining exercise on Twitter using qualitative and quantitative indicators (defined by literature review) and identified an extensive list of potential micro-SMI accounts. I reviewed the accounts for authenticity and relevance, to eliminate spam accounts and those of individuals who had celebrity status before or separate from their social media accounts. It was also important for the study to gain an understanding of different industries and genders while remaining focused on Australian residents. Much scholarship is focused within the cultural context of the United States; we know little about the similarities or differences for micro-SMI in Australia.

Participants were interviewed in 2018, either in person or via video conferencing. I collected 600 minutes of interview data from twelve participants of various backgrounds, industries, and motivations. Table 3.1 includes a list of participants and their Twitter bios. The interviews showed further essential aspects that need to be integrated with the initial theoretical model to offer a more thorough and rigorous construct. Figure 1 provides a visual summary of the key themes that arose across the interviews, overlaid onto the model developed from the literature review. There is no particular order for the dimensions and sub-dimensions; rather, this is a high-level overview of the themes that define micro-SMI. It is important to recognize that an individual need not meet all the dimensions to be considered a micro-SMI but provides a model for best practice.

INTERVIEW FINDINGS

It was interesting to find most participants were surprised and humbled by the prospect of being recognized as a micro-SMI. IL said, "I feel embarrassed because you're doing a significant project and I don't feel I've got much substance to add." By contrast, BL initially declined the invitation saying:

> Thanks for thinking of me. Sadly, I don't think I'll be able to help, because I find the idea [that] I'm a micro-SMI or have a brand a little icky. I know I have a following, but I don't attach myself to products.

Table 3.1 Interview Participant Information[1]

	Code	Full Name	Twitter Profile Description
1	MK	Mel Kettle	Communication & social media expert. Works with associations. Speaker. Author of The Social Association. Mentor. Cooks. Reads. Loves Shaun. Lives life.
2	AA	Anthony Agius aka decryption	Author of The Sizzle, a daily tech e-mail newsletter. North Melbourne Kangaroos supporter
3	BL	Ben Law	Writer, entrepreneur & local homosexual
4	MR	Matthew Rimmer	MR: Professor of IP & Innovation Law
5	KR	Kimberley Ramplin	BMA (Int'l Relations) UNSW. Holder of unpopular opinions, sometimes paid to share them. RT = smart people. Poetry, procycling,
6	JJ	Jocelyn Seip	media comms gal, i love sport & australian idol. find my hot takes on
7	KK	Keith Keller	TWITTER VIDEO MARKETING SPECIALIST @ BeSeenTV2020 Featuring @SheenaAlexandra Supportive Online Community #BeSeenTV2020 Sharing Your Story With The World.
8	S	Stilgherrian	Word-whore. I write 'em. I talk 'em. • Cybers, politics, media. • Signal +0000000000 • Wickr S • All hail Eris! Vive les poissons rouges sauvages!
9	IL	Ian Lawton	Life is short, love fiercely, do stuff that matters, be real.
10	MN	Mark Newton	Overopinionated geek. It turns out the other guy rusted first. Opinions are mine, all mine. Get a goddamn warrant. he/him/his
11	SS	Sam Sheppard	#Leadership #Diversity #Women#KeynoteSpeaker #ThoughtLeaderAmbassador @IndustryWomen Licensed Housing Builder
12	MP	Mark Pesce	Futurist, inventor, author, educator, speaker & broadcaster. Award-winning columnist @ TheRegister. Podcasts @nextbillionsecs + @ twistartupsaus. VRML/MRS. ENFJ.

[1] Profiles accessed April 16, 2018.

BL highlights a typical concern of micro-SMI that they wish to avoid being associated with the potential of commercial gain from their SMP identities. BL agreed to contribute when I clarified the project was not related to marketing, but the use of SMP, the individual, and their networks. Perhaps the reluctance of some participants to be identified as micro-SMI may be because of the shift from traditional advertising to trusted micro-SMI. Users do not want to be sold to, and participants are concerned that commercializing their profile could devalue their social capital as a micro-SMI. By contrast, marketing consultant MK, tech journalist ST, and futurist MP were not surprised to be asked to take part in the project, which may be because of their backgrounds in media and their appropriation of SMP as a tool of their trade.

Participants use SMP as self-expression, which reflects their sense of identity. Participants discussed using different SMP for different aspects of their lives and create sub-SMP-identities to manage this process. BL said his Twitter profile is "completely public," whereas his Facebook page is kept for more intimate relationships with friends and family. This was also the case for SS, KR, and MN. AA confessed his dislike of Facebook but uses Facebook Business Pages to support his business model. MK uses most of the popular SMP and said she is working on building a LinkedIn profile to market her business. The complex maze of channels, profiles, and communities means that separating personal and professional worlds (context collapse) is challenging. ST noted that the blur between his personal self and SMP identity is not a new thing:

> For people working in the media, particularly the journalists and news/information/current affairs producers and so on, that has always been a blurry boundary. Part of your job is knowing about the world and learning things about many things, so it's always been blurry.

The tension between creating a sustainable career and the risk of commercialization is further complicated by authenticity, a common concern among the participants.

All participants were busy, motivated individuals and agreed that SMP added another layer of complexity to their lives. Most participants knew their own sensibilities and not only have practical strategies in place to manage the new stressors of engaging on SMP, such as time management, but also have been more assertive. ST summed it up when he told me about a recent lecture, he presented to journalism students. A student asked ST, "Where should the line be drawn on being assertive or controversial on Twitter?" ST replied, "Students need to know what works for them. Having an awareness of self allows the participants to engage on social media from an empowered position." A position reflected by most participants: "I've always stood up for what I believe in and I've always backed myself," said MK.

The publicness of SMP is at the core of micro-SMI and essential for visibility, but balancing this against oversharing was also a challenge for the participants. BL said:

> I write columns about my life, I've written a memoir about my life, I've got a TV show out there based on my life. I guess it's like I'm not too wary of sharing personal stuff, but I'm not going to over-share because I think that's gross and vomitus.

Participants accept the positive and negative consequences of publicness on SMP, from building a network, meeting new clients, and/or friends to limiting their opportunities by association with these same networks. ST said, "If they don't like my content/opinions, then I don't want to engage with them anyhow." While we may see this as arrogant, for ST it is a practical strategy for selecting when to engage. MN mentioned that his public profile was scrutinized when interviewed for a new position.

Some participants admitted to using a personal filter to manage this challenge and choose a conservative approach. SS describes her experience:

> I'm careful with opinions now. If you've got a thick skin, that's great, but if you don't have a thick skin, you're best not to ruffle people's feathers, I guess. Have an opinion but keep to yourself and keep it to your friends.

The fine line here for participants is sharing the not-so-happy alongside celebrations and accomplishments while remaining humble. If an individual does not get this balance right, it can backfire, so it is important to know what details to share and what to leave out. This is not about being fake, but understanding personal boundaries, the audience, and platform etiquette.

AA, BL, MK, SS, and JS admit using SMP all of the time. Some participants were pragmatic in their time management and suggested that without time management strategies in place, having a visible SMP identity can overwhelm and lead to mental health challenges, particularly when events such as trolling can consume emotional capacity. Most participants had a routine and a process they go through every day, while others were more reactive or even unconscious of their strategies, depending on their schedules and what is happening around them. For example, MN said, "I'll be waiting for the computer to do something, if I'm waiting for a code to compile or something like that and it's easy just having a file to tweet." Sometimes, participants disengaged with their audiences as a matter of self-empowerment. This action then created another tension for the participants: not using SMP could trigger emotions and the "fear of missing out" (FOMO), but this more an acknowledgement than a primary concern.

Participants spoke of making real-life connections that started on Twitter but became something more. Participants' shared stories of exchanging ideas and knowledge through content, to prove themselves as authoritative and trustworthy. BL added:

> I've made real life connections whether they're professional or personal, some of the closest friends that I've got in Sydney are people that I met through Twitter. I don't think that would happen as often because Twitter has gotten so big.

Based on the notion of face-to-face networking, the participants knew who, what, and when to engage with other users to create a value exchange and increase in social capital. BL said his "value system drives how he uses social media; he wants to be helpful, and also be helped."

All participants were early adopters, and they started by experimenting with forums and message boards. ST joined Twitter in 2007 less than twelve months after launching, so by association he is an early adopter. IL added that:

> being an early adopter, every now and again you get lucky, we had Julian Lennon shared a post of ours a couple of years ago, and we grew by 100,000 followers in the course of about six months; you can't make that happen.

Curiosity is the most common reason the participants started using SMP— interestingly an important characteristic of entrepreneurship. Friends encouraged them or they saw this new, interesting technology in the media and wanted to know more about it. MP said the reason he enjoyed Twitter so much was he found it "experimental in terms of the kinds of temporary communities." SS explained, "I had heard about Twitter in the media and things like that, so I thought well, that might be an interesting one." MR confessed to creating an SMP identity because of curiosity and has kept his profile relevant by using a process of experimentation, stating "there's always a process of experimentation with all forms of new technology." KK calls himself a kinesthetic learner, a theme common among the participants, who all have a pragmatic approach to developing their tacit knowledge for managing their SMP identity.

Objectives for the participants were flexible and evolved depending on the individual's motivations. Some participants spoke of joining Twitter to discuss political or social issues, some see it as a business opportunity, and others for personal branding. MP was clear about using SMP to control the social graph. IL showed flexibility with his objectives. He started out using social media as part of a social enterprise, then incorporated a business model, and now it is about community. His motivations have always been about his community but outside forces mean objectives may not be as realistic as they initially were. He said, "I grew a community organically through the platforms (without paid advertising) but social media has changed so much since."

Most participants had a high level of expectation from their SMP; they spoke about being reflective and analyzing their strategies. Strategies ranged from data-driven analysis to implied and intuitive processes showing entrepreneurial characteristics. AA told me he is improving his use of the platforms to adapt to his customers/audience, yet was vague about his reasoning for wanting to do so. KK identified SMP as a marketing and branding tool early on and continues to approach SMP in this way. The participants are time-poor and driven by perfection; they are motivated to ensure their profiles provide a return on investment. "Good investment" for the participants implies not only commercial but also personal gain (knowledge, network, or social). An interesting insight from MR was that his social media profile also has historical value, and he saw digital legacy as an archive.

When discussing strategies for visibility, IL approaches his profiles by "not worrying about it." He acknowledged that if he paid for advertising, followed the algorithms, and was more strategic about it, he would achieve more. This was not the approach of all participants; JS said, "it just takes a couple of scrolls once it's updated to figure out what's going on." Thus, implying that JS's tacit knowledge of the SMP means her adaptation to any changes in the algorithms has become an unconscious response.

Throughout the interviews, a gender-based disparity emerged about issues affecting participants' mental health and how they managed both practically and emotionally. The male participants found it easier to separate their SMP identity from their self. The female participants spoke of feeling objectified as they were more likely to attach emotions to SMP identity. Participant's all agreed this is a gendered phenomenon and a complex cultural discourse, and it is not only afforded to labor practices. MP said, "I have never been trolled in the way I've seen other people trolled, particularly women." JS shared a story about the abuse attracted by an insignificant update to her profile picture:

> It just comes with the territory of being a woman on the internet. It's just that they want to like scream at you when you have opinions. For example, when my photo was a child, less people were tweeting me awful stuff and I'm like, Okay, you think I'm a child. But my picture's just me and I know men think it's fun to comment awful stuff, so sometimes I change it back. I think about, maybe I should just go private, maybe it's not even worth it especially when sometimes a tweet goes a little bit viral, but I'm a strong person I can hack it most of the time.

Even though the participants said women tend to be more vulnerable to trolls, it does not mean men are unaffected. BL is open about his sexuality as a gay man and has also been targeted by trolls: "Trolls who will say racist homophobic things and try anything." BL also admitted to trolling and enjoying the experience. He said, "I've been both the victim and the perpetrator of online shaming and it can feel good to online shame people. Right? Because they're so wrong and they need to know it."

It is not only trolls that impact well-being. Participants described having the urge to check in and respond to followers quickly. KR described using social media as "crack cocaine" and JS said, "it's an addiction." The expectation of participation and the want to be seen in a positive light are just some of the pressures described by female participants. Having a clear strategy and not getting bogged down in "the little stuff" is how SS keeps a balance. She deleted her Instagram account because she felt herself becoming depressed by it, in terms of the pressure to take the right picture, with the right filter, wearing the right outfit, and in the right location. She elaborated by saying it can also be a positive experience when approached with the right mindset. KR said mental health was the reason she had to quit Twitter on couple of occasions and related it to Stephen Fry (an English comedian) deactivating his Twitter account because of a nasty trolling incident in 2016.

The interview insights support aspects of current scholarship, such as authenticity, aspirational labor, and contextual collapse. It also highlights aspects of micro-SMI that have limited scholarship, such as engagement strategies, mental health, gender disparity, entrepreneurship, and tacit knowledge. The following begins to define a complex model of five dimensions for understanding micro-SMI, and how it may be identified for further research or emulated by digital citizens to support their professional development.

FIVE DIMENSIONS OF MICRO-SMI

Micro-SMI is a phenomenon that is multidimensional comprising of conscious and subconscious behaviors, personality attributes, personal motivations, and outside forces. The following theoretical model (Table 3.2) introduces five interrelated fundamental dimensions of micro-SMI: personal attributes, content attributes, outcomes generated, strategy, and network characteristics. Established using current scholarship and interview data the dimensions provide a narrative of micro-SMI practice/s, skills, knowledge, how/why they became a micro-SMI, how they think about themselves in the role of micro-SMI, and how they juggle the challenges of an unprecedented and evolving paradigm. By introducing the five dimensions, this chapter contributes to many fields of knowledge as a starting point for further research into SMP identity and how it relates to literacy, community, personal identity, professional development, and many more societal repercussions. In the following sections, I will investigate these dimensions in more detail, pointing to more specific research.

Personal Attributes

The first of the five dimensions conceptualizes the skills, knowledge, and abilities of individuals beyond niche content knowledge and gained from experience. These characteristics make the micro-SMI a unique individual and are defined in five sub-dimensions: perception, identity, reciprocity, entrepreneurship, and motivation. Quantification of personal attributes is precarious as we try to articulate how a micro-SMI perceives themselves and how others

Table 3.2 Five Dimensions Social Media Influence: Theoretical Model

		QUALITATIVE INDICATORS		QUANTITATIVE INDICATORS	
PERSONAL ATTRIBUTES	Perception (public/self)	Perceived positively, as credible, trustworthy, knowledgeable or expert.	user sentiment	Number of followers (across various platforms)	platform metrics
	Reciprocity	Contribute an authoritative and trustworthy viewpoint Considered altruistic, philan-thropic and a leader Collaboration	network survey	Regularity of posts Reciprocal engagement with followers	platform metrics
CONTENT ATTRIBUTES	Entrepreneurial	Early adopter, competitive, curious, recognises opportunity, commercial motivations, reflective	SMI interview	N/A	
	Visibility	N/A	content coding / close reading	High visibility for SMI's content on search results	search engine ranking
	Topic	Content quality, originality, consistency of topics, debate, knowledge sharing	user sentiment	N/A	
	Relevance	Entertaining, distinct perspective on topic, addressing audience needs		N/A	
OUTCOMES GENERATED	Inspire Action	Perceived impact on follower activities.	user sentiment	Quantity of follower responses received, increased wom on products / services / causes	platform metrics
	Generate Public Debate	First point of call when looking for advice, guidance or suggestions on a given topic.	SMI interview	Quantity of personal endorse-ments received	platform metrics
	Endorsements	N/A		Consistency of follower responses received; quantity of personal endorsements received	platform metrics
STRATEGIES	Engagement Strategy	Engagement strategy, considered platforms, clear understand-ing & manipulation of platform affordances, algorithms, and analytics.	SMI interviews	Scheduling Observable and consistent implementation of content / engagement strategies	platform metrics
	Commercial Strategy	Labour as a commodity, ROI Conscious strategy generating income from promotion of products / services SMI role as substantive employment, represented by influencer agency	SMI interviews	Receives income from SMI activities	SMI interviews
SMI NETWORK ATTRIBUTES	Network Size	Tipping point Managing arguments	user sentiment	Quantity of followers and ratio between followers and followees Content reach, Engagement reach	platform metrics
	Network Quality	SMI engagement with other SMI	qualitative assessment of accounts	Network metrics of followers / respondents	platform metrics
	Network Structure	i. Bonding (Homophily) iv. Bridging (Diversity) Indicator/s Network positioning of followers/ respondents.	network analytics (cluster mem-bership)	N/A	

Source: Created by the author.

perceive them. It is also important to consider the ambiguity of social cues on SMP compared to interacting in person. Additionally, Duffy (2016) identifies problematic constructs of gender and class subjectivities, as traditional stereotypes of celebrity endure. The dimension considers other questions, such as what motivates the micro-SMI to invest large amounts of time in self-education and labor to build and maintain their influence. The interview data also supported the fact that micro-SMIs are aware of the need to implement strategies for ensuring personal well-being and to protect their mental health.

Social capital as defined by Pierre Bourdieu (1986) as an aggregate of resources linked to a relationship within a network that offers benefits because of membership. According to Robert Putnam (2001) reciprocity and trustworthiness contribute to social capital in the context of individuals and groups. Digital social capital further extends the work of Bourdieu (Julien, 2014) and Putnam, referring to connections among individuals online, including social networks, reciprocity, and trustworthiness within the network (Lin et al., 2001). Social media has had a direct impact on how social capital allows individuals to expand their network beyond face-to-face relationships. Tom Postmes et al. (1998) reminds us that even in computer-mediated communication "people will use the identities and boundaries they build to interpret the social environment and guide them in it" (p 710). All participants invested a lot of time and effort in curating their SMP identity it increases social capital. They approached their SMP identity strategically while being adaptable depending on how the micro-SMI wanted to be perceived and how they think others might perceive them (Cunningham, 2013).

Entrepreneurial and reflective practice takes the personal attributes dimension a step further and highlights the innovative processes micro-SMI use to achieve their personal or professional ambitions. Micro-SMIs are driven by a want to know or learn something new, curiosity. Curiosity and experimentation were the top two skills considered essential for a micro-SMI by the participants. The relationship between SMP and publicity is a well-studied phenomenon, and publicity is the organizing element of democratic politics in an infotainment society (Dean, 2001). The competitive nature of the participants took different forms of attention seeking from wanting to be the first or have the scoop (news or technology updates), competing with the algorithms, getting the attention of a more influential user, or monetizing their digital identity. Although the motivations of the interview participants were well intended, it is also important to acknowledge this will not be true for all micro-SMI.

Content Attributes

Individuals have become produsers, a term introduced by Axel Bruns (2008) to describe social media users who share and cocreate user-generated content, therefore, increasing visibility on their chosen topic. This dimension highlights large changes in the way information and knowledge are disseminated and has three sub-dimensions: visibility, topic, and relevance.

Micro-SMIs publish, share, and network in the public domain of SMP, thus increasing visibility. Digital content can have massive reach and power for a micro-SMI (Marwick and Boyd, 2011), but can only inspire action if read and seen. The participants were active and spent most of their day on the SMP investing time and creating content that appeals to the network and SMP algorithms. They create content that sparks conversations around mutual interests at scale and publish it consistently to enhance relationships and establish new connections.

There is a balance between sharing too much personal information to engage the network authentically and topic-specific personal content (Huang, 2016). Participants spoke of wanting to share content, information, or knowledge on topics they are interested in, and of being able to tell people something new, fresh, and/or more extraordinary to standout. The immediacy of SMP provides micro-SMI opportunity weighing in as an expert on a topic to establish thought leadership and boost engagement in real-time. BL recalls, "My most successful Instagram—I mean successful in terms of likes—was steps to proceed in the same sex marriage survey, which was enrol to vote." Participants also suggested mixing serious subjects with humor as a strategy for increasing online engagement.

Participants resonate with their network through digital content that is relevant and keeps followers engaged: it is a matter of knowing their followers and how to speak to them (Marwick, 2013). Content must capture followers' attention by appealing to their interests and behaviors, creating currency or a meaningful value exchange. Micro-SMI can create breakthrough moments by informing, amusing, intriguing, or shocking their network. JS said, "my Twitter is a stream of consciousness, but it's more directed towards the things I know people are following me for."

Outcomes Generated

This dimension considers the value a micro-SMI has within their digital networks as they increase their social capital. Usually classified using quantifiable data models, such as number of followers, click-through rates, and so forth, this model considers network sentiment for added rigor. Micro-SMI who are focused on commercial gain and incentives use data to contribute to business proposals for marketers. Three sub-dimensions of the outcomes generated dimension include inspire action, generate public debate, and endorsements as social capital.

The participants did not become micro-SMI by creating more Internet noise; instead, they use content elements that are useful, engaging, and most importantly inspiring their followers to action, encouraging the network to continue to follow, engage, and share. IL said he asks his audience questions and posts inspiring messages and finds this strategy works well. BL the self-professed "high school debater" challenged his audiences' perceptions of politics and social issues.

Generating public debate was not discussed by all participants, for those that engaged in debate they described it as a double-edged sword as digital debates regularly digress to become an aggressive discussion quicker than personal interactions. Social movements, politics, and religion were common topics of debate described during the interviews. Alternative feedback is a natural part of any discussion, and the participants are not averse to debate to prove their point. BL declared he has a drive to wrestle with relevant issues and is not afraid of controversy. He said, "being averse to controversy might lead to a more conservative approach which audiences might find interesting or boring."

Endorsements are the contemporary form of word-of-mouth, occurring when individuals endorse the micro-SMI using various tools specific to the SMP. SMP endorsements can range from "likes" to written testimonials and offer varying degrees of social capital. SMP endorsement provides opportunity for network growth through SMP algorithms that promote popular content. Promoting popular content is a strategic business model used by SMP to engage users for longer and make them more likely to come back, providing opportunities to sell advertising space.

Strategy

With limited formal education available for micro-SMI, this project found that participants use a combination of innate and/or acquired skills gained from curiosity, experience, and experimentation. MN admitted that he does not have a strategy. By contrast, MK, KK, MR, and SS are motivated by business or branding objectives and were analytical and structured when managing their SMP identity. Two sub-dimensions of the strategy dimension are engagement and commercial strategy. It is interesting to note that not all participants were financially motivated.

The participants have ambitions guided by their motivations and are pragmatic about meeting objectives. While some participants claimed not to have a strategy for their SMP identity, it can be argued that they do. Some participants did not consciously strategize but developed a less rigid approach from increased tacit skills and knowledge developed over time and regular SMP use. For example, when asked if he had a strategy AA claimed, "it's just a coincidence rather than the actual aim of why I use social media." Yet as we got further into the interview, his objectives were clear—he wanted to sell more subscriptions to his daily tech news e-mail. "It's a daily e-mail newsletter full of tech news, people pay $5 a month to read it." To clarify his position on social media, I asked him if he saw potential in growing subscriptions through using social media. He responded:

> Yes, I have to say social media is an important part of that because people just need to spread the word and people are looking at social media. If you want to let people know about something, social media is a vital way to do that.

Across all interviews, engagement was a fundamental aspect of using SMP for micro-SMI. This is not a new concept, as engagement or being social is how SMP came into existence. ST said, "It's just about just being human. That is why the word social is in social media." JS said she relies on engagement to grow her network, "it's like a spider web grows and it gets bigger and bigger." AA said he has learned the importance of engagement and that repetition of the message has helped him grow his paid subscriptions:

> You can't just put it on the Internet and hope people find it, you have to be involved in sharing and telling people about it and convincing them, almost to the point of knocking them on the head with it . . . they get the message eventually and sign up. That's been a valuable lesson. You think you're being annoying, you're probably not.

Consistency is reflected in many elements of the micro-SMI strategy, such as a posting, messaging, tone of voice, and so forth. Being consistent is how micro-SMI build a recognizable, influential SMP identity. Their followers want to engage, and if they see they have not posted in weeks, it will decrease their relevance, or the algorithms will penalize them by decreasing their visibility. Discussing and sharing knowledge consistently and accurately gave participants the opportunity to be viewed as an expert on a topic, particularly if they started around ten years ago. ST said, "Follows go up each time I post."

Collaboration was suggested as an effective strategy used by participants to increase micro-SMI. Cross-promotion not only grew reach but also formed relationships with other micro-SMI and audiences. This approach was more complicated than other strategies as participants had niche audiences, which meant they found it challenging to make sure the collaboration was the right fit for them. MK said, "When collaborating it is important to have a consistency of values, message and audience. My biggest asset is the audience; when that audience grows, it brings more opportunities for partnerships." This perspective highlights the need for the participants to protect their SMP identities. None of the participants were willing to associate their SMP identity with topics, products, or people they do not have a synergy. They described this as inauthentic and suggested it could jeopardize the trust built with followers. The last thing they want to do is to alienate the followers who enable them to be micro-SMI.

Time, a limited commodity contrasted with the reach of social media, is a duality that challenges all participants. Throughout the interviews, the tension between time management and labor practices were revealed as a constant battle. Combining this with a strategy that requires engagement and network growth and not having a time management plan leads to unsustainable practices and processes. Participants' approaches ranged from accepting the pitfalls of SMP to quitting SMP altogether.

Commercial investment by large companies to engage a micro-SMI as part of their marketing strategy is increasing. A Google search of "social media micro-influence" returns countless news articles and blogs sharing the secret to becoming a micro-SMI and showing individuals who are earning attractive incomes because of their micro-SMI status. As discussed earlier, some participants in this study were tentative about associating themselves with this discourse, viewing authenticity as an asset to increase social capital. Participants have built their networks by increasing their digital social capital and being authentic. Any transgressions can harm relationships with their network which, when combined with the need for financial security, highlights a tension between entrepreneurship and authenticity. That tension becomes problematic when the micro-SMI is perceived by the network as inauthentic.

Henkel (2008) observes, "practitioners and entrepreneurs in creative industries are increasingly self-managing their careers rather than relying on employers or corporations" (p. 145). KK and MK value their independence from corporate structures or working for "the man" as KK put it. He then added that the goal is being financially self-supporting. JS is motivated by having a career in the media and started her podcast as an investment toward a profession in the media. She maintains financial stability with a "nine-to-five" administrative position until she can support herself as a micro-SMI. Here we see complex social structures impact the level of authenticity and therefore micro-influence. As all participants displayed entrepreneurial skills, they had a natural tendency to pursue business opportunities. They balance commercialization (enterprise), authenticity, and social capital. For the sake of authenticity, BL, AA, MR, and JS tell their network of their intentions. MK said that when/if she commercializes her digital profile, the product or service will be congruent with her SMP identity.

Network Characteristics

This dimension focuses on the network (followers and who the micro-SMI is following) of the micro-SMI. The size of a network cannot be solely relied on as a data point to identify micro-SMI, rather the quality and structure of those in the network also need to be considered. Three subdimensions of the network characteristics dimension include network size, quality, and structure.

On average, the participants have been using SMP for seven years, and this time period has contributed to the size of their networks. Participant's network size varied from 2,500 to 100,000. The common factor was that they all started their digital profiles by connecting with friends, family, and those with similar interests. JS said, "Mostly just our friends helped in starting our podcast, we were like, 'hey, we're both doing this thing, give it a listen,' and then it just blew up because it was all the people we know."

Micro-SMI are valued for sharing ideas, information, and opinions. They have a quality network that drives political and social issues, such as racial issues, to greater national and international attention (Brooks, 2013; Francalanci et al., 2015; Kapitan & Silvera, 2015; Khamis et al., 2017; Reid, 2014). Data points that drive visibility, such as comments, shares or retweets, followers, and the level of engagement, leading to increased digital.

There are two schools of thought when discussing micro-SMI network structures, those that engage with followers like themselves (homophily) and those who cross over different domains (bridgeblogger). Homophily describes participants who engaged with followers with perceived similarity (McPherson et al., 2001). Users of SMP build and expand their social relationships with other users of similar interests and preferences by mutually confirming a friendship (Kim & Tran, 2013). A "bridgeblogger" is a specific type of micro-SMI (Zuckerman, 2007). MR is an example of this in action as he strategically engages with different communities. He said he considers himself a hybrid because he crosses a lot of domains, and feels this a unique approach:

> It's a global village, I've become very internationalised, aware of what developments are happening in other jurisdictions. Sometimes when translating developments from Australia to overseas, you're learning about what's happening in other jurisdictions and then translating that to Australian audiences. There are a series of different communities associated with the topics I'm interested in, not everyone has the same set of interests.

The sub-dimensions of micro-SMI, network quality, structure, visibility, and reciprocity are interdependent and a subject for further study.

DISCUSSION

Social media have become a major form of public communication in their own right (Bruns & Burgess, 2016), the question of what defines micro-SMI arises, leading to further enquiry regarding the definition of influence, and the motivation and skills required to become influential using SMP. This chapter identified an area for further knowledge development in the current research, defining theoretical approaches to micro-SMI as technology and society evolve. Of particular interest are topics raised in the interviews that have limited scholarship. Topics such as micro-SMI well-being, and how they manage pressures such as government regulations, economical, FOMO, mental health, and trolls, have limited research, conflicting, and lacks rigor (Elhai et al., 2016; Hampton et al., 2015). Well-being and mental health are crucial considerations for most of the participants, indicating a gap in the literature that needs to be explored. In the interviews, I found that as the participants became more familiar with the nuances of SMP, they developed strategies to ensure positive mental health, but were left to their own curiosity and experimentation.

The desire for authenticity has existed for hundreds of years (Grayson & Martinec, 2004). Authenticity creates a safe space for people to engage and has a positive effect on relationship quality (Fritz et al., 2017). Interrogation of authenticity was a common theme for the participants. For example, KK said, "the real power of social media is in authenticity." In a commercially driven world, people expect authenticity. In a recent study, Kowalczyk and Pounders (2016) discussed the role antecedents of authenticity play in online connections with celebrities. Participants believed that being authentic shows the followers of micro-SMI that they are vulnerable, raw and real, honest and true, and unashamed of being themselves, whether sharing the good or the not-so-good.

Participants used their SMP identities to increase followers motivated by achieving their objectives. Those objectives were varied, at times, aspirational (Abidin, 2015a) and complex but always related to participants' motivations. Scholars such as Abidin (2016), Baym (2015), and Duffy (2016) are bringing to light the disparity of reward verses investment. Described in the literature as aspirational labor (Abidin, 2016; Duffy, 2016), the motivations of participants had a direct correlation with how the participants engage with their network on social media. Duffy (2016) highlights the gender gap in aspirational labor. The article "The Romance of Work" (Duffy, 2016) draws on interviews and blogger discourses to conceptualize creative practices promising social and economic capital within a gender-biased reward environment. She argues that while digital workspaces have provided a flexible employment structure, social inequalities and hierarchies endure.

CONCLUSION

This chapter provides a framework for current discourse of micro-SMI as a nuanced digital subculture, how it is operationalized—theoretically and practically. The model includes a systematic list of dimensions that can identify micro-SMI and a set of questions to interrogate their practice, which offers the beginning of a theoretical approach for understanding micro-SMI. The model comprises of five dimensions: personal attributes, content attributes, outcomes generated, strategies, and network characteristics. When operationalizing the dimensions, we must also consider the elements of SMP that are not openly shared in public forums. This research identified individuals who are micro-SMI in the public sphere of Twitter. The study attempts to gain an understanding of micro-SMI of different industries and genders while remaining focused on Australian residents.

The future for digital marketing, social media, digital literacy, and education in Australia will be a turbulent one as our understanding evolves through a combination of actionable and applicable knowledge. Motivation/s for creating and maintaining a SMP identity have a complex, interchangeable role in participants' lives (Al-Menayes, 2015). Platforms are constantly changing, so it will be important to keep revisiting these criteria to ensure their relevance to ongoing discussion and analysis moving into the future. The express purpose of this project is to narrow the knowledge gap and identify opportunities in academic scholarship and education, and more generally, the use of SMP as communication tools. In the Australian Digital Inclusion Index (2018), the authors acknowledge the growing gap in digital literacy and stated that "digital inclusion is now fundamental to full participation in our economic and social life and an ever-increasing number of essential and community services and other communications are going digital (p. 03)." By understanding and learning from those who have led the way as micro-SMI, we can then offer structured programs for the inclusion of all, regardless of circumstance (Dezuanni et al., 2019).

REFERENCES

Abidin, C. (2015a). Communicative intimacies: Influencers and perceived interconnectedness. *Ada: A Journal of Gender, New Media, and Technology*, *8*. http://bit.ly/38jkyf0

Abidin, C. (2015b). Micromicrocelebrity: Branding babies on the internet. *M/C Journal*, *18*(5). http://bit.ly/2Hg1CBC

Abidin, C. (2016). Visibility labour: Engaging with Influencers' fashion brands and #OOTD advertorial campaigns on Instagram. *Media International Australia*, *161*(1), 86–100.

Al-Menayes, J. J. (2015). Motivations for using social media: An exploratory factor analysis. *International Journal of Psychological Studies*, *7*(1), 43.

Bakshy, E. (2011). *Information diffusion and social influence in online networks* (Doctor of Philosophy: Information). University of Michigan.

Bargh, J. A., & McKenna, K. Y. A. (2004). The internet and social life. *Annual Review of Psychology, 55*, 573–590.

Barnes, R. (2018). Hitch up the Wagon: Charting the online commenting landscape. In R. Barnes (Ed.), *Uncovering online commenting culture: Trolls, fanboys and lurkers* (pp. 1–26). Springer International Publishing.

Baym, N. K. (2015). *Personal connections in the digital age.* John Wiley & Sons.

Bourdieu, P. (1986). The forms of capital. In *Handbook of theory and research for the sociology of education* (pp. 241–258). Greenwood.

Boyd, D. (2007). Why youth (heart) Social network sites: The role of networked publics in teenage social life. *MacArthur Foundation Series on Digital Learning— Youth, Identity, and Digital Media, 7641*(41), 1–26.

Brooks, S. L. (2013). *Social media usage: Examination of influencers and effects.* Washington State University.

Bruns, A. (2008). The future is user-led: The path towards widespread produsage. *Fibreculture Journal, 11.* http://bit.ly/2Hh2Bl2

Bruns, A., & Burgess, J. (2016). Methodological innovation in precarious spaces: The case of Twitter. In S. Roberts, H. Snee, C. Hine, Y. Morey, & H. Watson (Eds.), *Digital methods for social science: An interdisciplinary guide to research innovation* (pp. 17–31). Palgrave Macmillan UK.

Cunningham, C. (2013). *Social networking and impression management: Self-presentation in the digital age.* Rowman & Littlefield.

Dean, J. (2001). Publicity's secret. *Political Theory, 29*(5), 624–650.

Dezuanni, M., Marshall, A., Cross, A., Burgess, J., & Mitchell, P. (2019). *Digital mentoring in Australian communities: A report prepared for Australia Post.* Australia Post.

Duffy, B. E. (2016). The romance of work: Gender and aspirational labour in the digital culture industries. *International Journal of Cultural Studies, 19*(4), 441–457.

Elhai, J. D., Levine, J. C., Dvorak, R. D., & Hall, B. J. (2016). Fear of missing out, need for touch, anxiety and depression are related to problematic smartphone use. *Computers in Human Behavior, 63*, 509–516.

Farrugia, D. (2018). Youthfulness and immaterial labour in the new economy. *The Sociological Review, 66*(3), 511–526.

Francalanci, C., & Hussain, A. (2015). Social influence and influencers analysis: A visual perspective. *Communications in Computer and Information Science, 178*, 81–98. https://doi.org/10.1007/978-3-319-25936-9_6

Fritz, K., Schoenmueller, V., & Bruhn, M. (2017). Authenticity in branding— Exploring antecedents and consequences of brand authenticity. *European Journal of Marketing, 51*(2), 324–348.

Fukuyama, F. (2001). Social capital, civil society and development. *Third World Quarterly, 22*(1), 7–20.

Grayson, K., & Martinec, R. (2004). Consumer perceptions of iconicity and indexicality and their influence on assessments of authentic market offerings. *Journal of Consumer Research, 31*(2), 296–312.

Hampton, K. N., Rainie, L., Lu, W., Shin, I., & Purcell, K. (2015). *Social media and the cost of caring.* Pew Research Center, Washington, D.C. https://pewrsr.ch /2SyGVX4

Henkel, C. (2008). Creative regions in the digital era: Screen and creative industries in the northern rivers region of NSW. In *Making meaning, making money: Directions for the arts and cultural industries in the creative age*. Cambridge Scholars Publishing.

Huang, L.-T. (2016). Flow and social capital theory in online impulse buying. *Journal of Business Research, 69*(6), 2277–2283.

Julien, C. (2014). Bourdieu, social capital and online interaction. *Sociology, 49*(2), 356–373.

Kapitan, S., & Silvera, D. H. (2015). From digital media influencers to celebrity endorsers: Attributions drive endorser effectiveness. *Marketing Letters, 27*(3), 553–567.

Katz, E., & Lazarsfeld, P. F. (1964). *Personal influence* (2nd ed.). Free Press.

Khamis, S., Ang, L., & Welling, R. (2017). Self-branding, "micro-celebrity" and the rise of social media influencers. *Celebrity Studies, 8*(2), 191–208.

Kim, Y. S., & Tran, V. L. (2013). Assessing the ripple effects of online opinion leaders with trust and distrust metrics. *Expert Systems with Applications, 40*(9), 3500–3511.

Kowalczyk, C. M., & Pounders, K. R. (2016). Transforming celebrities through social media: The role of authenticity and emotional attachment. *Journal of Product & Brand Management, 25*(4), 345–356.

Kwon, K. H., Stefanone, M. A., & Barnett, G. A. (2014). Social network influence on online behavioral choices: Exploring group formation on social network sites. *The American Behavioral Scientist, 58*(10), 1345–1360.

Lin, N., Cook, K. S., & Burt, R. S. (2001). *Social capital: Theory and research*. Transaction Publishers.

Marwick, A., & Boyd, D. (2011). To see and be seen: Celebrity practice on Twitter. *Convergence: The International Journal of Research into New Media Technologies, 17*(2), 139–158.

McPherson, M., Smith-Lovin, L., & Cook, J. M. (2001). Birds of a feather: Homophily in social networks. *Annual Review of Sociology, 27*, 415–444.

Phillips, W. (2015). Defining terms: The origins and evolution of subcultural trolling. In *This is why we can't have nice things*. MIT Press.

Postmes, T., Spears, R., & Lea, M. (1998). Breaching or building social boundaries?: Side-effects of computer-mediated communication. *Communication Research, 25*(6), 689–715.

Reid, S. (2014). Knowledge influencers: Leaders influencing knowledge creation and mobilization. *Journal of Educational Administration and History, 52*(3), 332–357.

Senft, T. M. (2008). *Camgirls: Celebrity and community in the age of social networks*. Peter Lang.

Senft, T. (2013). Microcelebrity and the Branded Self. In *A Companion to New Media Dynamics* (pp. 346–354). Wiley-Blackwell. https://doi.org/10.1002/9781118321607.ch22

Turner, G. (2004). *Understanding celebrity*. SAGE Publications Ltd.

van Laer, T. (2014). The means to justify the end: Combating cyber harassment in social media. *Journal of Business Ethics: JBE, 123*(1), 85–98.

Zuckerman, E. (2007). Meet the bridge bloggers. *Public Choice, 134*(1–2), 47–65.

Chapter 4

Evaluation of Brand-Sponsored Influencers and Tactics Across Industries

Ronda Mariani

We have all been there, surfing our favorite social media platform, video channel, or news outlet, and behold, something catches our attention. Usually, an individual uniquely positioned to create further curiosity for us. The next thing we know, we are watching some beautiful young girl explaining the dreadful process of applying false eyelashes, in order to look our best for that special night out. We now realize this is something that they do regularly, and we subscribe to their channel. We then go on to purchase and try the same products these individuals demonstrated. Innocently enough, we now know, or maybe not, that we have been influenced and completed the intended cycle of influencer to purchase.

Social media is an excellent avenue for influencers to create dialog and relationships with consumers. Social media platforms have a wide variety of users, yet create microenvironments which in return produce communities that can be led by influencers. Communities are mostly an audience with a common interest (Montgomery, 2019). These individuals come together to share, communicate, and learn. These communities' environments are built on trust and commitment. Furthermore, there is a great deal of human engagement, which is what most social media users seek when using these networks. The growth of social media has enabled the evolution of what was once considered brand sponsors or spokespersons to the current day "social media influencer."

Social media influencers (SMIs) use their unique ability to communicate to an audience their viewpoint (Stubb & Colliander, 2019). In return for this unique voice, brands compensate SMIs for being their brand advocates. However, many times, the birth of an influencer is no more than a passionate viewpoint for a particular subject, product, service, or brand. This generated content provides an agreeable and trusted appeal to followers creating positive perceptions of ideologies and brands, which SMIs support. A study conducted by Nielsen (2013) found that consumers who followed and viewed SMIs' content saw these individuals as more trustworthy. Therefore, these influencer–consumer relationships create an avenue for brands to connect with consumers through an environment that is founded on existing confidence. Research has revealed that consumers are more likely to purchase a product that is advertised or endorsed by a familiar face, such as a celebrity, friend, or family member within a social network (Zeljko et al., 2018).

TRUST AND BANNER BLINDNESS

Evaluating trust can be difficult and time-consuming. The meaning of trust can be interpreted differently from one individual to the next; therefore, understanding the impact of trust in regards to purchasing behavior can be complicated. With that said, brands have learned over time and acknowledged how vital consumer trust is. A great deal of money and research has been spent uncovering factors that increase consumer trust and how this may be a gateway to purchasing. With more consumers undertaking their purchasing online, trust is a critical component, which needs to be established between the brand and the consumer. One might ask, "How do consumers establish online trust leading to stronger purchasing?"

Today, consumers no longer follow a linear process when deciding their purchase intent. There are many avenues a consumer can take to validate their purchasing decisions including online reviews, social media communities, and SMIs. This form of electronic word of mouth has changed the way consumers interact with each other and the buying process (Olabarri-Fernández et al., 2015). Complicating purchase intent further is the clutter of advertising that consumers are exposed to daily. Clutter is not a new problem, but it is a problem that consistently impacts brands and their return on investment when it comes to advertising dollars. For decades, scholars have researched and presented many findings promoting the lack of impact that online advertising has on consumers (Cho, 2003; Ha, 2004; Resnick et al., 2014; Zouharová et al., 2016). Terms such as banner blindness, in which consumers tend to "ignore and avoid display advertisements" (Cho, 2003, p. 203) has been a concern at the center of all advertising placement and effectiveness.

Measures taken to combat the lack of online advertising effectiveness have been demonstrated through the implementation of multiple online advertising tactics such as catchy banner design and formulated banner placement. Research has supported some of these methods as being optimistic. For example, Chtourou and Abida (2010) found positive effects when utilizing banner animation and rich media characteristics in online environments. Sigel et al. (2008) found that display advertising styles, including size and location of display advertising, had an impact on click-through rates. Moreover, the utilization of programmatic advertising and geofencing has become popular because of its ability to target consumers directly and more accurately. Although there are many tactics and tools available, advertisers and marketers still seem to fall short of meeting expectations. These shortcomings have led advertisers to seek more appealing avenues when connecting with consumers. One such avenue is the employment of influencers.

BRAND ADVOCATES AND THE CUSTOMER JOURNEY

Brand advocates are consumers who genuinely believe in the product or the service they support (Social Media Glossary, 2019). These individuals advocate for the brands they are passionate about and will defend the integrity and reputation of these products or services. We can see this debate readily among cell phone users, iPhone and Android. As a professor, many times, I will use these two powerful cell phone giants as examples in my classes. It seems very easy to bait users and create everlasting and passionate conversations as to why one uses an iPhone over an Android phone, and vice versa. Consumers have a personal connection to their phones. Their life would be incomplete if something were to happen to their cell phone device. In many ways, these same students that participate in classroom debates about their cell phone brand loyalty are in their own right a brand advocate. Take this cell phone loyalty a step further and start talking about it on a YouTube channel. Grow and obtain one hundred thousand followers, and you are now a social media sensation, or what one may call an "influencer."

Brand advocates communicate with people using a variety of activities (Aquino, 2013). As consumers endorse our products and services, we also know that word-of-mouth marketing is the Holy Grail for marketers (Aquino, 2013). The ability to share information today comes easily with the available social media platforms. Consumer decision-making has also changed when it comes to the process of purchasing. The ability to access online reviews, recommendations, social posts, which are shared or liked, and video, has changed the way consumers go about their decision-making and purchase intention. Consumers now have the ability to weave through the many elements of technology before making a final purchasing decision, whether to buy or not to buy. Since technology contributes to the disruption of marketing and advertising, consumers at all stages of the customer's journey can leave behind a digital trail of information, which in return, can become a wealth of knowledge for others.

In order to understand the digital trail and its impact on consumer purchasing today, one must understand how we got here. Traditionally, when brands approached consumers, marketing and advertising strategies were very straightforward. The practice of implementing sales funnel strategies such as the AIDA Sales Funnel, which was developed by St. Elmo Lewis in 1898, was a common practice. The acronym AIDA stands for awareness, interests, desire, and action. Lewis was a well-known successful sales professional and utilized these four levels of consumer cognitive behavior. He felt each stage was a cognitive phase that illustrated a path to consumer buying. In order for a brand to achieve a sale, in this case, represented by "action," Lewis felt most consumers would need to proceed through each of the other cognitive stages first, creating what we understand today as a sales funnel approach to consumer buying(see figure 4.1).

Lewis explained that specific marketing strategies could be developed and strategic advertising served to these consumers through each stage of the funnel in hopes of coercing a sale. The AIDA Sales Funnel approach is still used today, but may not always be the best approach. Essentially, the AIDA Sales Funnel enables brands to attract a high number of possible customers at the

Figure 4.1   AIDA Sales Funnel. *Source:* Created by St. Elmo Lewis in 1898.

awareness stage but at the same time, does not take into account the many choices and forms of media, which impact consumers. Moreover, the cognitive behaviors of consumers as they move through each stage of the funnel can become disrupted when approaching a purchasing decision. As a result, the well-known traditional sales funnel has transitioned into a new circular process, referred to as the customer's journey, while also adding further cognitive stages impacting consumer purchase intent.

To illustrate the customer's journey further, it can be seen that the process is still similar to the traditional sales funnel. However, because of technology, the consumer's cognitive process has become more complicated in regards to purchase intention and decision-making. When referring to the AIDA Sales Funnel, there are four stages in the cognitive process. On the other hand, when evaluating today's customer's journey, five stages appear and each stage grows with complexity. By contrast, many elements remain the same, but it is the digital aspects of the brand to consumer communication that changes the dynamics of consumer cognition when approaching purchasing today. The diagram below illustrates the five stages and demonstrates at each stage where consumer cognition may lie. The diagram also presents where the consumer may be in each stage of the process concerning the brand, moving from stranger to brand advocate. Brand advocates can be compelling for brands, influencing other consumers (see figure 4.2).

In the past, digital marketing was considered only a component of the overall marketing mix. Today, this has changed. Digital marketing may be the number one tool connecting brands to consumers. The traditional method of acquiring customers used a funnel approach, or what I like to call the "tunnel" approach. Digital communication channels have changed marketing and the methods brands use to create sales conversions. Moreover, attempts to utilize

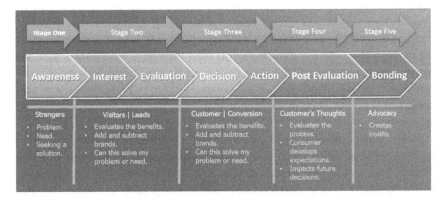

Figure 4.2   Customer's Journey. Demonstrating How Consumers Move through the Cognitive Process of the Customer's Journey. *Source:* Created by author.

the traditional marketing funnel may no longer be relevant. Undoubtedly, it is essential to understand the impact of technology on consumer decision-making and how this has created a customer journey that may no longer be perceived as a linear process. Consumers may move in and out of the buying process before actually making a purchase. Let us take a look at an example.

When consumers are in need of a computer, most will engage in an element of research before making a decision and purchase. When approaching this journey, the consumer, who is in need of a new computer, enters the awareness stage. Here the consumer has a problem or a need—in the case of our consumer, they are in need of a new laptop. At the awareness stage, consumers may be strangers to the brands that offer laptops to purchase. Here the consumer will engage in research. Research may consist of consumer reviews, ratings, and brand comparisons. Therefore, a brand needs to have the appropriate messages and advertising available to connect with the consumer in this stage and build brand trust.

As the consumer begins to research and acknowledge the variety of brands that offer laptops, then interest and evaluation begins to develop. Here consumers may learn about the differentiating attributes between laptop brands. This could be price, how fast the processor is, and the weight of the laptop. Whatever the differentiating factors, the more attributes that solve the consumer's problem will lead the consumer to the evaluation of a brand. Once our consumer feels they have adequately evaluated what is available, this will lead to a decision, which usually follows with an action. This action is known as a conversion or sale. Our consumer has made a decision to purchase a laptop that they felt met their expectations.

The postevaluation stage is very important. This is when the consumer thinks about their purchase, the process, and engages with the product. If the experience was positive, this is also the stage in which the brand begins to build a strong relationship that should lead to consumer and brand bonding. This is the beginning of the customer relationship management stage. The bonding stage is the last stage of the journey. This is where our consumer is happy with their choice and the relationship they have established with the brand. The consumer will let their friends know how great their experience was and how the brand met all expectations. This is brand advocacy. Our consumer is an advocate of the brand, or we may also call this person a brand influencer.

Keeping in mind once again, the customer's journey is not a linear process such as the traditional sales funnel. It is important to understand that this journey can start at any stage, although it is very unlikely that action would be taken without some previous decision-making, such as evaluation. But consumers can enter and exit the circle at different points in their journey. For example, a consumer can enter the interest and evaluation stage by placing the laptop in their online shopping cart, but at the same time, take a minute to read another review, which may lead them to abandoning the shopping cart and no purchase. A week may pass, and the consumer may receive a coupon for the same laptop and go straight to action and complete a purchase. A good strategy is to keep the consumers within the circle and have them become a continuous advocate of the brand revolving in and out of each stage of the customer journey (see figure 4.3).

Another essential element is the digital trail that consumers now leave behind for others to see. This digital trail, or what marketers refer to as "earned media" provides more than name recognition for a brand; it provides consumer trust. Earned media is a part of what marketers call the digital marketing trifecta, which consists of paid, owned, and earned media strategies. The trifecta provides brands the opportunity to implement its communication channels throughout the customer's journey. Paid media consists of marketing and advertising in which the brand has paid. Examples can be programmatic advertising, television commercials, paid per click, paid influencers, and social media advertisements. Owned media consists of marketing and advertising that a brand owns. Examples can be the brand's website, mobile app, and social media pages. Earned media consists of marketing and advertising that the brand does not solicit. Examples can be social mentions, shares, likes, reposts, and online reviews. This is what is also known as a digital trail created by consumers, advocates, and influencers (see figure 4.4).

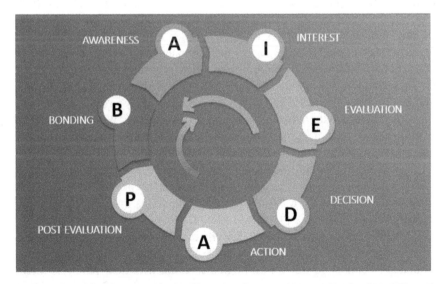

Figure 4.3   New Customer Journey. The New Customer Journey Moving from a Funnel to a Circular Process. *Source:* Created by author.

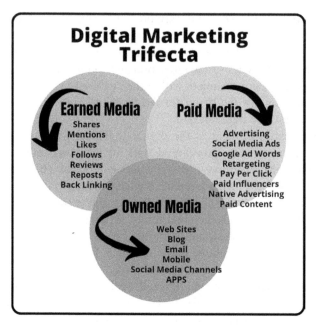

Figure 4.4   Digital Marketing Trifecta. *Source:* Recreated by author from Titan Growth figure.

Earned media is considered one of the most "trusted and influential sources of information" among consumers (Stebbins, 2015, para. 3). Nielsen (2013) found that 84 percent of consumers surveyed saw earned media as the most trusted form of advertising. MDG Advertising (2014) found that 70 percent of consumers wanted to learn more about products employing content rather than traditional advertising approaches. ODM Group found that "74% of consumers rely on social networks to help with their purchasing decisions, and HubSpot reported 71% of consumers are more likely to make a purchase based on social media referrals" (Garvin, 2019, para. 2). With statistics like these, one can make a safe assumption that earned media is a game-changer and marketers will need to rethink their marketing strategies to include such prominent and influential media sources. Moreover, marketers will need to seek out brand advocates who can build the bridges needed to connect brands with consumers through a variety of earned mediums that can demonstrate success.

The customer's journey, as we have read, is a very complicated process. Consumers not only have more product choices but also have multiple means available to collect pertinent information to assist with their purchase intent and decision-making. Brand advocates, also known as influencers, play a critical role in communicating to consumers the benefits of a brand. Brands are now considering influencers as a serious component of their marketing strategies. Influencers can create relationships, built on established trust, between the brand and the consumer furthering the success of brand loyalty.

THE BEAUTY INDUSTRY AND INFLUENCERS

The beauty industry has changed quite a bit over the past decade or so, moving from the faces of supermodels adorning television commercials and magazines to now, unknown faces with large social media followings promoting products. In the past, this industry was dominated by only a few popular brands, such as Cover Girl, Maybelline, and L'Oreal. These same brands also paid millions of dollars to try and capture their audiences. Now, brands are seeking more innovative channels, such as Instagram and YouTube, with less familiar faces to lead the way for their cosmetic and beauty lines. For example, Estée Lauder is planning to spend 75 percent of its advertising budget on digital marketing, particularly SMIs (Pearl, 2019). The brand is even looking to hire a global director of global influencer marketing and customer engagement to work with influencers of all sizes, both mainstream and well known (Weiss, 2019). Cosmetic and beauty brands are beginning to realize that famous people and large amounts of money do not necessarily mean brands will sell makeup. Consumers know what they like and want when they see it, and they do not need a celebrity or supermodel to reaffirm this.

The cosmetic industry offers not only familiar faces, such as celebrities we all know, but also partners with SMIs who are new and do not hold celebrity status. When evaluating SMIs, brands look at the number of followers these individuals have as well as their methods of interaction and engagement with audiences. Brands also recognize how vital "trust is between influencers and their audiences; knowing this is paramount and can impact their bottom lines" (Sharma & Albus, 2018, p. DE13).

Becca Cosmetics

An example of this is the partnership between Becca Cosmetics and Jaclyn Hill. Becca Cosmetics is a line of cosmetics that caters to all women, both young and old, and its focus is on a variety of shades that offer a natural glow and radiance when applied. Jaclyn Hill is an Internet celebrity and SMI who gained her following through her YouTube channel, featuring cosmetics. Becca Cosmetics saw the popularity of Jaclyn Hill as a cosmetic influencer and decided to collaborate with Hill to develop the Jaclyn Hill Champagne Collection, which consisted of a face palette inspired by cocktails of color, highlights, and radiance (Sharma & Albus, 2018, p. DE14). There were

41,000 units of this palette created through this partnership, and these units sold out in two hours, while also receiving one billion social media impressions (Sharma & Albus, 2018, p. DE14).

Coty's Rimmel London

Coty's Rimmel London is another beauty company that partners with celebrities and beauty influencers. The brand sees itself as unique and not like a typical beauty line. It challenges the users of its products to be daring when experimenting with its cosmetics, to engage in street beauty, meaning to have a desire for authenticity, and challenges consumers to be an edgier self. Coty's Rimmel London wants to reflect these characteristics: daring, street beauty, and edgier self, when it communicates with its audience. Chandra Coleman, vice president of U.S. marketing for Sally Hansen, indicated that Coty's Rimmel London understood that their consumers are not the only females. Coleman went on to say the brand wanted to encourage all people to have the confidence to experiment and embrace edgy makeup looks (DSN, 2017). The brand continually reaches out to up-and-coming and unique SMIs who speak to Coty's Rimmel London consumer base. These SMIs create content featuring Coty's Rimmel London products to share with their followers. The idea for Coty's Rimmel London is to use SMIs to create a diverse community that celebrates differences.

Henry Giddins Jr., Coty's Rimmel London head of insights for global color cosmetics, stated: "He has seen a massive shift in trust among its consumers with the brand" (Rao, 2018, para. 3). Giddins went on to say, "Peer-to-peer recommendations bring a level of objectivity to consumers, and we cannot replicate that with celebrities and paid influencers completely. We view this strategy as having more value now" (Rao, 2018, para. 3). This reiterates the importance of trust between a brand and its audience, which can be facilitated by SMIs.

Coty's Rimmel London's approach to working with SMIs is organic. The brand does not rely on a paid approach when, incorporating SMIs in their advertising campaigns, but instead the brand uses an organic approach to its strategy. Organic marketing is a method in which customers and influencers are obtained naturally and slowly over time (Thiefels, 2018). Instead of paying SMIs for Coty's Rimmel London, influencers are provided with products in exchange for endorsements. It takes time for these product exchanges to take place, and many times the SMIs who represent Coty's Rimmel London are individuals that received no compensation at all. It is the passion that the SMI has for the product that begins these relationships and soon grows over time between the company and influencer.

For example, Coty's Rimmel London worked with the platform Influenster and sought out everyday women to promote its summer Wonder Ombre

Holographic eyeliner launch. Influenster created two thousand VoxBoxes containing the eyeliner and sent the boxes to women between the ages of eighteen and thirty residing in two U.S. cities, Dallas and San Francisco, which were known as vast markets for the brand (Rao, 2018). Women who received the product began to blog as well as post on Instagram and YouTube about their experiences with the product. One blogger, "Mary" who describes herself as just another friendly, beauty-crazed blogger and self-confessed perfumista (Mary, 2018), also noted a disclaimer on her blogging site, stating that she was provided with the free VoxBox of Wonder Ombre Holographic eyeliner, and what the viewer was about to read was purely her opinion on the product. She went on to provide a testimonial for the product, explained its ease of use, and ended with high recommendations for her audience to try the new eyeliner.

This type of collaborations has paid off for the Coty's Rimmel London brand. Giddins Jr. reported that the Influenster campaign drove sales for Coty's Rimmel London eyeliners 69 percent higher than usual, thus demonstrating a grander halo effect among consumers and users (Rao, 2018, para. 3).

As both of these examples illustrate, influencers can be a potent instrument in the digital marketing toolbox. Both Coty's Rimmel London and Becca Cosmetics turned to regular people who would demonstrate their products online in a way that traditional advertising methods could not achieve. For these brands, employing SMIs created a more personal connection between the brand and the consumer. Instead of brands using the push approach, such as programmatic advertising, which advertisers and marketers would typically employ, these brands connected with their audiences using the pull approach. Specifically, having SMIs with large followings create YouTube and Instagram content about their beauty products. This method generated more buzz for the brand, and therefore, the consumer sought out the product more readily.

THE OPTICAL INDUSTRY AND INFLUENCERS

The optical industry in another industry that has taken full advantage of SMIs and their audiences. SMIs communicate to the consumer the practicality and functionality of eyewear as both a medical device and a fashion statement (Wilson & Sengwe, 2018). Through storytelling, SMIs create content that is appealing to a brand's audience. Storytelling is the ability to create narratives, which convey facts about the brand and its offerings (Schäferhoff, 2018). "Your story is what the world believes about you based on the signals you send through all of your brand assets" (Gutman, 2018, para. 4). Creating compelling brand stories many times leads to influencer advocacy.

Warby Parker

A brand that was successful in combining storytelling and SMIs is the prescription glasses retailer Warby Parker. Warby Parker's marketing strategy has several unique characteristics. Rather than choosing very well-known SMIs, Warby Parker chose individuals who were creative and possessed a need for a quality and stylish eyewear (Kix, 2020). Through the use of social media platforms such as Instagram, these artistic and creative SMIs led other creatives who were needing prescriptive eyewear to the Warby Parker experience.

Gutman (2018) a writer who is a fan of books and literature, recalled his shopping experience with Warby Parker. He noted how well the brand created a story based on the brand's promise, which is the ability for consumers to purchase stylish, cost-effective eyewear with minimum hassle. Gutman (2018) went on to illustrate his customer journey experience with Warby Parker when visiting one of the brand's stores. He discussed his encounters when entering a Warby Parker store, and how he was greeted by opticians and smiling store employees providing all the necessary information about choosing the correct eyewear. He went on to describe the ambiance as creative, stylish, and the motif was books and literature. Gutman (2018) felt a creative connection and realized that by the "brand telling him who they were, at the same time, the brand was telling him who he was" (para. 13). By choosing Warby Parker eyewear, the brand wanted Gutman (2018) to feel smart, stylish, and even savvy, slowly making him feel part of the brand's tribe (para. 14). Every step of the buying process included Gutman (2018). After he left the store, he was sent continued updates about the status of his ordered eyewear. When the eyewear arrived at his home, even the packaging was colorful and contained prints of famous artists. Upon opening the box, once again, another connection to the brand was made, a stylish microfiber cleaning cloth containing the brand's story in less than 100 words (Gutman, 2018). Warby Parker just gained another fan, or what we refer to as an influencer, to tell others about their brand story experience.

Eastern States Eyewear and Optical Transitions

Eastern States Eyewear (ESE) and Optical Transitions are two well-known eyewear brands that have partnered with SMIs Coco and Breezy to create content that is unique and tells the brand's story. Coco and Breezy are twin sisters who are of Puerto Rican and African descent. Growing up in Minnesota presented them with many challenges, one of which was bullying. During this time, these sisters discovered their love for sunglasses and the protection, they felt when wearing a pair. Sunglasses provided them a sense of security and allowed them to present their alter-egos, "which were fearless young women who could conquer the world" (Morad, 2019, para. 1). To avoid bullying, the twins turned to social media to make friends. The sisters used Myspace as a place to show off stylish and cutting-edge eyewear, they had created from existing do-it-yourself sunglasses while connecting and making friends. Their audience were always "bedazzled by their creations" (Morad, 2019, para. 2). With 30,000 followers, Coco and Breezy continued to make and embellish their sunglasses and founded their company Coco and Breezy in 2009. Celebrities also began to take notice and wear their creations. In their small Bushwick apartment on an air mattress, their glasses were eventually worn by big stars such as Lady Gaga and Prince (Morad, 2019). Today, with over 80,000 followers on Instagram, eyewear brands such as Optical Transitions and ESE have partnered with Coco and Breezy to launch the duo's latest unisex sunglass collection (News, 2017). While these brands know traditional marketing methods are essential, they believe that using SMIs is also an effective strategy to enhance their brand image (Yeh, 2017).

Influencers have demonstrated a positive return for Warby Parker, ESE, and Optical Transitions. However, these eyewear brands are not only ones to incorporate SMIs into its brand communication strategy. Less-expensive brands such as J+S Premiums and Kent Wang have also incorporated SMIs into its brand communication strategy. Their sunglasses may not have the price tag of Ray-Ban, Oakley, or Dolce and Gabbana, contributing to their massive marketing budgets, but through influencer marketing, these less-expensive brands can reach potential consumers in a more cost-effective manner. Since less-expensive brands may be somewhat unknown in the optical industry, SMIs can provide the needed trust that is important to capturing market share (Lou & Yuan, 2019). After all, SMIs have grown their followings, knowing what their audience likes and dislikes.

THE FINANCIAL INDUSTRY AND INFLUENCERS

American Express

American Express is a brand that understands the power of SMIs and storytelling. As mentioned earlier in the chapter, brand storytelling connects the consumer to the brand's promise and value through narrative. In the past, brands would advertise their products or services in the hopes of gaining a sale. The presentation of coupons, discounts, and bundling are just some of the ways brands would persuade existing and new customers to purchase what they were offering. The goal of each dollar spent was to create a sale. However, in the present moment, this may not be the case for many brands. In today's "fast-paced, overly-automated, and digitally-driven society, humanity is becoming the new premium" (Costa, 2019, para. 1). Creating content that tells a story is something that many brands, both big and small, are engaging in today. Therefore, the conversion that was once the sale is not necessarily the only goal anymore. Although selling is the end intention for brands, the creation of relationships in today's digital world is equally as important. Consumers remembering the brand and what it represents seem to be increasingly critical to business success today. Brands want to engage with the consumer with a purpose and enable consumers to feel part of this purpose. For example, through storytelling, Apple taught consumers to think differently and Tesla's consumers needed to feel that they support a sustainable environment (Costa, 2019). This storytelling is something brands are trying to achieve, including American Express.

American Express knew that authentic stories were the most impactful to consumers (Moltz, 2014). American Express worked with and continues to work with bloggers, SMIs, and celebrities to create expression behind what the brand offers. For example, when American Express launched OPEN in 2007, the brand created a narrative that was dedicated to the expression of small-business owners. Today, OPEN is a content-driven forum for small businesses, which includes growth stories, local business stories, and built-in America stories (Roque, 2015) all of which resonate among small-business America Express cardholders.

American Express implemented a storytelling campaign, which included a series of YouTube videos called "My Travel Style" (Bjornson, 2018). During this series, American Express partnered with SMIs such as Marcus Troy, Krystin Lee, and Adam van Koeverden, and asked them question about their travel style (Bjornson, 2018). The idea was to learn more about how SMIs travel and what essentials they bring with them every time they travel. Responses were fun and warm creating an authentic atmosphere and connecting to people who travel or have an interest in travel. The video ends with each SMI booking their travels with American Express and how if the user saved enough points they can travel the world for free.

American Express has also done well utilizing SMIs on Instagram. A recent campaign named AMEX Ambassadors used the hashtag #AMEXAMBASSADORS to promote the American Express Platinum Card and to signify long-term partnerships with specific SMIs (MediaKix, 2019). Knowing how vital their rewards program was to their current audience, and in retaining and acquiring new customers, the brand felt influencer marketing would be perfect when connecting and engaging with these individuals. These influencers would promote lifestyles instead of the actual product, the platinum card. The focus would be on "inspirational influencers leading the luxury lifestyle that American Express can offer" (Seavers, 2018, para. 15).

American Express has partnered with Instagram accounts of all sizes ranging from celebrities like Shaquille O'Neal (who has over five million followers) to micro-influencers like Corrine Stoke (who has under 100,000 followers) (MediaKix, 2019). The followers of SMIs working with American Express get second-hand experience of a lifestyle of the American Express card users and the rewards they can obtain through the card. The following is an example post on Instagram by the SMI and American Express brand ambassador Adam Gallagher. The picture shows Gallagher on his way to attend an American Express event to celebrate the opening of two new Centurion Lounges in Philadelphia and Hong Kong (MediaKix, 2019). American Express Platinum Cardholders such as Adam Gallagher receive free access to Centurion Lounges around the world with benefits that provide travelers with free wi-fi, workspaces, and gourmet food (letsinfluence, 2020). Posts like these clearly show the perks of owning and using an America Express Platinum Card (see figure 4.5).

American Express has consistently worked to integrate SMIs into its marketing DNA (Bullas, n.d.). The brand has realized that working with SMIs provides an opportunity to personalize brand communication messages to a variety of audiences (Bjornson, 2018). These methods of influencer

Figure 4.5   American Express Influencer Post. Adam Gallagher attending an American Express event in Philadelphia.

engagement provided the brand with authenticity and therefore, attract new consumers while retaining existing consumers.

BEST PRACTICES FOR WORKING WITH SMIS

The previous sections discussed how brands have integrated SMIs into its marketing efforts. It is also important to note that although this is a compelling method of advertising, as well as capturing and retaining customers, knowing if it is an effective strategy can be a challenge. However, studying how existing brands have integrated SMIs into its brand communication can help us uncover some of the best practices for working with influencers.

It is important for brands to first determine its objectives and if SMIs are a good fit, can provide a brand with transparency, and subsequently obtain data to measure success (Kuligowski, 2019). Authentic Brand Group (ABG) recommends using SMIs who have an organic following or in other words influencers who have followers that were not purchased or incentivized monetarily in some way (Zeman, 2018). Instead, brands should seek out SMIs who have a genuine following that is active and engaged with the influencer. Remember, it is not the number of followers, but it is the activity and relationship that the followers have with the influencer that makes it successful.

Another strategy for brands working with SMIs is to develop relationships with influencers. Just because an influencer has a large following, that does not mean that their following or content style is a good fit for the brand. It may be more impactful to work with fewer SMIs, which the brand has developed a relationship with and knows whether or not the influencer aligns appropriately with the brand and its message. In return, SMIs better understand the brand and the message they should convey about the brand. The brand-influencer relationship should be collaborative and focus on telling "authentic stories and collaborate with individuals that want to create content for the brand" (Conick, 2018, p. 42). A strong brand-influencer relationship will allow SMIs to be part of the voice of the brand and have uncanny expertise about the brand.

Karen Koslow, cofounder and managing partner of Wellness Amplified, a health and wellness influencer agency, suggests there is not enough strategy or discipline in influencer marketing; instead, there is a lot of people-chasing (Conick, 2018). As such, brands should consider developing an influencer-focused strategy and seek out quality SMIs with an active following who aligns with the brand's values and aesthetic. Brands should select SMIs who are able to create an authentic and memorable content experience for followers. Once the brand has found the best SMIs to work with, it is the brand's responsibility to clearly communicate expectations to the influencer. It is also important to enable SMIs to be creative and to incorporate their perspective and voice into the brand's communication. Brands need to trust in the creativity of the SMIs to get the most out of this strategy. Again, this is why proper communication of expectations and the formation of agreeable ground rules are always needed between the brand and the influencer.

Another best practice for brands working with SMIs is for influencers to use the product or service offered by the brand. Trust, as discussed previously in this chapter, is essential for consumers, especially in an online environment. It would be disingenuous for an influencer to promote a product or a service having never used it. This also promotes transparency between the brand, influencer, and followers. However, it is important to remember that transparency includes legal disclosures. This means if there is an exchange of any kind between the brand and the influencer, this should be revealed to the audience.

Warer Bros. is a prominent example of what happens when there is no disclosure. Warner Bros. reached millions of people with its new video game "Middle Earth: Shadow of Mordor." The game received many positive reviews, most from video game influencers. The Federal Trade Commission accused Warner Bros. of paying for these reviews (Conick, 2018). Findings revealed that Warner Bros. did "pay each influencer and provided them with a free advance-release version of the game and asked the gamers to promote the game positively" (Commission, 2016, para. 1). It was not the point that Warner Bros. paid for these reviews, it was the fact that the company did not disclose this information to the consumer, these reviews were actual paid independent reviews from reviewers (Conick, 2018).

Related, it is the brand's responsibility to make sure that the federal regulations are properly incorporated into content created by SMIs. More specifically, the Federal Trade Commission requires a brand to disclose the relationship it has with SMIs. This disclosure needs to be in plain view, above the fold, and be present first before the reader continues through the content (Commission, 2019). According to Truth in Advertising (n.d.) using one of the following marker's is appropriate for transparency and disclosing the brand's relationship with the influencer:

- #ad or Ad:
- Advertisement
- Sponsored
- Promotion
- Paid ad
- Thanks [COMPANY NAME] for the free product
- Thanks [COMPANY NAME] for the gift of [NAME] product
- #[COMPANY NAME]Ambassador
- #[COMPANY NAME]Partner

If a brand is going to claim something, the brand will want to make sure it can back the claims up with facts. Disclosing side effects, FDA warnings, and other important consumer information should always be present when using influencers. Avoid misrepresentation of facts, and do not use gimmicks to get the brand's message across.

EVALUATING INFLUENCER SUCCESS

As previously mentioned, it is challenging to measure the success of influencer marketing because it is a relatively new strategy; however, there are a few tactics a brand should try to utilize. The Association of National Advertisers (ANA) recommends measuring the following: engagement; the number of users who engage, impressions; impact of brand awareness, impressions, and sentiment, website views; utilizing a landing page or unique URL, posting; are users engaging by posting content, increase in conversions, such as a sale, again this can be done by utilizing landing pages, Facebook Pixel, and/or unique URL, sharing; are users engaging by sharing the content (Conick, 2018, p. 43).

CONCLUSION

SMIs are an essential component for communicating the brand's purpose and value to consumers. Influencers complete a vital role in creating trust between the brand and the consumer. Brands understand the benefits of employing influencers in their marketing and advertising tactics. Through storytelling, influencers can bring consumers into a world that champions the brand and its messages. Moreover, influencers can be present in all aspects of the customer's journey. However, full disclosure and choosing influencers that achieve the goals of the brand are necessary when delivering the brand message to its followers.

REFERENCES

Advertising, M. (2014, April 21). *The shift to native advertising in marketing [Infographic]*. Retrieved from MDG Advertising: https://www.mdgadvertising .com/marketing-insights/infographics/the-shift-to-native-advertising-in-marketing -infographic/.

Advertising, T. I. (n.d.). *The scoop on social media influencer disclosure require-ments*. Retrieved from Truth in Advertising: https://www.truthinadvertising.org/ social-media-influencer-disclosure-requirements.

Aquino, J. (2013, January 1). *Boost brand advocates and social media influencers.* Retrieved from https://www.destinationcrm.com/Articles/Editorial/Magazine-F eatures/Boost-Brand-Advocates-and-Social-Media-Influencers-86675.aspx?pageN um=2.

Bjornson, L. (2018, July 15). *A lesson in influencer marketing with american express.* Retrieved from Press Board Media: https://www.pressboardmedia.com/influencer -marketing-american-express.

Bratu, S. (2019). Can social media influencers shape corporate brand reputation? Online follower's trust, value creation, and purchase intentions. *Review of Contemporary Philosophy, 18,* 154–160.

Bullas, J. (n.d.). *How American Express is integrating social media into its marketing DNA.* Retrieved from Jeff Bullas: https://www.jeffbullas.com/how-american-expre ss-is-integrating-social-media-into-its-marketing-dna/.

Cho, C. H. (2003). Factors influencing clicking of banner ads on the WWW. *Cyber Psychology and Behavior, 6*(2), 201–215.

Chtourou, M., & Abida, F. (n.d.). What makes one animation more effective than another? An exploratory study of the characteristics and effects of animation in internet advertising. *International Journal of Internet Marketing and Advertising, 6*(2), 107–126.

Commission, F. T. (2016, July 11). *Warner Bros. Settles FTC charges it failed to adequately disclose it paid online influencers to post gameplay videos.* Retrieved from Federal Trade Commission: https://www.ftc.gov/news-events/press-releases /2016/07/warner-bros-settles-ftc-charges-it-failed-adequately-disclose-it.

Commission, F. T. (2019, November). *Disclosures 101 for social media influencers.* Retrieved from Federal Trade Commission: https://www.ftc.gov/tips-advice/bus iness-center/guidance/disclosures-101-social-media-influencers.

Conick, H. (2018, August 12). *How to win friends and influence millions: The rules of influencer marketing.* Retrieved from https://www.ama.org/marketing-news/how-t o-win-friends-and-influence-millions-the-rules-of-influencer-marketing/.

Costa, C. D. (2019, January 31). *3 reasons why brand storytelling is the future of marketing.* Retrieved from Forbes: https://www.forbes.com/sites/celinnedacosta /2019/01/31/3-reasons-why-brand-storytelling-is-the-future-of-marketing/#4178 24f155ff.

DSN. (2017, July 12). *Coty taps social influencers, beauty shoppers for new Rimmel campaign.* Retrieved from Drug Store News: https://drugstorenews.com/beauty/qa -cotys-chandra-coleman-discusses-rimmel-londons-newest-marketing-effort.

Garvin, R. (2019, May 11). *How social networks influence 74% of shoppers for their purchasing decisions today.* Retrieved from Awario: https://awario.com /blog/how-social-networks-influence-74-of-shoppers-for-their-purchasing-decis ions-today/.

Glucksman, M. (2017, Fall). The rise of social media influencer marketing on lifestyle branding: A case study of Lucie Fink. *Elon Journal of Undergraduate Research in Communications, 8*(2), 77–87.

Golbeck, J. (2013). *Analyzing the social web.* Boston: Morgan Kauffman.

Gutman, M. (2018, March 23). *Warby Parker brand story audit.* Retrieved from Wildstory: https://www.wildstory.com/warby-parker-brand-story-audit/.

Ha, Y. H. (2004). Factors influencing consumer perceptions of brand trust online. *The Journal of Product and Brand Management, 13*(4/5), 329–342.

Huhn, J. (2019, Spetember 8). *Influencer marketing best practices: Harness the power of influencer marketing.* Retrieved from Referral Rock: https://referralrock .com/blog/influencer-marketing-best-practices/#7-Use-influencer-marketing-soft ware-to-pinpoint-the-right-influencers-for-your-brand.

Kix, M. (2020). *Case study: Glasses brand Warby Parker partners with eye-conic Instagram influencers.* Retrieved from Media Kix: https://mediakix.com/blog/warb y-parker-influencer-marketing-case-study-instagram.

Kuligowski, K. (2019, April 15). *Measuring success when working with influencers.* Retrieved from Business News Daily: https://www.businessnewsdaily.com/12012- measure-success-social-media-influencers.html.

letsinfluence. (2020, January 14). *American Express: Using brand ambassadors on Instagram.* Retrieved from letsinfluence.io: https://letsinfluence.io/american-e xpress-using-brand-ambassadors-on-instagram/.

Lou, C., & Yuan, S. (2019). Influencer marketing: How message value and credibility affect consumer trust of branded content on social media. *Journal of Interactive Advertising, 19*(1), 58–73.

Mariani, R., Price, F., & Gumbs, J. (2019). The influence of political messages on user engagement with social media environments. *Journal of Management Policy and Practice, 20*(2), 100–113.

Mary. (2018, February 20). *Rimmel's Wonder Ombre holographic eyeliners can freshen up your look for Spring 2018.* Retrieved from Beauty Cooks Kisses: https://www.bea utycookskisses.com/2018/02/rimmels-new-wonder-ombre-holographic.html.

Mechem, B. (2018, September 21). *The ROI of influencer marketing [Infographic].* Retrieved from GRIN: https://www.grin.co/blog/the-roi-of-influencer-marketing -infographic.

MediaKix. (2019). *Case study: How American Express works with top Instagram influencers.* Retrieved from Media Kix: https://mediakix.com/blog/american-expre ss-marketing-instagram-case-study/.

Moltz, B. (2014, July 16). *The power of storytelling for your business.* Retrieved from American Express: https://www.americanexpress.com/en-us/business/trends-and -insights/articles/the-power-of-storytelling-for-your-business/.

Montgomery, H. (2019, March 7). *What is an online community? The basics & ben- efits.* Retrieved from Higher Logic All Together.

Morad, R. (2019, July 9). *From bullied to bosses: How sisters Coco and Breezy launched their designer sunglasses brand.* Retrieved from NBC News: https://ww w.nbcnews.com/know-your-value/feature/bullied-bosses-how-sisters-coco-breezy -launched-their-designer-sunglasses-ncna1027761.

News, L. (2017, March 10). *Eastern states to distribute coco and breezy eyewear in U.S.* Retrieved from Vision Monday: https://www.visionmonday.com/latest-news/ article/eastern-states-to-distribute-coco-and-breezy-eyewear-in-us-1/.

Nielsen. (2013a, September 17). *Global trust in advertising and brand messages.* Retrieved from Nielsen Media: https://www.nielsen.com/us/en/insights/report /2013/global-trust-in-advertising-and-brand-messages/.

Nielsen. (2013b, September 17). *Under the influence: Conumer trust in advertising, media, and entertainment.* Retrieved November 2019, from Nielsen Insights: https ://www.nielsen.com/us/en/insights/article/2013/under-the-influence-consumer-trus t-in-advertising/.

Olabarri-Fernández, M., Monge-Benito, S., & Usín Enales, S. (2015). Young internet users' evaluation of online consumer reviews: The case of the students from the University of the Basque Country (UPV/EHU). *Revista Latina de Comunicación Social, 70,* 703–725.

Pearl, D. (2019, August 23). *75% of Estée Lauder's marketing budget is going to digital and influencers.* Retrieved from Adweek: https://www.adweek.com/brand -marketing/75-of-estee-lauders-marketing-budget-is-going-to-influencers.

Rao, P. (2018, November 20). *Inside Rimmel's revamped influencer strategy.* Retrieved from Glossy: https://www.glossy.co/new-face-of-beauty/rimmel-is-decr easing-its-reliance-on-paid-influencer-marketing.

Resnick, M., & Albert, W. (2014). The impact of advertising location and user task on the emergence of banner ad blindness: An eye-tracking study. *International Journal of Human-Computer Interaction, 30*(3), 206–219. https://doi.org/10.1080 /10447318.2013.847762.

Roque, C. (2015, April 8). *How Amex raised the bar for longform brand storytelling.* Retrieved from Contently: https://contently.com/2015/04/08/content-express-how -amex-raised-the-bar-for-longform-brand-storytelling/.

Schäferhoff, N. (2018, December 4). *Storytelling – Why and how to use it for your content marketing.* Retrieved from Torque: https://torquemag.io/2018/12/storyt elling-content-marketing.

Seavers, D. (2018, November 13). *7 top influencer campaigns.* Retrieved from Talkwalker: https://www.talkwalker.com/blog/top-7-influencer-campaigns-2018.

Sharma, S., & Albus, T. (2018). Influencer marketing strategies for Indie, mass and luxury brands. How to drive conversions among the frivolous millennials and tech savvy boomers. *Global Cosmetic Industry Magazine, 7,* DE11–DE14.

Sigel, A., Braun, G., & Sena, M. (2008). The impact of banner ad styles on interaction and click-through rates. *Issues in Information Systems, 9*(2), 337–342.

Social Media Glossary. (2019). Retrieved from Sprout Social: https://sproutsocial .com/glossary/brand-advocate/.

Stebbins, C. (2015, July 14). *Why earned media belongs in your content strategy. 50 Stats to prove it.* Retrieved from Conductor, Spotlight: https://www.conductor.com /blog/2015/07/earned-media/.

Stubb, C., & Colliander, J. (2019). This is not sponsored content: The effects of impartiality disclosure and e-commerce landing pages on consumer responses to social media influencer posts. *Computers in Human Behavior, 98,* 210–222.

Tapinfluence. (2015, June 2). *What is influencer marketing?* Retrieved from Tapinfluence: http://www.tapinfluence.com/blog-what-is-influencer-marketing/.

Thiefels, J. (2018, July 18). *The difference between paid and organic marketing and why it matters.* Retrieved from Salceforce: https://www.salesforce.com/blog/2018/07/paid-organic-marketing-strategy.html.

Weiss, G. (2019, August 23). *Beauty Giant Estée Lauder now allots 75% of its digital marketing budget to influencers.* Retrieved from Tubefilter: https://www.tubefilter.com/2019/08/23/lauder-75-percent-digital-spend-influencers.

Wilson, J., & Sengwe, S. (2018). Social influencers: How optical is leveraging followers, clicks and pics for marketing. *Vision Monday, 32*(3), 54–62.

Yeh, C. (2017, July). *Twinning combination.* Retrieved from 20/20 Magazine: https://www.2020mag.com/article/twinning-combination.

Zeljko, D., Jakovic, B., & Strugar, I. (2018). New methods of online advertising: Social media influencers. In B. Katalinic (Ed.), *29th DAAAM international symposium* (pp. 0041–0050). Vienna, Austria: DAAAM International.

Zeman, K. (2018). Powerful influencer: Authentic brands group unveils Winston, a proprietary social media influencer network that powers influencer programs across ABG's portfolio. *Retail Management, 58*(5), 14–17.

Zouharová, M., Zouhar, J., & Smutný, Z. (2016). MILP approach to the optimization of banner display strategy to tackle banner blindness. *Central European Journal of Operations Research, 24*(2), 473–488. https://doi.org/10.1007/s10100-015-0398-3.

Chapter 5

LushUK Goes "All In" on Influencers

Adrienne A. Wallace, Regina Luttrell, and Kylie Torres

Lush Cosmetics (Lush), a popular bath and beauty retailer across the UK and North America, famous for the origination of the "bath bomb," eliminated all of their UK social media accounts in April 2019. In a company statement LushUK noted, "We are tired fighting with the algorithms, and we do not want to pay to appear in your newsfeed" (Lush, 2019). Following this bold move, LushUK announced their new approach to digital media was to focus on their existing market of "Lush Personalities," "brand advocates," and empowering employee spokespeople, which the marketing community took as a nod that LushUK was going "all in" on influencers. Can the Lush Cosmetics influencer-only strategy succeed?

THE LUSH BRAND

In the early 1970s, Mark Constantine and Liz Weir came together to create a line of natural and nonanimal tested beauty products called Constantine & Weir, and later, Cosmetics to Go ("Our Fresh Handmade Story," n.d.). The duo created new products never seen before in the cosmetic and beauty industry, such as bath bombs, solid shampoo bars, and the massage bar. Within six years of developing their businesses, the pair had found themselves bankrupt. They had depleted their capital due to their aggressive strategy of innovation; creative, social-first model which would seem was not quite ready for the open market. (Lush "Our Fresh Handmade Story," n.d.). Constantine and Weir recovered from this setback and opened the first Lush shop in Poole, England. They eliminated the eccentric packaging used at Cosmetics to Go in order to scale back on production costs. The new business model revolved around simple design, minimal packaging, and fresh ingredients. The Lush brand positioned itself on the values of sustainability, no animal testing, and social justice as well as promising to include using only fresh and high-quality ingredients in all of the cosmetic products (Lush "Ethical buying policy," n.d.).

In 1995, while on vacation in London, business partners and security traders, now cofounders of Lush North America, Mark Wolverton and Karen Delaney-Wolverton discovered Lush on a trip to Europe and fell in love with the fresh products and bright colors. The couple loved the unique shop as well as Constantine and Weir's business philosophy. Despite knowing nothing about retail or manufacturing, the Wolvertons worked with Constantine and Weir to open a Lush shop in Vancouver, Canada. The new shop opened in 1996 (Lush "Our Fresh Handmade Story," n.d.). In the decade that followed, 931 Lush shops were opened in in forty-nine countries around the world, and the company was valued at approximately $900 million. In 2015, Lush was ranked thirty-forth among the top beauty companies by Beauty Inc., which was up from forty-sixth in 2012 (Loeb, 2017).

LUSH'S MARKETING STRATEGY

Since its inception, Lush instituted what they call a global "no advertising spend" policy, which means the company maintains a $0 external advertising budget. Instead, the company claims that its advertising strategy is internal; often relying on creating brand advocates, in-store staff, relying on user-generated content (UGC), and cultural authenticity to create loyal audiences (Witton & Miller, 2017; Jones & Manktelow, 2017). In a podcast interview with LushUK's Brand Communications Manager, Natasha Ritz, she discussed how a "zero advertising spend" is possible:

> We don't advertise above or below the line. We don't spend money on TV campaigns, on celebrity endorsements. We don't promote social media posts. So, everything we do is organic. Every Facebook post is organic. We have no budget to push behind it. (Witton & Miller, 2017; Jones & Manktelow, 2017)

In the interview, Ritz goes on to say,

> We've got internal brand advocates, which are our staff, and they are our customers, too. They buy our product and we help service them as a communications department to know what other great messages they can be sharing. And then they create brand advocates on the shop floor by sharing those messages, pampering people, making them feel really good about coming in. (Witten & Miller, 2017)

Eliminating Social Media

On April 2019, on the heels of the thirtieth anniversary of the bath bomb, LushUK announced they would no longer maintain a central social media account for the brand. This included the LushUK Instagram, Facebook, and Twitter accounts with a combined following of 1.2 million users (Petter, 2019). In 2018, Lush's Facebook and Instagram channels garnered more than ten million video views. Furthermore, these accounts had an average month-to-month growth of 42 percent, indicating success in reaching audiences with its content (McCarthy, 2019a). In addition to the previously mentioned social media accounts, LushUK announced they will close the brand's other accounts including Lush Kitchen, Lush Times, Lush Life, Soapbox, and Gorilla. Local UK store accounts were to remain open (Benjamin, 2019).

The statement from LushUK's Twitter account (@LushLTD) reads:

We're switching up social.

Increasingly, social media is making it harder and harder for us to talk to each other directly. We are tired of fighting with algorithms, and we do not want to pay to appear in your newsfeed. So we've decided it's time to bid farewell to some of our social channels and open up the conversation between you and us instead.

Lush has always been made up of many voices, and it's time for all of them to be heard. We don't want to limit ourselves to holding conversations in one place, we want social to be placed back in the hands of our communities—from our founders to our friends.

We're a community and we always have been. We believe we can make more noise using all of our voices across the globe because when we do we drive change, challenge norms and create a cosmetic revolution. We want social to be more about passions and less about likes.

Over the next week, our customer care team will be actively responding to your messages and comments, after this point you can speak us via live chat on the website, on email at wecare@lush.co.uk and by telephone: 01202 930051.

This isn't the end, it's just the start of something new.

#LushCommunity—see you there." (April 8, 2019, 5:24 PM, Tweet)

The breakup with social media only affected the LushUK brand. On April 8, 2019, Lush Cosmetics posted the following message on its North American accounts:

Our dearest Lushies: You might have noticed that our @LushLTD friends across the pond are making a fresh and exciting change to their social channels. We are happy to share that the North American @LushCosmetics channels aren't going anywhere! #lushcommunity #lushlife. (April 8, 2019, 3:01 AM, Tweet)

Experts hypothesize that it seems this LushUK division social experiment was limited with a control group as the audience is much smaller than the North American audience on social media. In that vein (Viveiros, 2019), perhaps Lush believed that their UK audience would take to the concept better, perhaps they chose to use a smaller sample size rather than risk a loss in a larger population.

CAN INFLUENCERS REPLACE ALL ADVERTISING?

Influencers are usually considered an expert in their field, fit into a social media niche, and have an active relationship with their followers (Newberry, 2019; Dhanesh & Duthler, 2019). Influencers who have amassed a large following or have a specific niche following are able to leverage that following into brand partnerships where they have the opportunity to showcase and endorse products for their followers (Dhanesh & Duthler, 2019). If someone endorses a product through social media, the endorsement message should make it obvious when a relationship is present ("material connection") with the brand. A "material connection" to the brand includes a personal, family, or employment relationship or a financial relationship—such as the brand paying the influencer or the influencer is receiving free or discounted products or services (Federal Trade Commission, 2019). Aspiring influencers may promote products because they genuinely like the product, they hope to get sponsored by the brand, or at least receive something free from the company they are promoting (Influencer Marketing Hub, 2019b).

LushUK is not the only brand to focus its online marketing strategy on influencers (Dhanesh & Duthler, 2019). In a recent campaign, vegan and fruit snack Lärabar, reported that is cost £700,000 ($905,000) to promote online in the UK, and around £230,000 ($298,000) of it went to its influencer marketing strategy (Joseph, 2019). General Mills spends 33 percent of its advertising budget on social media influencers. Speaking at an Oystercatchers event in London on May 14, 2019, Arjoon Bose, head of marketing for Europe at General Mills, said the decision to spend more on influencers came from the need to show his bosses how effective influencers are compared to other forms of marketing (Joseph, 2019). While tough to nail down a return on investment for influencers in either of these brands, during the fourth quarter, Brad Hiranaga, chief brand offer at General Mills discussed at the Brand Masters Conference (Marney, 2019) that

Partnerships with influencers bring us innovation and experiences for people that we would not be able to do on our own. Partnerships like these result in increased brand relevancy and sales for our brands, but they also result in fostering creativity and inspiring innovation. There's huge value in that for our consumers and us. (para. 8)

LushUK Turns to Influencers

Of particular interest to note is the part of the LushUK statement that reads, "We are tired of fighting with algorithms, and we do not want to pay to appear in your newsfeed." Instead, it seemed that LushUK's new approach to social media would be to focus on the existing marketing strategy of "no spend advertising" and to recruit "Lush Personalities" (social media users who are brand advocates) and empowering employee to be spokespeople for the brand. In other words, LushUK appeared to be "going all in" on influencers (Petter, 2019). Prior to making this move, the LushUK brand had a group of dedicated, popular brand advocates on Facebook and Instagram. The brand also had active relationships with influencers such as AllThingsLushUK on Instagram, who posts product reviews and runs a LUSH product-dedicated blog (Wright, 2019.).

Regarding the incorporation of influencer content, Natasha Ritz said:

People like to take pictures of [our products] in their shower. We get lots of nude butts . . . shared. People love it. Bums make impact. It creates an opportunity for creativity. And it means that we invest in things that are more important, like our ingredients and our supply chain and where we source things from. And our people. We've got internal brand advocates, which are our staff, and they are our customers, too. They buy our product and we help service them as a communications department to know what other great messages they can be sharing. And then they create brand advocates on the shop floor by sharing those messages, pampering people, making them feel really good about coming in. (para. 3–8)

A statement by LushUK highlighted this new emphasis on influencer marketing in place of the centralized social media: "You'll start to see the rise of Lush personalities online. This isn't a replacement for the brand channels but an opportunity for our customers to connect one-on-one with people within Lush based on the various categories" (McCarthy, 2019a).

Risks with influencers are plenty (Confessore et al., 2018) Social Media Today (Iurillo, 2019) lists the top dangers of influencer marketing as follows: (1) influencer engagement is nearing an all-time low; (2) brands use inauthentic partnerships and content; (3) Federal Trade Commission (FTC) regulations are cracking down; (4) morality conflicts are present with brand relationships to spokespersons; (5) follower farms falsely inflate follower and engagement numbers; and (6) ethical implications of influencer labor. This final point is one that is often overlooked. Influencers being treated more like a commodity than a human being runs the risk that social media influencers and brand personalities can simply quit without obligation as unless contracted, these influencers have no obligation to Lush or any other company for that matter (Confessore et al., 2018; Owens, 2019).

In order to fully understand LushUK's decision to rely on influencers, it is necessary to look at the benefits, risks, and costs associated with decentralized social media.

BENEFITS OF DECENTRALIZED SOCIAL MEDIA

Decision fatigue is a physiological phenomenon that is getting worse as people's use of technology grows (Hodas & Butner, 2016; MacKay, 2018; Seo et al., 2019; Dhir et al., 2019). The concept of decision fatigue refers to a phenomenon where individuals are presented with so many decisions during their day that they actually become overwhelmed and then cannot make educated decisions (Schwartz, 2016; MacKay, 2018). The decision by LushUK to eliminate its algorithm-based advertising may help fight the fatigue. By eliminating a "push" concept for social media and developing a more influencer-based culture, consumers can connect with LushUK's marketing efforts in a more organic and entertaining way through first person UGC of those actually using the products. Use of influencer marketing, particularly that micro-influencer level, creates relationship-driven choices (Joseph, 2019). People are inherently social, and frequently will turn to client testimonials, like those offered through social media accounts, when they are deciding about buying a product. Social media influencers can become one such trusted source of information. For example, an influencer can promote a LushUK product and provide information related to the product with the potential consumers, then LushUK has a good chance of making a sale (Massenz, 2016).

THE RISKS OF DECENTRALIZED SOCIAL MEDIA

By not engaging with this growing audience and emphasizing a decentralized space for them to engage, LushUK could be losing this high visibility. Brands can use social media to create more personal encounters with customers, and these social media accounts become, in effect, part of the brand's properties through a unified voice and brand standards. The risk with going all-in on influencers is that it places the responsibility on the consumer to connect with the brand on its own terms.

Brand uniformity and consistency with influencers can be difficult (Patel, 2018; Jackson, 2019). Brand uniformity, across all communication channels, is how consumers start to recognize and develop a loyalty to a brand (ThriveHive, 2019). Without consistent and monitored messaging, a brand can easily lose its identity (Jackson, 2019). Losing control over the messaging is, in fact, the risk LushUK was taking with relying on influencers and closing its centralized social media accounts.

For example, without a centralized social media presence, LushUK consumers are at risk of potentially being deceived by fraud and counterfeit accounts. Additionally, the lack of a centralized social media account with consistent brand messaging creates confusion over the brand's values. Inconsistent brand messaging can create a breakdown of consumers' ability to recognize the brand, which can have implications for consumer-brand trust. Similarly, well-meaning influencers and brand ambassadors can have potential harmful effects on a brand. For example, if a consumer follows a influencers' account and thinks it is an official LushUK page, but then the influencers posts something unethical, the customer could potentially associate unethical practices with LushUK and have a negative feeling toward the brand.

THE COST OF BRAND DECENTRALIZED SOCIAL MEDIA

Social media represents a new communication paradigm (Kent & Li, 2020). For much of its time being examined by researchers, social media has borrowed context and importance from theories and practices associated with mass communication but rarely studied upon its own merits as a new social media paradigm for public relations, marketing, or advertising (Kent & Li, 2020). Even with this background, relying completely on social media influencers is not a strategy often used among major brands due to a litany of issues from not being able to control the content, to the inability to provide customer service, and the inability to listen to the needs of social media users in a target audience; the risks of "social media stars" or influencers is real (Moore, 2020). Though some companies, such as tech giant Apple, tobacco company Marlboro, and mega-media investor SevenVentures, have managed without a defined social media presence, it is rare and not "the normal." LushUK's statement on Twitter indicated the company noted that the cost of appearing in a newsfeed was too much (Bowden, 2019); however, the problem with this statement is that all forms of advertising and marketing costs money. Moreover, influencer marketing is not free, as the brand will have to compensate influencers and staff members to monitor the influencers' content. Compensating influencers, through payment or otherwise, to push out content is, in fact, another way of paying to reach consumers through their newsfeeds.

Generally speaking, it is free to create and maintain accounts on social media, but for major brands there are some overhead costs including staff, graphic designers, copywriters, and so on. The more significant point is that LushUK did not have to shut down its social media feeds all together to achieve a goal of less overhead cost, the brand could have just stopped paying for placed ads or promoted content in order to decrease their budget in this area and moved to organic content.

Social media is not just a "push" business; it instead allows for two-way communication for brands and consumers. Therefore, not having a centralized social media account for a brand can likely impact the brand's ability to listen to its consumers.

Unless LushUK is switching to a more environmental scanning approach than content approach, they will get lost in the noise of social as other brands capitalize on their branded hashtags meant to assist the Lush community. A quick search on Twitter or Instagram for two of the brand's committed hashtags, #LushCommunity or #FirstLookLushies you will see that it is over-run with knock offs, sponsored posts of competitors, and the general noise that comes with an unmonitored and unattended social media. Consumers have been conditioned to look to social media for customer service or for a way to engage with brand's they love, and so they will look for LushUK's official social media pages and instead be driven to, at best, unclear and cluttered hashtags for "resources."

Without brand social media accounts, it leaves a lot to be desired. Particularly, for a cosmetics brand, not having a centralized social media account is a risky step to take. Among beauty brands, 96 percent had an Instagram account in 2016 (Clement, 2019). That same year, a survey by Statista found that female social media users were more likely to interact online with a beauty brand than any other industry including clothing, personal care, or retailers (Gesenhues, 2019).

Another cost of decentralizing a social media presence includes the risk of social media influencers shutting down their accounts. One of LushUK's largest influencers, All Things Lush, closed her Lush social media account in October 2019, just seven months after the company implemented the influencer strategy. Jen Wright, who maintained the All Things Lush account, has been writing about LushUK since 2013. In her final blog, she wrote:

It was almost seven years ago that I made the choice to dedicate my time and energy into creating the most definitive Lush blog that I possibly could. Little did I know just how much money and time would be needed to fulfil this dream, and create something that has grown and flourished as much as it has over the years. (para. 2–3)

[I] reached a stage in my life where I want to explore far more of this world, and in doing so dig far deeper into my own consciousness. This means that I need to let go of the things that are no longer serving me and begin to walk a new, exciting path, and see what life has to offer me when I do. For this reason, I will be stepping away from updating this blog completely and will no longer be reviewing Lush products on this platform. This blog will remain out there to hopefully inspire and inform new, wide-eyed Lush fans who are looking for a solid reference point to start from, as well as serve as a memory of my time over the last seven years. (para. 4–5)

ASSESSING THE DECENTRALIZED
SOCIAL MEDIA STRATEGY

Company-authored data obtained by The Drum, a global media platform and the biggest marketing website in Europe, shows that since closing its owned social media channels, LushUK social traffic has only dropped by 4.8 percent (McCarthy, 2019b). Independent data obtained by The Drum however, showed that traffic on Lush.co.uk dropped by 7.2 percent from April 2018 to August 2019 (McCarthy, 2019b). However, even though there was a drop in website traffic, there was an increase in site engagement with the average customer spending 10.6 percent more time on Lush.co.uk and pages per visit went up by a quarter (McCarthy, 2019b). Organic searches for the Lush website went up 2.6 percent. Additionally, the #LushCommunity hashtag, that was promoted during the dropping social media announcement, had more than 171,976 posts as of October 2019 (McCarthy, 2019b).

With the focus moving to organic search strategies not inclusive of paid social strategies, comparisons from January to March 2019 and from April to August 2019, show that organic search was increased by 2.6 percent (McCarthy, 2019b, para. 11). Furthermore, a Google Trends reports on brand interest over time, from April 2018 to December 2018 and April 2019 to December 2019, seemed to indicate that in 2019 search results for LushUK improved in the UK. See figures 5.1 and 5.2.

Similarly, year-to-year data from January 2018 to December 2018 and January 2019 to December 2019 indicates a rise and drop during holiday season 2018 in contrast to 2019 where the interest over time has continued to trend positively surpassing organic search interest in 2018 (see figures 5.3 and 5.4).

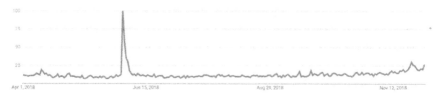

Figure 5.1   Google Trends Interest Data over Time: April 2018 to December 2018.

Figure 5.2   Google Trends Interest Data over Time: April 2019 to December 2019.

Figure 5.3   Google Trends Interest over Time (2018).

Figure 5.4   Google Trends Interest over Time (2019).

An examination of the brand's history shows that the holiday season is when most online sales happen. Sales numbers will be a key indicator whether or not the company's sales are increasing (McCarthy, 2019b).

THEORETICAL PERSPECTIVES ON DECENTRALIZED SOCIAL MEDIA

The study of social media, from a brand perspective, draws on theories from a number of other fields including mass communication, psychology, sociology, and strategic communication disciplines such as public relations, advertising, and marketing plus add in the idea that social media is ever-changing, sometimes morphing overnight, you have a real recipe for confusion or a lens for great opportunity, depending on your personal perspective (Couldry, 2012; Leask & Bridge, 2013; Langaro et al., 2019; Kent & Li, 2019; Hall, 2019; Sipling, 2020). In this section, we draw on theories from the aforementioned disciplines to examine the decision made by LushUK to close its centralized social media accounts and focus on influencer marketing.

Social Impact Theory

From a psychology perspective, social impact theory provides one way to look at this strategy. Social impact theory provides a framework for understanding how individuals are impacted by their social environment and is the belief that impact on individual feelings, thoughts, or behavior is wielded by actual, implied, or the fictional actions of others (Latané, 1981). This theory describes social impact as a social force that acts on individuals and is considered as powerful as a physical impression, pushing individuals to think or behave in a particular way. Relevant to this chapter, the theory has expanded to include how individuals are influenced and can influence others in a group setting (Diao et al., 2014; Mikulincer & Shaver, 2012). This theory provides a framework for how individuals are impacted by their social environment. On social media, if one sees a friend, individual, or an influencer that they find particularly smart, interesting, or intelligent, then one is more likely to believe what the person is posting (Changa et al., 2018; Friedman, 2019). One study, which examined influencer marketing affects consumers via social media proposes that "the informative value of influencer-generated content, influencer's trustworthiness, attractiveness, and similarity to the followers positively affect followers' trust in influencers' branded posts, which subsequently influence brand awareness and purchase intentions" (Lou & Yuan, 2019, p. 58), supporting the role of influence in sales directly.

Based on social impact theory, LushUK's influencer strategy could be effective. According to the theory, customers are more likely to purchase a product endorsed by an influencer if they find that influencer to be credible. For example, if a consumer feels like they have bonded with the influencer and trusts them, the customer will be persuaded to purchase the product being promoted. This would be easier to achieve with a LushUK personality versus just a centralized LushUK social media account because it is providing consumers with a real person they can trust along with the product.

Social Networking Theory

From media effects research, we can also consider, social network theory to better understand the LushUK strategy. This theory was developed in the 1960s and focuses on how the structure of a social network connections gives individuals access to new information (Kadushin, 2004; Stone, 2019). Strong social network ties and weak social network ties exist within social networks, and the theory explains the role of social relationships in transmitting information, channeling influence, and enabling attitudinal or behavioral change (Liu et al., 2017; Stone, 2019). A strong tie between two individuals is likely to return more favors and create trust over time. Weak ties still bridge information, though not as effectively as strong ties. A mixture of strong and weak ties creates the ideal social network structure as relational networks can create a sense of belonging online that can transform ordinary physical boundaries (Merchant, 2012).

Based on social network theory, LushUK's influencer strategy assumes there are strong ties between Lush personalities (products) and their followers (consumers). Individuals can become loyal to social media influencers and start to feel like they know them on a personal level, thus creating a strong tie. However, weak ties are also part of this theory which means that a LushUK run social media account would form that weaker tie with a potential client. As the theory suggests, weak and strong ties would make the ideal social networking environment for LushUK by creating strong ties with personalities and weak ties with the corporate account. This would give the consumer multiple links and reminders of the brand, creating a strong and trustworthy network.

Uses and Gratifications Theory

Uses and gratifications developed by Katz and Blumler in 1974 is an audience-based theory that centers on what individuals do with media versus what the media does to people (Katz & Blumler, 1974). This theory seeks to explain why people seek out media and what they use media for. Uses and gratifications focuses on the idea that individuals have control over their own media uses, as opposed to individuals being indifferent bystander consumers of media. Uses and gratifications help us understand why people seek out media to fulfill needs such as entertainment, relaxation, socializing, among others (Ruggiero, 2009).

According to uses and gratifications, individuals choose what media they will consume. Some studies suggest that it can be used to determine what media users are inclined to choose based on their favorite online websites to fulfill their needs and wants, for example, if they love a brand online, they will be willing to experience it offline—online presence matters (Harun & Husin, 2019). Based on this, LushUK having both influencers and a centralized LushUK account would help consumers, so long as the content produced fulfills the consumers' needs. If a consumer is not getting their needs met by the LushUK central social media account, then they have the choice to follow an influencer account. Some consumers may want to follow both accounts or even none at all—this is the consumer's choice and they will follow the accounts that fulfill their needs. Uses and gratifications suggest having multiple platforms to provide more choices for consumers is most beneficial to the consumer and brand.

Media Ecology Theory

Media ecology theory is the study of media and how they affect human environments and impact society (McLuhan, 1964). This theory examines how media, technology, and communication affect a person's perception as well as an individual's understanding, feelings, or values on a subject or matter. The theory also suggests that a person's perception of media, and its effects on one's feelings, facilitates an individual's chance of survival. Media ecology theory illustrates the role media plays in how we structure and see everyday life (Islas & Bernal, 2016).

Though this theory sounds a bit dramatic stating "chance of survival," when dealing with social media, the idea of survival represents social survival for the consumer within the medium of social media through a digital society; however, LushUK personalities can provide media for individuals that can give them a sense of purpose and feelings. Additionally, LushUK's account can provide structure, understanding, and values for individuals. Both types of accounts have the potential to affect individual perceptions through social media. In media ecology, this media presented through Lush channels would be an extension of the human senses in the era of communication and technology being used by many brands, like Lush to advance social change.

Social Exchange Theory

Social exchange theory suggests that people seek out rewards and avoid punishments. According to social exchange theory, people want to gain maximum rewards and do so with minimal cost or issues (Cook et al., 2013). The theory seeks to understand or answer "what is in it for me" (Cook et al., 2013) Additionally, the theory suggests, individuals will understand that the value of the reward will vary from person to person (Emerson, 1976; Ekeh, 1974).

A centralized LushUK social media account and content created by influencers could have potential positive rewards for consumers. Sometimes influencers are given promotional codes to give to consumers, which is all reward, and limited risk. LushUK accounts provide rewards through promotions and sale information. Additionally, both types of accounts provide the reward of information and entertainment. A potential negative or risk that might cause unfollowing is if an individual sees themselves spending too much money on LushUK products.

Social Identity Theory

Social identity theory posits that a person's sense of self is based on group membership (Stets & Burke, 2000; Davis et al., 2019). Every day people interact with others and create relationships, which shape the way that they make sense of what is happening around them (Bergstrom, 2019). The idea of social identity theory is that group membership gives an individual a social identity. In other words, a person's social identity is derived from their membership in social groups, which can include online groups, social status, community involvement, affinity groups such as sports teams, TV shows, celebrity fan groups, and much more. If you like something, a social group exists for it. Social identity theory maintains that groups give individuals a sense of pride, self-esteem, purpose, and belonging in the social world (Stets & Burke, 2000).

DISCUSSION

Influencer marketing is an industry with a valuation of somewhere between $4.85 and $16.6 billion if we are using the earned media value of sponsored posts as a measure of overall budget—just in the last twelve months, 320 new platforms and influencer-based agencies have surfaced (Influencer Marketing Hub, 2019a). Popular social media influencers generate a dedicated, sometimes cult-like fan following allowing brands, fans, and customers to engage in real time, sometimes transposing traditional brand management ideas into a virtual community even becoming a "brand" themselves (Helal, 2019; Hultman et al., 2019); however, this can also work against a brand if a brand's social media stars actually repel consumers (Moore, 2020). Individuals often choose to identify with social media influencer. For LushUK's strategy, using the #LushCommunity gave consumers a place to turn to where they can find their social identity with other Lush brand enthusiasts.

Discussion in the 2019 Influencer Marketing Hub (2019b) survey, 63 percent of respondents admit to having some concern about influencer fraud and report finding appropriate influencers moderately difficult to find for their brand. The business of influencers is already an ambiguous area wrought with issues, but likewise full of possibility. Embracing the opportunities available through social media rather than seeing it as battle against algorithms would serve LushUK better. Even a more thoughtful consideration of "right ad, right channel" could improve the brand reach on digital mediums (Briggs, 2018)

LushUK's decision to decentralize its social media accounts created a chaotic environment for its consumers, violating all sorts of tried and true brand ideals from messaging to consistency and everything in-between (Neidlinger,

2014; Hutchinson, 2017; Simpson, 2019; Jackson, 2019). Decentralized social media alone doesn't solve the issue that LushUK left for, but policy does. A better strategy would be to pursue policies that are proalternatives to advertising via digital media where this more organic LushUK idea could thrive (Barabas et al., 2017). In this way, there is a clear understanding in the direction for the common user to understand if a social media page is an official page run by LushUK or not.

When LushUK launched its new website in 2014, they put social media at the heart of it—then digital managing director said the aim was to "clean up Lush's global brand identity, starting with the website launch in the UK, before taking on misconceptions of the cosmetics industry as 'celebrity-endorsed and over-advertised.'" And the brand sought out "a consistency that we need to establish so people understand that [the website] is Lush and not some dodgy copycat. We are pulling together our global digital presence into one that clearly conveys what Lush is as a brand" seemingly understanding the need for social media for authenticity and even bucking the industry refusing "celebrity-endorsed and over-advertised" cosmetics (Vizard, 2014, para. 1–4).

As we see through theory, there are many ways in which to influence consumers from trust and influence, to media and environment. There are no rules that say they must purchase social media advertisements, LushUK could continue post original content on its accounts and still manage influencers all while maintaining brand standards and the product support and customer service that Lushies have come to expect—these are great first steps for LushUK to transition back to having a centralized social media account, nonpaid ads. Decentralizing social media is possible, but the costs and benefits should be weighed carefully. The entire strategy seems like they are staying on brand while being "authentic," but does the muddiness of decentralization make it worthwhile from a profitability standpoint? That is yet to be determined as Lush is a privately held company, its earnings reports are voluntarily offered when they decide for them to be released. From a social media strategist perspective, we would expect that Lush would use digital assets to inspire the coveted Lush in-store brick-and-mortar experience that was given a total renovation circa 2015 where customers can touch, feel, smell, play with the innovative and socially conscious product in big, bright, and engaging physical environment just as the director of brand communications, Brandi Halls mentioned in a 2017 interview with Fashionista's Stephanie Saltzman,

> Social media has had a significant impact on our business. Long before social media, our fans were very active on online forums and other online communities, so we are well versed in listening to, engaging with and learning from our customers. Of course, with the growth of social media, all of those opportunities have been enhanced. Not only are we hearing from fans more often and about more

things, but we're also seeing a bigger impact on sales when those discussions go viral. The shareability of the Lush experience has certainly inspired our product inventors to continue to push the boundaries around things like our bath bombs, which are creating more beautiful and shareable experiences" and "of course, they're fizzy, sparkly and fun, begging to be shared via social media. (If you don't Instagram your bath bomb, you're doing it wrong) (Saltzman, 2017, para. 13)

Appealing to a New Generation

Demographics of those shopping at Lush include mostly those under the age of thirty-five (late Millennial and Generation Z or Gen Z as it's commonly referred), female, college-educated, "regulars" (those shopping monthly to semi-monthly for products), with channel affinities of beauty, pet, and health (Numerator, 2020). Researchers Luttrell and McGrath refer to Gen Z as the "Superhero" generation (2020), so it is no surprise that Lush's dedication to advocacy and social responsibility resonates with Gen Z who respects the company's values of transparency in its supply chain, social conscientiousness related to product sourcing, dedication to sustainability, and its generalized inclusion messaging built into the brand featuring all types of people (Hill Holliday, 2019).

The decision to remove decentralized social media accounts for LushUK also coincides with what some experts refer to as a mass exodus of Gen Z users from mainstream social platforms. According to a study of over 1,000 Gen Z Americans (individuals born after 1994), 64 percent are taking a break from social media and 34 percent are quitting altogether (Hill Holliday, 2019). This generation makes up over 64 percent of consumers gaining spending power (Hill Holliday, 2019), and LushUK's move to cut back on social might be appealing to them based on the aforementioned qualities and their aggressive stance on social issues near and dear to their hearts (Luttrell & McGrath, 2016, 2020).

Furthermore, generational research suggests one-to-one communication can make an impact with younger target markets. Gen Z, in particular, is turning more to phone conversations and face-to-face small talk over online interactions (Stinson, 2017; Luttrell & McGrath, 2020). Thus, the push for customers to reach out to LushUK via a phone call may be intriguing to some; however, that doesn't mean they are using their phones for calls, nor are they abandoning apps. For Gen Z, first phones are a major milestone, a life event, right up there with getting their first car; video rules on mobile, with Gen Z watching on average more than three hours of mobile video; Gen Z are mobile shoppers making most of their purchases off a phone app, and they stay connected via messaging apps, like GroupMe or WhatsApp (also owned by Facebook) (Google, 2017).

While Gen Z does show interest in a more personalized experience, this usually occurs mediated through apps and video calls like Facetime, and this idea of a "mobile-first" mindset involving private recommendations via something like group chats (Google, 2017). This idea, however, doesn't offset the range of needs discussed wherein most of their shopping is still done online, and they want to align themselves more with brands that speak to their own value-system (Durfy, 2019; Luttrell & McGrath, 2020). The average Gen Z consumer is still not going to want to e-mail or call Lush on the phone for answers; they are going to post their question on a social page or join a chat or Reddit thread for custom opinions, and they want their voice to be heard (Durfy, 2019).

REFERENCES

Barabas, C., Narula, N., & Zuckerman, E. (2017, September 8). *Decentralized social networks sound great. Too bad they'll never work.* Wired. https://www.wired.com/story/decentralized-social-networks-sound-great-too-bad-theyll-never-work/

Benjamin, K. (2019, April 10). *Lush ditches UK social media accounts.* PRWeek. https://www.prweek.com/article/1581596/lush-ditches-uk-social-media-accounts

Bergstrom, J. (2019). *Social identity theory and the #vanlife movement.* [Master's thesis, The University of Maine]. DigitalCommons@UMaine. https://digitalcommons.library.umaine.edu/etd/3101/

Bowden, J. (2019, April 9). *Beauty brand Lush shuttering some social media accounts: We are "tired of fighting with algorithms."* The Hill. https://thehill.com/policy/technology/438088-beauty-brand-lush-shuttering-some-social-media-accounts-we-are-tired-of

Briggs, R. (2018, October 17). *Why brands need to shift the focus on putting the right ad in the right channel.* AdWeek. https://www.adweek.com/brand-marketing/why-brands-need-to-shift-the-focus-on-putting-the-right-ad-in-the-right-channel/

Changa, J.-H., Zhu, Y.-Q., Wang, S.-H., & Li, Y.-J. (2018). Would you change your mind? An empirical study of social impact theory on Facebook. *Telematics and Informatics, 35*, 282–292. https://www.sciencedirect.com/science/article/abs/pii/S0736585317304938?via=ihub

Clement, J. (2019, September 2). *Leading beauty brands ranked by number of Instagram followers as of September 2019 (in millions).* Statistica. https://www.statista.com/statistics/536991/leading-beauty-brands-instagram-followers/

Confessore, N., Dance, G. J. X., Harris, R., & Hansen, M. (2018, January 27). *The follower factory.* New York Times. https://www.nytimes.com/interactive/2018/01/27/technology/social-media-bots.html

Cook, K. S., Cheshire, C., Rice, E. R., & Nakagawa, S. (2013). Social exchange theory. In *Handbook of social psychology* (pp. 61–88). Springer.

Couldry, N. (2012). *Media, society, world: Social theory and digital media practice.* Polity.

Davis, J. L., Love, T. P., & Fares, P. (2019). Collective social identity: Synthesizing identity theory and social identity theory using digital data. *Social Psychology Quarterly*, *82*(3), 254–273. https://www.doi.org/10.1177/0190272519851025

Dhanesh, G. S., & Duthler, G. (2019). Relationship management through social media influencers: Effects of followers' awareness of paid endorsement. *Public Relations Review*, *45*(3). https://doi.org/10.1016/j.pubrev.2019.03.002; https://www w.sciencedirect.com/science/article/abs/pii/S0363811118305216

Dhir, A., Kaur, P., Chen, S., & Pallesen, S. (2019). Antecedents and consequences of social media fatigue. *International Journal of Information Management*, *48*, 193–202. https://www.doi.org/10.1016/j.ijinfomgt.2019.05.021

Diao, S. M., Liu, Y., Zeng, Q. A., Luo, G. X., & Xiong, F. (2014). A novel opinion dynamics model based on expanded observation ranges and individuals' social influences in social networks. *Physica A: Statistical Mechanics and Its Applications*, *415*, 220–228. https://www.doi.org/10.1016/j.physa.2014.07.072

Durfy, L. (2019, February 21). *Millennials vs generation z on social media*. Post Beyond. https://www.postbeyond.com/blog/millennials-genz-social-media/

Ekeh, P. P. (1974). *Social exchange theory: The two traditions*. Heinemann.

Emerson, R. M. (1976). Social exchange theory. *Annual Review of Sociology*, *2*(1), 335–362.

Federal Trade Commission. (2019, November 1). *Disclosures 101 for social media influencers. Federal Trade Commission protecting America's consumers.* https:// www.ftc.gov/tips-advice/ business-center/guidance/disclosures-101-social-media-i nfluencers

Friedman, R. (2019). *Fullscreen's Stu Smith on new marketing secret: Millennials trust influencers more than brands.* Newstex.

Gesenhues, A. (2019, April 11). *Lush UK bids farewell to social. Will other brands follow suit?* Marketing Land. https://marketingland.com/lush-uk-bids-farewell-to -social-will-other-brands-follow-suit-259391

Google. (2017). *Think with Google: Generation Z—New insights into the mobile-first mindset of teens.* https://www.thinkwithgoogle.com/interactive-report/gen-z-a-l ook-inside-its-mobile-first-mindset/#dive-deeper

Hall, J. A. (2019). On founding human communication & technology. *Human Communication & Technology*, *1*(1), 1–3. https://journals.ku.edu/hct/article/view /12072/11366

Harun, A., & Husin, W. H. R. (2019). Is the purchasing behavior of suburban millennials affected by social media marketing? Empirical evidence from Malaysia. *Kome*, *2*, 104–127. https://www.doi.org/10.17646/KOME.75672.38

Helal, G. (2019). Social media managed brand communities. In W. Ozuem, E. Patten, & Y. Azemi (Eds.), *Harnessing omni-channel marketing strategies for fashion and luxury brands* (pp. 157–209). Universal-Publishers.

Hill Holliday—Origin. (2019). *Meet gen z: The social generation part 2. A report on the first true generation of social natives and the next generation of mass-market consumers.* http://387c234b056784d14ee9-444ab69a763c675d9d74b1fe398cebbd .r57.cf5.rackcdn.com/factsheets/2019-Gen-Z-Report.pdf?__hstc=16060841.b01d5

e37365ed9dfdb9e181f0ff82f7c.1575210704248.1575210704248.1575210704248.
1&__hssc=16060841.1.1575210704248

Hodas, N. O., Butner, R., & Corley, C. (2016). How a user's personality influences content engagement in social media. In E. Spiro & Y. Y. Ahn (Eds.), *Social informatics* (pp. 481–493). Springer. https://doi.org/10.1007/978-3-319-47880-7_30

Hultman, M., Ulusoy, S., & Oghazi, P. (2019). Drivers and outcomes of political candidate image creation: The role of social media marketing. *Psychology & Marketing, 36*(12), 1226–1236. https://www.doi.org/10.1002/mar.21271

Hutchinson, A. (2017, January 24). *3 tips on the importance of visual consistency (from Twitter).* Social Media Today. https://www.socialmediatoday.com/social-business/3-tips-importance-visual-consistency-twitter

Influencer Marketing Hub. (2019a). *Influencer marketing benchmark report: 2019.* https://influencermarketinghub.com/IM_Benchmark_Report_2019.pdf

Influencer Marketing Hub. (2019b, February 1). *What is an influencer?* https://influen cermarketinghub.com/what-is-an-influencer/

Islas, O., & Bernal, J. D. (2016). Media ecology: A complex and systemic metadiscipline. *Philosophies, 1*(3), 190–198. https://www.doi.org/10.3390/philosophies1030190

Iurillo, O. (2019, July 11). *6 dangers of influencer marketing.* Social Media Today. https://www.socialmediatoday.com/news/6-dangers-of-influencer-marketing/558 493/

Jackson, S. (2019, January 8). *Importance of brand consistency: 7 key approaches for keeping aligned.* Clear Voice. https://www.clearvoice.com/blog/brand-consist ency-why-its-so-important-how-to-achieve-it/

Jones, M., & Manktelow, N. (2017, November 28). *How lush has grown without spending a dime on advertising.* Chief Marketing Officer. https://www.cmo.com/ interviews/articles/2017/11/9/the-cmo-show-natasha-ritz-brand-communications -manager-lush-cosmetics.html#gs.jy21ol

Joseph, S. (2019, May 16). *Why General Mills is spending more of its digital budget on influencers.* Digiday. https://digiday.com/marketing/general-mills-shifts-more -digital-budget-to-influencers/

Kadushin, C. (2012). *Understanding social networks: Theories, concepts, and findings.* Oxford: Oxford University Press.

Katz, E., & Blumler, J. (1974). *The uses of mass communications: Current perspectives on gratifications research.* Sage Publications.

Kent, M. L., & Li, C. (2020). Toward a normative social media theory for public relations. *Public Relations Review, 46*(1), 101857. https://www.doi.org/10.1016/j. pubrev.2019.101857

Langaro, D., de Fátima Salgueiro, M., Rita, P., & Del Chiappa, G. (2019). Users' participation in Facebook brand pages and its influence on word-of-mouth: The role of brand knowledge and brand relationship. *Journal of Creative Communications, 14*(3), 177–195. https://www.doi.org/10.1177/0973258619889404

Latané, B. (1981). The psychology of social impact. *American Psychologist, 36*(4), 343–356. https://doi.org/10.1037/0003-066X.36.4.343

Leask, B., & Bridge, C. (2013). Comparing internationalisation of the curriculum in action across disciplines: Theoretical and practical perspectives. *Compare: A*

Journal of Comparative and International Education, 43(1), 79–101. https://www
.doi.org/10.1080/03057925.2013.746566

Liu, W., Sidhu, A., Beacom, A. M., & Valente, T. W. (2017). Social network theory.
In P. Rossier (Ed.), *The international encyclopedia of media effects* (pp. 1–12).
John Wiley & Sons.

Loeb, W. (2017, April 7). *Lush beauty: Taking the industry by storm thanks to young
love.* Forbes. https://www.forbes.com/sites/walterloeb/2017/04/07/lush-beauty-ta
king-the-industry-by-storm-thanks-to-young-love/#4ed2f03d11c5

Lou, C., & Yuan, S. (2019). Influencer marketing: How message value and credibility
affect consumer trust of branded content on social media. *Journal of Interactive
Advertising, 19*(1), 58–73. https://www.doi.org/10.1080/15252019.2018.1533501

Lush. (n.d.a). *Ethical buying policy.* https://uk.lush.com/article/ethical-buying-policy

Lush. (n.d.b). *Our fresh handmade story.* https://www.lushusa.com/stories/article_a
-lush-legacy.html

Lush. [@LushLtd]. (2019, April 8). *We're switching up social. Increasingly, social
media is making it harder and harder for us to talk to each other directly. We are
tired of fighting with algorithms, and we do not want to pay to appear in your newsfeed.* [Tweet]. Twitter. https://twitter.com/LushLtd/status/1115147751648571392

Lush Cosmetics. [@lushcosmetics]. (2019, April 8). *Our dearest Lushies: You might
have noticed that our @LushLTD friends across the pond are making a fresh and
exciting change to their social channels. We are happy to share that the North
American @LushCosmetics channels aren't going anywhere! #lushcommunity
#lushlife pic.twitter.com/fzd8cppJQO.* [Tweet]. Twitter. https://twitter.com/lushc
osmetics/status/1115364719253016576

Luttrell, R., & McGrath, K. (2016). *The millennial mindset: Unraveling fact from
fiction.* Rowman & Littlefield.

Luttrell, R., & McGrath, K. (2020). *Generation Z: The superhero generation.*
Rowman & Littlefield.

MacKay, J. (2018, March 20). *Decision fatigue: What it is and how it's killing your
motivation.* RescueTime. https://blog.rescuetime.com/decision-fatigue/

Marney, G. (2019, December 3). *Transforming a legendary brand with General
Mills' Brad Hiranaga.* ANA. https://www.ana.net/blogs/show/id/mm-blog-2019
-12-general-mills-qanda

Massenz, M. (2016, December 31). *The psychology of sales.* Business. https://www
.business.com/articles/the-psychology-of-sales/

McCarthy, J. (2019a, April 10). *Lush abandons social media: It's getting harder to
talk to customers.* The Drum. https://www.thedrum.com/news/2019/04/09/lush-
abandons-social-media-its-getting-harder-talk-customers

McCarthy, J. (2019b, October 25). *Christmas "make or break" for Lush Uk's social
"switch up" strategy.* The Drum. https://www.thedrum.com/news/2019/10/25/
christmas-make-or-break-lush-uk-s-social-switch-up-strategy

McLuhan, M. (1964). *Understanding media.* Mentor.

Merchant, G. (2012). Unravelling the social network: Theory and research. *Learning
Media and Technology, 37*(1), 4–19. https://www.doi.org/10.1080/17439884.201
1.567992

Mikulincer, M., & Shaver, P. R. (2012). Attachment theory expanded: A behavioral systems approach. In K. Deaux & M. Snyder (Eds.), *Oxford library of psychology: The Oxford handbook of personality and social psychology* (pp. 467–492). Oxford University Press. https://doi.org/10.1093/oxfordhb/9780195398991.013.0019

Moore, T. (2020). *Bad influence: When a brand's social media stars repel consumers.* PRWeek. https://www.prweek.com/article/1671223/bad-influence-when-brands-social-media-stars-repel-consumers

Neidlinger, J. (2014, April 7). *Why visual brand consistency is important on your social media accounts.* CoSchedule. https://coschedule.com/blog/brand-consistency/

Newberry, C. (2019, May 2). *Influencer marketing in 2019: How to work with social media influencers.* HootSuite. https://blog.hootsuite.com/influencer-marketing/

Numerator. (2020). *Lush numerator retailer snapshot.* https://snapshot.numerator.com/retailer/lush

Owens, S. (2019, January 17). *Is it time to regulate social media influencers?* New York Magazine. http://nymag.com/intelligencer/2019/01/is-it-time-to-regulate-social-media-influencers.html

Patel, S. (2018, November). *How you can build a powerful influencer marketing strategy in 2019?* Big Commerce. https://www.bigcommerce.com/blog/influencer-marketing/#how-to-build-your-influencer-strategy

Petter, O. (2019, April 10). *Lush is quitting social media.* The Independent. https://www.independent.co.uk/life-style/fashion/lush-quit-close-social-why-accounts-gone-twitter-instagram-a8861836.html

Ruggiero, T. (2009). Uses and gratifications theory in the 21st century. *Mass Communication and Society, 3*(1), 3–37. https://doi.org/10.1207/S15327825MCS0301_02; https://www.tandfonline.com/doi/abs/10.1207/S15327825MCS0301_02?journalCode=hmcs20

Saltzman, S. (2017, August 28). *How Lush is winning at both online and brick-and-mortar beauty retail.* Fashionista. https://fashionista.com/2017/08/lush-cosmetics-business-strategy

Schwartz, B. (2016). *The paradox of choice: Why more is less (revised edition).* Ecco. https://wp.vcu.edu/univ200choice/wp-content/uploads/sites/5337/2015/01/The-Paradox-of-Choice-Barry-Schwartz.pdf

Seo, Y., Primovic, M. J., & Jin, Y. (2019). Overcoming stakeholder social media fatigue: A trialogue approach. *Journal of Business Strategy, 40*(6), 40–48. https://www.doi.org/10.1108/JBS-04-2019-0071

Simpson, J. (2019, February 11). *Why content consistency is key to your marketing strategy.* Forbes. https://www.forbes.com/sites/forbesagencycouncil/2019/02/11/why-content-consistency-is-key-to-your-marketing-strategy/#4ebc08b54ef5

Sipling, W. (2020). Bernays, Horkheimer, and Adorno: Theory in the age of social media. In *Political propaganda, advertising, and public relations: Emerging research and opportunities* (pp. 114–135). IGI Global.

Stets, J. E., & Burke, P. J. (2000). Identity theory and social identity theory. *Social Psychology Quarterly, 63*(3), 224–237. https://www.doi.org/10.2307/2695870

Stinson, L. (2017, June 3). *It's not just you-the lowly phone call is making a comeback.* Wired Magazine. https://www.wired.com/2017/05/phone-call-renaissance/

Stone, T. (2019, April 24). *Social network theory: A literature review for understanding innovation programs.* https://medium.com/swlh/social-network-theory-a-literature-review-for-understanding-innovation-programs-7f1c214e9a77

ThriveHive. (2019, January 17). *The importance of brand and marketing consistency.* https://thrivehive.com/the-importance-of-brand-and-marketing-consistency/

Viveiros, B. (2019, April 10). *Lush UK closes social media accounts.* Chief Marketer. https://www.chiefmarketer.com/lush-uk-closes-social-media-accounts/

Vizard, S. (2014, April 1). *Lush positions itself as "more than a soap shop."* MarketingWeek. https://www.marketingweek.com/lush-positions-itself-as-more-than-a-soap-shop-2/

Witton, C., & Miller, E. (Producers). (2017, November 9). The CMO show: The organic growth of Lush cosmetics with Natasha Ritz (Show #66) [Audio podcase episode]. In *The CMO show.* https://thecmoshow.filteredmedia.com.au/lush-cosmetics-organic-growth/

Wright, J. (2019, October 24). *Let the good times roll.* All Things Lush UK. http://allthingslushuk.blogspot.com/2019/

Chapter 6

#OhSnap! Using Current Students as Influencers in Higher Education

Alisa Agozzino

Higher education institutions aim to set themselves apart from other universities in order to build their brand. Image is and has always been exceptionally important. However, social media plays a larger role in that process now than a decade ago with perpetual motion and little room for brand control. Social media is based on the notion of creating social relationships through individualized platforms. Higher education institutions can lose control over what is said about its brand on any social media platform not owned by the brand. Anyone has the ability to post about the college on their individual account. Fifteen years ago, a college might have spent a hefty sum of its marketing budget on brand-building in traditional media and disseminating those printed materials at both college fairs and high school visit days. With the evolved technology and slashed budgets, new digital strategies have been infused to create a more integrated marketing approach. This targeted approach has allowed for data points to be tied to different parts of the admissions funnel, allowing those using the platform to test messages in order to evaluate what is working and what isn't.

The admissions funnel, or enrollment funnel, has been used as a metaphor to categorize the stages prospective students typically move throughout from the moment of inquiry to the moment of enrollment. As campaigns are set to recruit incoming classes, the admissions funnel is carefully planned, and different strategies are put in place to incite students to continue through the decision-making process to the end result of enrollment. While there is not a cookie-cutter answer to move prospective students through the funnel, institutions understand it must tailor its messaging to reflect what each group needs to hear at each stage of the process. The end goal usually dictates budget considerations and the survival of the institution—butts in seats, better known as enrolled students.

Overall, the Internet has changed the way people connect. Furthermore, social media platforms on the Internet have allowed individuals to develop online communities to connect and interact with others on a large scale. Pew Research Center began tracking social media use in 2005. Back then, it was reported only 5 percent of American adults used social media. By 2011, that percentage jumped to 50 percent, and in 2019, 72 percent report using social media (Social Media Fact Sheet, 2019). With the growth of social media, colleges are finding ways to utilize this tool in the admissions process. Social media platforms can help universities create an online community that helps represent and fulfill the institution's mission.

Included within this chapter is a case study highlighting a Snapchat campaign conducted by the undergraduate admissions office at Ohio Northern University. The pros and cons of using student ambassadors as content creators and influencers with the campaign are highlighted. Colleges across the country are creating social media campaigns and engaging with prospective students through Snapchat. Research has supported that the platform will provide the opportunity for prospective students to feel more connected to the university community. Prospective students value and seek opinions of current students who share their on-campus experiences to help inform their admissions decisions. The trust and transparency of the current students help solidify their influencer status, while prospective students engage on a platform, they are already comfortable and ready to connect in order to deepen their relationship and commitment to the university.

COLLEGE ADMISSIONS MARKETING

The online Wild West has made university marketing efforts a lot more complex. The ever-changing landscape has made it increasingly difficult to stay current with best practices. In the first year of *The Internet and Higher Education* academic journal, Michael Harris made this statement: "For, by all the evidence available to us, it seems clear that IT is sweeping across campuses everywhere, and while development still remains uneven, it proceeds with remarkable speed" (Harris, 1998, p. 243). And sweep across it did. Harris spoke to some of the same challenges we speak of today over two decades later—administration leery to participate in the revolution. Nearing the twentieth century, those fears consisted of internet and e-mail. Now that same resistance can pertain to the vast amount of social media platforms that beckon on our university doors.

Finding and collecting data on students is nothing new in the admissions process. Done to make connections stronger with students, collecting said data helps admissions teams personalize communication with prospective students. "Analyzing in real time which parts of your recruiting message hit home can help you better tailor and personalize future communication" (Stegmeir, 2019, p. 33).

In 2013, Davis et al., with funding from the Bill & Melinda Gates Foundation, conducted a comprehensive literature review on the use of social media technology in higher education. Their findings can be summarized in the following:

> Nearly all of what is widely known about types of social media technology use in higher education has been documented in literature describing four year colleges and universities, where it tend to be utilized as a la carte communication tools for stand-alone departments, administrative offices, and individual faculty rather than being part of a larger, more systemic institutional commitment to the use of SMT. (Davis et al., 2013, p. 4)

While institutions have come a long way with grappling with the new tools, social media strategy within higher education has become more of a must-have within the marketing playbook. In addition to being active on various digital platforms, it is also important for brands to tactically integrate the various platforms into its comprehensive communication strategy. One strategy is to create a synergy among the social media tools by making sure links to all available social media networks are easily found and accessible on a variety of communication channels—both traditional and social. Cromity (2012) speaks to the by-product of adopting social media, noting, it can "help to enhance user experience which can have a ripple effect of strengthening branding, extending communication, improving work flow, and keeping users connected" (p. 31). Cromity posits social media tools can help facilitate building sustainable user communities, which is a fundamental characteristic of building and maintaining mutually beneficial relationships between an organization and its key publics.

SOCIAL MEDIA AND HIGHER EDUCATION

While e-mail is still a tool used by colleges and universities to reach prospective students, studies have provided evidence that students are accessing their e-mail much less frequently (Goral, 2009; Judd, 2010; Straumsheim, 2016). EAB (2017) surveyed 5,580 college-bound high school students regarding a range of college communication concerns and found that over half of them preferred to be contacted via a myriad of different channels. Students are turning to social media and texting on their smartphones to build relationships with brands. Higher education isn't turning its head, but instead realizing the potential of connecting with prospective students through social media platforms. When social media began to hit mainstream, Barnes and Jacobsen (2012) made a call to college and universities to be on the lookout to match students' communication preferences to channels that would best resonate with them. "Just as marketers have long looked to satisfy consumer preferences, social media provides an opportunity for academia to relate to its 'customers' in the way they are most comfortable" (Barnes & Jacobsen, 2012, p. 117). Looking for right channel to connect with the needs of prospective students only helps solidify brands wanting to build mutually beneficial relationships with key audiences.

Over the past decade, social media platforms such as Facebook, Twitter, YouTube, Pinterest, Snapchat, and countless others have grown exponentially. Thus, public relations and marketing practitioners have moved through the discovery stage and into the application stage of social media management. No longer is simply being present on these mediums enough, instead utilizing best practices to successfully build mutually beneficial relationships with target audiences is a necessity. From devising social media goals and objectives, to monitoring channels, to evaluating outcomes, social media is now deeply integrated into many brands and organizations.

Defined by Kaplan and Haenlein (2010), "social media is a group of Internet-based applications that build on the ideological and technological foundations of Web 2.0, and that allow the creation and exchange of user generated content" (p. 61). Davis et al. (2013) defined social media as the "web-based and mobile applications that allow individuals and organizations to create, engage, and share new user-generated or existing content, in digital environments through multi-way communication" (p. 1). Both definitions share common core elements. In combining and simplifying the two aforementioned definitions, Agozzino (2014) defined social media as "applications that allow the user to create and share user-generated content" (p. 70).

Social media allows users to create and share their content, thus making it an attractive tool to place in the higher education institution's admissions toolbox. A variety of tactics can lead to a successful admissions recruitment campaign through social media platforms. "Social media has incredible power in today's increasingly digital world. It's a way to relate with your students, connect with your colleagues all over the world, and find your community" (Cox, 2018, p. 28). From knowing your target audience, to the use of photos and videos, to implementing filters to be utilized at special visit days, best practices for using social media in higher education are constantly being tweaked in order to use each platform to its fullest potential. Even with all the filters, live features, and picture-perfect photos, the key to building a successful recruiting class at a college or university through a social media platform seems to include enticing them through the content posted to make a personal visit to campus. Porterfield (2010) shares, "Contests, promotions, and special offers are all great ways to invite new fans to come in and check things out" (para. 18). Porterfield goes on to suggest through examples that having your target audience actually visit your establishment and take a picture of themselves to post to the organization's social media platform is an excellent way to have the audience visit and feel a connection.

While every prospective student is different, establishing that this younger demographic enjoys using the social media platforms is supported. A deeper look into the research uncovers that social media offers some unique opportunities to reach underrepresented students. EAB's (2017) research indicates underrepresented students are more likely than their counterparts to rely on social media platforms. "First-generation students are 7% more inclined to 'like' a post and 5% more likely to 'share' content from a college on Facebook. Results regarding Snapchat—now surpassing Facebook as the most popular forum for social media—are similar" (EAB, 2017, p. 4).

Whether it is having them post content or engage with the brand's content through social media platforms, ultimately the goal of using social media is to have an engaging relationship that is authentic. Transparency and authenticity are buzzwords within the industry when speaking of social media use. Changing attitudes from whether it is appropriate or not to look at applicants' social media accounts has been in flux over the past decade from college officials. As for the 2019 recruiting class, research has found while a majority (68 percent) of college officials and students find it legitimate to examine applicants' social media accounts, a continuous decline (29 percent) of admissions officers actually do so (Jaschik, 2018). In an article by Gewetz (2019), the author states how difficult it is to track how many colleges had to rescind an admission offer based on applicants' social media. Yet even if it is difficult to track how often it happens, she goes on to say that many colleges have policies in place to protect its right to withdraw offers of admission if they learn of behaviors that call into questions student's character or integrity. It is safe to say that using social media platforms to attract, recruit, and even dismiss prospective students can happen within the college admissions process.

SNAPCHAT

Started in 2011 as a platform where users could communicate through photo, video, and text messaging that would disappear once viewed (hence the ghost logo), Snapchat quickly boomed as a trendy social media platform. As parents fretted over what was disappearing, young tweens flocked to the new app. Snapchat defines itself as a camera company, "we believe that reinventing the camera represents our greatest opportunity to improve the way people live and communicate" (Snapchat, 2019, para. 2). While Snapchat touts the camera functionary, there is no doubt prospective students are attracted to and using this tool for a variety of reasons. In research conducted by Pew Research Center, those ages eighteen to twenty-four who say they use Snapchat checks in at 73 percent. Furthermore, 77 percent of Snapchatters say they use the app every day, including 68 percent who say they do so multiple times day (Perrin & Anderson, 2019). Another study conducted by SCG advertising and public relations confirmed the Snapchat popularity adding, "71% say they use Snapchat more than six times per day, and 51% says they are on Snapchat more than 11 times per day" (SCG, 2019, para. 2). Noted on Snapchat's Business Ad (2019) webpage, the largest audience focus is on Millennials and Gen Z, reaching 219 million people on average who use the platform every day.

Building your brand story is an important part of connecting with target audiences. With a robust internal business help center, Snapchat enables brands to create a campaign, review ad policies, customize audiences, and understand analytic measurement on the platform. One of Snapchat's prime functions is contributing to the brand story. "It leverages geofencing technology to ensure contributions are coming from users who are physically located at your event, adding an element of authenticity that is extremely important to the Snapchat community of users" (Elliott, 2019, p. 19).

Authenticity is a buzzword that many of those within the prospective student demographic are drawn (Farrington, 2019; Koh, 2019). Scrutinizing motives of brands and organizations, the student demographic aims to understand what a university stands for and why it exists. Additionally, prospective students look to make sure that whatever is outlined as authentic to the university is indeed true throughout its social media space. While requiring more resources, in the sense of both time and expertise, designing a custom geofilter on Snapchat can be an engaging promotional resource for prospective students. Not only does the student use the filter and interact with the institution's Snapchat account, but also additionally the prospective student's friends view the filter and increasing the reach of the institutions marketing effort.

Takeovers are also a popular strategy to use within Snapchat. This is when an individual, or group of individuals, become the focus of the content shared. Like any social media strategy, the more strategic the better. SCG (2019) offers advice to brands to preplan all content in advance with takeovers to ensure the content aligns to the brand's specific goals. While this is sage advice, sometimes the best content generated within a takeover is organic and transparent, allowing for the viewer to feel like they are really getting a true view of what is taking place within the snap.

Defining Terms of Snapchat

Snap. A photo or video that the user sends to another user or publishes to their Story, which typically disappears after it is viewed. Some devices allow for Long Snaps, which is a continuous video Snap, allowing the user more than the traditional ten seconds.

Snap Code. A QR code that allows Snapchatters to add you as a friend and follow your Story.

Snap Score. A Snapchat score is determined by an algorithm set by Snapchat. This special equation combines the number of Snaps you've sent and received, the Stories you've posted, and a couple other factors that Snapchat doesn't share with the public.

Filters. Added to countless Snaps a day, filters are artistic overlays that appear when you take a Snap and swipe left or right.

Lenses. An AR experiences to add 3D effects, objects, characters, and transformations to Snaps. Lenses become available to Snapchatters at different times, and they can change from day to day.

Stories. Can be viewed an unlimited number of times in a twenty-four-hour period, My Story is a collection of the user Snaps that play in the order you created them. If you mention a particular friends name in a story, they receive a notification in their chat box.

Context Cards. Designed to help you learn more about a place, or plan your next visit. Shares information on brand—from reviews to contact information to directions.

Spectacles. Share your perspective anywhere, even under shallow water. Glasses that are specifically made to pair with Snapchat app, three versions of the Spectacles exist. The most recent version offers a new perspective—3D.

SNAPCHAT AND COLLEGE ADMISSIONS

Setting up a brand social media strategy starts with defining its goals, objectives, strategies, and tactics. What social media platform(s) a college decides to be present and engage on is left up to each institution. Once goals and objectives are defined, identifying the target audience is key to know where to focus your attention. With limited resources in many college admissions offices, institutions can't (and shouldn't) be on every social media platform and run each effectively for every target audience. It is wise to instead choose what works best for the brand and then build a strategy that makes sense to attract and engage the defined target audience effectively on that platform.

With social media platforms and prospective student usage of the platforms constantly in flux, determining which platforms yield the best results is a huge challenge (Turner, 2017). As we look specifically at social media within the admissions process, Snapchat is the new kid on the block. For the last decade, institutions have been utilizing social media to help in its marketing efforts for the university (Goral, 2009; Judd, 2010; Stoner, 2013). While we can find a surplus of support throughout literature that prospective students are engaging with social media platforms, the best practices for attracting, recruiting, and retaining students, specifically with Snapchat, are still unclear. EAB (2017) reported in its study that less than 20 percent of the over 5,000 students asked had followed a school on Snapchat. Yet a few sentences later, it stated students appear to be using Snapchat almost exclusively to interact with their friends. So what's stopping higher education institutions from tapping into this gold mine? One guess would be they didn't know a brand could be so savvy. While students might not follow a school immediately upon learning it exists, once a stronger relationship is built and more insight or information is needed, Snapchat could be the tool to reach the student. When the relationship is built with the college, or more likely an admissions counselor, a friendship may blossom. Thus, Snapchat does indeed become a virtual place to interact with their friends.

Scholars have identified social media usage patterns of prospective students, yet it is worthwhile to go one step deeper and identify distinctions between how prospective students use social media versus where they go to find college information. "Social media is not as useful for increasing student awareness as it is for influencing college choice" (Turner, 2017, p. 32). This important distinction should be identified early on within the admissions funnel. By recognizing this fact, Snapchat strategy can be targeted toward the final section of college choice. This becomes increasingly important when contemplating timing of introducing the tool and the content or messaging within snaps and stories placed.

While building relationships is foundational, and timing and strategic content are pivotal to any campaign, tactical attributes of Snapchat can be game changers. Geofilters are one of those unique attributes of Snapchat that admissions offices can capitalize on by tying to the university brand. SCG (2019) backed the enjoyment of students using geofilters when it surveyed students about their use of Snapchat, and 90 percent confirmed they enjoyed the platforms' geofilters. That same sample also responded they also enjoyed Snapchat's lenses (85 percent). Furthermore, Bauer (2019) expanded on research that maintained during college visit day, geofilters yielded 328 swipes, with prospective visitors posting the geofilters at a 32 percent rate. Compare that to the engagement rate on Facebook advertisements, which checks in at a 6.4 percent. When taken together, this supports the notion that prospective students are hungry and willing to participate and engage in recruitment practices within Snapchat. Moreover, another encouraging statistic that help to support the use of Snapchat geofilters in enrollment efforts was that friends of the user viewed clients' geofilters an average 2,300 times during college visit days (Bauer, 2019).

Student Influencers and Snapchat

Another strategy that shouldn't be overlooked when developing an admissions Snapchat campaign should be to target those who haven't been campus, or want a deeper look into the everyday life of being on campus. A student takeover strategy can give a more complete look into college life. Within the admissions funnel the decision-making process can be daunting for the student. After all, they are deciding where they'll spend their next several years growing as a young adult and scholar. Many times, students rely on how they picture themselves within the campus life. In making the difficult decision of where to attend college, students lean on a variety of influencers who help shape the future choice. Turner (2017) states, "Facebook and Twitter are great for answering students' questions, while Instagram, Snapchat, and YouTube help students picture themselves on campus" (p. 32). Student takeovers can be an insightful and creative way to give prospective students a taste of campus life. Joly (2019) suggests, "Student takeovers of a school's social media account are among the most interesting types of social media content for 44% of seniors and sophomores and for 47% of juniors" (p. 32). Furthermore, remember that authenticity we spoke of earlier? This generation eats this up. Student takeovers are the epitome of authenticity and give prospective students a real glimpse of what it is like to be a student at the institution.

So how does this work? Walking out into the quad and handing over the university Snapchat account doesn't sound like a good idea. To fuel engagement on all social media platforms, EAB (2017) suggest dedicating and fully integrating a team of digital experts. This could be your brand ambassadors, or in this case current students, who work to create content on Snapchat that is visually compelling while being informative. By customizing messages as prospective students move through the admissions process, capturing and engaging them to enroll can be a #snap. For example, Southwest Wisconsin Technical College (SWTC) enhanced its social media recruitment efforts with six student social media ambassadors. Rather than intuitional messages from college administrators, SWTC found that prospective students preferred to learn about the college from a current student. These campus influencers were using social media to provide prospects with a peer's perspective, something that resonates with this demographic (Expert Insight, 2016).

Implementing an admissions Snapchat campaign can be exhilarating and exhausting at the same time. The University of Michigan claims it was the first to strategically implement a Snapchat campaign geared toward attracting and recruiting students. Director of Social Media for the university, Nikki

Sunstrum said, "Snapchat allows current students or young alumni to connect immediately with prospective students, sharing their own experiences directly in a personal way" (Zarling, 2017, para. 24). Because of University of Michigan's success with the platform, other universities have followed suit.

Colleges across the country are creating Snapchat accounts for prospective or admitted students to engage through the platform. Admissions officers feel the platform can make students feel connected to the college so they are more likely to apply and enroll. The University of Wisconsin-Green Bay bypassed the traditional acceptance letter in the mail and instead delivered acceptances via Snapchat. When the student screenshotted the message or sent the university a selfie back, this further engaged the accepted student with the university platform (Price, 2016). While this tactic garnered plenty of media attention, prospective students acquired their own attention on the platform selflessly promoting their college of choice.

PEERS AS INFLUENCERS

Consumers have always valued others' opinions; this is not a new phenomenon. However, with the booming popularity of social media, peer recommendations have seen increased likeness as the ease of recommendations can span across the globe. Social media users like to seek peer recommendations on different social media channels. Social media has empowered consumers to share their opinions and experiences with more than those who live next door, but around the world (De Veirman et al., 2017).

When thinking of social media influencers, many high-profile names may come to mind. While these initially nonfamous people grew quickly to become influencers by their sizeable followers and smaller price tags than celebrities, their accessibility as experts in their niche are ideal for many brands to tap into. Specifically, within the higher education digital space, student influencers can own a large chunk of territory. Communication and marketing directors for colleges should take note. Nguyen (2019) writes, "Search any college's name and you're likely to see a student-produced dorm-room tour or move-in day video among the top hits" (para. 5). Not owning the content, yet having a high stake in the return, can be frightening for admissions and university marketing departments. However, the quicker college administrators appreciate the power of the peer as influencer, the more comfortable they may become in relinquishing some control. This doesn't mean turn them loose, but instead understand the importance of properly training brand ambassadors/influencers and monitoring the university social media channels.

The 2019 Edelman Trust Barometer revealed trust had profoundly changed within the past two years. President and CEO of Edelman, Richard Edelman, noted how the research supported that people have lost confidence in the social platforms that fostered peer-to-peer trust globally (Edelman, 2019). Adversely, Wissman (2019) spoke to higher education's bread-and-butter, Millennials and Gen Z, and their interest more in authenticity and not so much salesmanship. "They have diminished brand trust compared to past generations, and they want insights from people whose lives are like theirs—not from people who have additional privileges. And that's opened the floodgates for peer-to-peer marketing" (para. 2).

Freberg et al. (2011) define social media influencers (SMIs) as "independent third-party endorser who shape audience attitudes through blogs, tweets, and the use of other social media" (p. 90). With the evolution of social media platforms and their attraction to the digital natives, aka the younger generations, have opened up a new channel for brands and organizations to connect with their key audiences more directly and organically. Social media peer influencers have been infused into many different industries, and university recruitment is no different.

A decade ago, Johnston (2010) examined if peer-to-peer marketing via social media platforms, and the role of influential peers was used to make decisions about college selection. While his study found that social media tools used as a source of information was comparable to that of paper mail at the time, he realized that we were on the frontend of a paradigm shift of how universities would market to the digital native in the future. Ringing true a few years later, Horvath-Plyman (2018) found that most valuable social media content for students is the perspectives and lived experiences of other current students (peer influencers), which helped provide insight into the authentic student life at each college.

MAKING A CASE FOR PEER INFLUENCERS AND SNAPCHAT FOR HIGHER EDUCATION

Set among cornfields in Northwest, Ohio, Ohio Northern University (ONU) is a private university devoted to developing students who are ready to immerse themselves in high-impact learning. In spring 2017, the ONU Admissions Department needed a new and unique way to reach prospective students. They were looking for something beyond the typical direct mail list and phone outreach tree. They needed something *unexpected* (part of the university branding catch phrases) that would resonate with high school students and exemplify the high-impact learning environment the university had worked hard to establish.

Secondary research supported and set forth three guiding themes. One, a majority of high school students were checking their Snapchat several times per day. Two, prospective students were utilizing social media as a primary tool to research colleges. And three, prospective students were looking for an authentic, uncensored view of life on campus. Primary research via focus groups also explored current ONU student's social media habits and recruitment process to help gain a deeper understanding on how to effectively reach prospective students. Finally, a thorough competitor analysis was conducted with the top twenty-five competitors within higher education and found their strategies utilized on six platforms.

After defining the measurable objectives, strategies and tactics were put in place to implement for the 2018–2019 school year. Three objectives were set:

1. To gain 25 percent of the ONU prospective student incoming class as followers by March 2018.
2. To reach an average of 600 Snapchat filter views by March 2018.
3. To post content at least three times per week in order to drive an average of 50 percent total unique views by March 2018.

Within the academic school year, a campaign took place to implement tactics that would help to meet these three objectives.

The results were empowering. In the eight months after launching the account, 30 percent of the ONU prospective student incoming class followed the university on Snapchat. The account garnered an average of 9,600 filter views at each of the two prospective student events. The unique views per story checked in at 72 percent. Furthermore, with the help of student influnecers, the account maintained a consistent schedule of five days of diverse content posted per week.

Evaluating the ONU Snapchat Campaign

One challenge when trying to implement a social media strategy is distinguishing what content would be best geared to engage. Initially setting up the account, there was lengthy discussions with both admissions and university marketing administration about finding a balance for all university audiences. It was determined that the demographic who was most active was prospective and current students, so the content would cater to those audiences.

Additionally, a major concern among administrators was relinquishing control of the university Snapchat account, particularly with student takeovers. Finding a balance between the two continues to raise concern, particularly when a university account and password is accessed many times run by the current students. While there is not a blanket answer to help relieve or calm university administrators, brands can certainly help by developing and enforcing a social media policy. A Google search supplies a host of examples;

so then each campus can develop one that works best. If the institution does not have some sort of social media policy in place, it is encouraged to consider developing one to share with administrators.

A third recommendation to best implement a social media campaign, such as the one outlined above, is to first develop a strategy for attack. Knowing that you want to implement a plan isn't enough. Adopting a social media platform is easy, maintaining them is a different story. By developing a social media comprehensive plan, users are better equipped to have success. This includes everything from the research stage to implementation to evaluation. Many seem to want to forgo the research or evaluation stage, as the implementation is the fun stuff! However, forgoing these all-important steps can leave the process to chance and little data to support whether or not the campaign worked.

For ONU's Snapchat campaign, a key component of success was the purchase of spectacles. Three pairs were purchased for the admissions office to use with campus tours and special visit days. Not only did this give an opportunity for prospective students to tell their ONU campus story while visiting, it also allowed current students to take over the account and tell their authentic, noncensored ONU story. In turn, this allowed for more transparency, thus those viewing the snaps, using the filters or lens, or watching the stories felt more connected to ONU's campus. Watching peer-to-peer stories or snaps also allowed users to connect with who they deemed influencers in their college selection process.

If needed to come up with one big take-way from this case—engaging with students through social media platforms is worth it. Developing, implementing, and evaluating a well-strategized Snapchat campaign is worth the time, resources, and energy. Even with challenges for the adoption of a social media plan in higher education, the interaction and collaboration that social media can offer is worth the effort. While every platform is different, Snapchat has a way of connecting the right target audience (prospective students) with the right set of influencers (current students). Supporting previous research (Johnston, 2010; Horvath-Plyman, 2018) that examined peer influencers via social media within college recruitment, prospective students valued the social media content that is conducted through the Snapchat channel. The authenticity of the student takeovers and prospective students being able to experience student life at each college through the current students was reinforced on Snapchat.

CONCLUSION

Higher education institutions will continuously aim to set itself apart from other universities in order to build its brand and recruit the ideal student class each year. Social media platforms can help universities create an online community that helps to represent and communicate the institution's mission, while staying authentic to its brand.

Within the social media sphere, peer influencers play a role in prospective student college decision-making. By utilizing social media platforms, such as Snapchat, higher education institutions are able to bring its story to prospective students around the globe via a communication channel the digital natives prefer. Employing student takeovers and allowing influencers to share their experiences with prospective students can be frightening for college administrators. Relinquishing control of the brand for fear of influencers posting content that is off-brand messaging makes many college officials ultra-conservative in sharing university accounts and passwords with current (peer influencer) students. However, that fear can be turned into opportunity when prospective students look to these forward-thinking institutions to connect and share content with their followers, while gaining a deeper understanding of the college during the recruitment process.

When the social media efforts are evaluated and measured, those in higher education administration can demonstrate how two-way communication with key audiences can not only help build meaningful relationships but also contribute ultimately to the bottom line. #OhSnap!

REFERENCES

Agozzino, A. (2014). Building and maintaining relationships through social media. In J. Bauer & C. Stevenson (Eds.), *Building online communities in higher institutions* (pp. 69–90). IGI Global.

Barnes, N., & Jacobsen, S. (2012). Fish where the fish are: Higher-ed embraces new communications tools to recruit the wired generation. *Journal of Higher Education Theory & Practice, 12*(1), 108–118.

Bauer, E. (2019, May 27). Gen Z wants an authentic experience: Use these Snapchat and Instagram feature to deliver it. https://eab.com/insights/blogs/enrollment/gen-z-wants-an-authentic-experience-use-these-snapchat-and-instagram-features-to-deliver-it/

Cox, S. (2018). #CONNECTWITHUS. *Journal of College Admission, 240*, 28–29.

Cromity, J. (2012). The impact of social media in review. *New Review of Information Networking, 17*(1), 22–33. doi: 10.1080/13614576.2012.673425.

Davis III, C. H. F., Deil-Amen, R., Rios-Aguilar, C., & González Canché, M. S. (2013). *Social media and higher education: A literature review and research directions.* Report printed by the University of Arizona and Claremont Graduate University. http://academia.edu/1220569/Social_Media_in_Higher_Education_A_Literature_Review_and_Research_Directions

De Veirman, M., Cauberghe, V., & Hudders, L. (2017). Marketing through Instagram influencers: The impact of number of followers and product divergence on brand attitude. *International Journal of Advertising, 36*(5), 798–828. doi: 10.1080/02650487.2017.1348035.

EAB. (2017). Student communications in the evolving digital era: Insights and implications from our 2017 student communication preference study. EAB. 2445 M Street NW, Washington, DC 20037.

Edelman. (2019, Jan. 20). 2019 Edelman trust barometer. https://www.edelman.com /trust-barometer

Elliott, J. (2019). Using Snapchat to connect with Generation Z and Millennials. *Parks & Recreation, 54*(7), 16.

Expert Insight. (2016, Sept. 16). How to use social media to drive enrollments. https ://eab.com/insights/expert-insight/community-college/how-to-use-social-media-to -drive-enrollments/

Farrington, A. (2019). Gen Z customers look for authenticity. *Duty-Free News International, 35*(6), 37.

Freberg, K., Graham, K., McGaughey, K., & Freberg, L. A. (2011). Who are the social media influencers? A study of public perceptions of personality. *Public Relations Review, 37*(1), 90–92. doi: 10.1016/j.pubrev.2010.11.001.

Gewetz, C. (2019, June 19). Yes, colleges can rescind admission offers. Here's What educators need to know. *Education Week.* https://www.edweek.org/ew/articles/ 2019/06/19/yes-colleges-can-rescind-admission-offers-heres.html

Goral, T. (2009). Being sociable. *University Business, 4,* 4.

Harris, M. H. (1998). Is the revolution now over, or has it just begun? A year of the internet in higher education. *The Internet and Higher Education, 1*(4), 243–251.

Horvath-Plyman, M. (2018). Social media and the college student journey: An examination of how social media use impacts social capital and affects college choice, access, and transition [ProQuest LLC]. In *ProQuest LLC.*

Jaschick, S. (2018, Apr. 23). Social media as "fair game" in admissions. *Inside Higher Ed.* https://www.insidehighered.com/admissions/article/2018/04/23/new-data-how-college-admissions-officers-view-social-media-applicants

Johnston, T. C. (2010). Who and what influences choice of university? Student and university perceptions. *American Journal of Business Education, 3*(10), 15–24.

Joly, K. (2019). Are you up on the digital habits of prospective students? Survey provides insight on student reaction to higher ed website and social media marketing (Hint: They like personalization). *University Business, 22*(6), 32.

Judd, T. (2010). Facebook versus email. *British Journal of Educational Technology, 41*(5), E101–E103.

Kaplan, A. M., & Haenlein, M. (2010). Users of the world, unite! The challenges and opportunities of social media. *Business Horizons, 53*(1), 59–68. doi: 10.1016/j. bushor.2009.09.003.

Koh, P. (2019). Want to attract millennials and Gen Z? Focus on authenticity, not fads. *Grocer.* https://www.thegrocer.co.uk/consumer-trends/want-to-attract-mille nnials-and-gen-z-focus-on-authenticity-not-fads/595450.article

Nguyen, T. (2019, February). Want to learn how the world sees your college? Look on YouTube. *Chronicle of Higher Education,* p. N.PAG. https://search-ebscohost-com .onu.ohionet.org/login.aspx?direct=true&db=tfh&AN=135186354&site=ehost-live

Perrin, A., & Anderson, M. (2019, Apr. 10). Share of U.S. adults using social media, including Facebook, is mostly unchanged since 2018. *Pew Research Center.* https://www.pewresearch.org/fact-tank/2019/04/10/share-of-u-s-adults-using-social-media-including-facebook-is-mostly-unchanged-since-2018/

Porterfield, A. (2010, Aug. 31). 10 top Facebook pages and why they're successful. http://www.socialmediaexaminer.com/top-10-facebook-pages/

Price, E. (2016, Dec. 2). This university is sending out acceptance letters via Snapchat. https://www.fastcompany.com/4026358/this-university-is-sending-out-acceptance-letters-via-snapchat?utm_content=buffer0d867&utm_medium=social&utm_source=twitter.com&utm_campaign=buffer

SCG. (2019). Survey: Snapchat, Instagram, Facebook in dead heat for student use. Whitepaper from *SCG Advertising & Public Relations.* https://bit.ly/2OBt7Ku

Snapchat. (2019). Snap, Inc. https://www.snap.com/en-US

Snapchat's Business Ad. (2019). Overview. https://forbusiness.snapchat.com/

Social Media Fact Sheet. (2019, June 12). https://www.pewresearch.org/internet/fact-sheet/social-media/

Stegmeir, M. (2019). Culture shift: How data science is changing the work of college admission offices. *Journal of College Admission, 245,* 30–33.

Stoner, M. (2013). Social media comes of age: Universities get results from social-powered campaigns. *Planning for Higher Education, 41*(4), 41–47.

Straumsheim, C. (2016, March 2). Read and unread. *Inside Higher Ed.* https://www.insidehighered.com/news/2016/03/02/study-explores-impact-social-media-texting-email-use#.XeRU8OhEIok.link

Turner, M. L. (2017). Like, love, delete: Social media's influence on college choice. *Journal of College Admission, 237,* 30–33.

Wissman, B. (2019). Peer-to-peer is the next wave of influencer marketing. *Entrepreneur.* https://www.entrepreneur.com/article/334472

Zarling, P. (2017). Institutions turn to Snapchat to recruit new generation of students. *Education Dive.* https://www.educationdive.com/news/institutions-turn-to-snapchat-to-recruit-new-generation-of-students/504986/

Chapter 7

Influencer Marketing

Is it Right for Your Brand?

Terri N. Hernandez

Collaborations between organizations and influencers are successful; however, there have been several instances when some of these collaborations do not work out, and a crisis unfolds for the business and influencer (e.g., #bloggergate, Fyre Festival, Kendell Jenner and Pepsi, Sunny Co. Clothing, etc.). Despite the merits of companies collaborating with social media influencers (SMIs), sometimes there are also merits for not creating a relationship with SMIs. As such, the main purpose of this chapter is to offer a research-based exploration of the difficulties that can occur when managing SMI-brand relationships and deciding if influencer marketing is an appropriate tool to use for an organization. Specifically, this chapter will explore factors to consider when deciding to employ influencer marketing, factors to consider when deciding to not employ influencer marketing, how to reject a collaboration proposal, and finally presents primary research on a detailed case study of one organization publicly rejecting a business proposal deal from a SMI and the theoretical underpinnings that caused the case to go viral.

TO USE SMIS, OR NOT TO USE SMIS?
THAT IS THE QUESTION

In recent years, influencer marketing has increased, as organizations seek to reach new audiences "through the social influencer's platforms from blogs, websites and social media profiles" (Sassine, 2017, para. 4). Collaboration between brands and SMIs has increased because word-of-mouth marketing influences sales—in fact, at a level that is double what paid advertising produces (Sassine, 2017). Research has also shown that influencer marketing can trigger eleven times more return on investment (ROI) than traditional forms of advertising (Woods, 2016; Kirkpatrick, 2016). *Forbes* magazine reported that approximately 92 percent of consumers trust SMIs more than traditional forms of advertising and celebrity endorsements (as cited in Sassine, 2017). Additionally, SMIs have strong persuasive power (Freberg et al., 2011). A study exploring the strength of SMIs revealed that SMIs were perceived as "smart, ambitious, productive, poised, power-oriented, candid, and dependable," and were preferred over a CEO as a source of "advice and reassurance" (Freberg et al., 2011, p. 91).

Due to the potential ROI on influencer marketing, approximately $255 million is spent on influencer marketing almost every month (Weinswig, 2016). In addition, approximately 65 percent of brands participate in influencer marketing (Morrison, 2015), because influencers "can teach consumers about your products, lend search-engine-optimization authority, counteract negative feedback with positive feedback, increase sales, and help with user-generated content" (Morrison, 2015, para. 6). Specifically, Ballantine and Yeung (2015) observed that this electronic word-of-mouth communication has changed "the way consumers interact with each other" and how they "buy products and services" (p. 508). It has been found that when SMIs follow and openly disclose they are following a brand, their fans will "form friendships with the brand," and this will generate "higher brand attitudes and brand purchase intentions" (Ballantine & Yeung, 2015, p. 510).

Therefore, the distinction between SMIs and the brand is becoming less clear, and the lines between what is a sincere endorsement and what is paid are becoming blurred (Weinswig, 2016; Woods, 2016). The key to successful influencer marketing is understanding that the influencer is an extension of the brand—it's about collaboration and not a transaction (Neale, 2016). In 2015, reports showed influencers could be highly persuasive, as consumers were more likely to trust SMIs more than traditional brand content (Morrison, 2015), and influencers were reported to be the third most consulted decision tool for consumers (Morrison, 2015). As such, brands are faced with the decision of whether to use influencer marketing or not. The following sections outline factors to consider when deciding to use influencer marketing and factors to consider when deciding not to use influencer marketing.

Factors to Consider: Deciding to Use Influencer Marketing

If an organization decides to use influencer marketing, there are a wide variety of differing opinions on how to find the right SMI and how to maintain that partnership. These factors include, but are not limited to, brand relevance, influencer engagement, frequency of interactions, and capabilities to create authentic or organic results. The following sections will explore each of these factors, presents case studies, and theoretical literature to showcase each factors' importance when deciding to use influencer marketing.

Brand Relevance

When identifying the "right" influencer, experts recommend first not looking at standard metrics, but rather the relevance of the SMI to your brand (Hamann, n.d.). An effective SMI could have thousands or only hundreds of social followers, but the "size of their following is not as important as their passion, authenticity and collective influence" (DeGruttola, 2019, para. 14). As such, looking at past posts could help identify the influencer's relevance to the organization's brand message. This is especially true when identifying how the influencer became popular to begin with.

For example, YouTube SMI Felix Arvid Ulf Kjellburg, or Pewdiepie, gained popularity through his early posts stirring controversy. Specifically, he would make "sordid commentary and jokes about rape in his videos" (Haplin, 2019, para. 10). Pewdiepie began to refrain from posts like these as he gained popularity, and as he gained popularity, he gained numerous brand partnerships. However, his controversial posts did not completely stop; issues about inappropriate language on his channel inspired #PewdiepieIsOverParty when he used the n-word, raising issues about racism. Additionally, Pewdiepie lost partnerships with Disney-owned Maker Studios when he laughed at "a sign held by two people he had staged on the side of a road and filmed to see people's reactions, which said 'death to all Jews'" (Haplin, 2019, para. 12).

To ensure that brand-influencer partnerships stay on-brand, professionals have recommended encouraging and communicating with SMIs as an ideal way to not only generate authentic consumer content but also keep the content on-brand. DeGruttola (2019) suggests, "Inviting your advocates into an organic influencer community, you can not only cultivate a 1:1 connection with them, but you can also open the lines of communication to help guide the types of content that they post about your brand" (para. 18). By looking through past posts, a brand can determine what type of consumer the SMI is and if their content aligns with brand messaging, and the strategic inclusion of transparent communication encourages the content created stays on-brand.

Influencer Engagement

Second, experts recommend looking at how SMIs engage their audience and how the audience engages with the SMI, in terms of responding, commenting, and sharing (Hamann, n.d.). Looking at engagement could give insight into the return rate incentive for followers, and how meaningful the relationships are between the SMI and their followers. Specifically, the more meaningful the relationship, the more credibility and sway the SMI has on its audience. As such, social presence, or clout, is the main predictor of positive electronic word-of-mouth, which explains why SMIs have the power to impact consumer attitudes, beliefs, and purchase intentions (Ruiz-Mafe et al., 2018). Similarly, interpersonal influence, which refers to "the effect of the opinion of friends, colleagues, etc.," has been shown to moderate the impact of social presence (Ruiz-Mafe et al., 2018, p. 29). In other words, the more personal information a SMI presents and shares with their followers, the more influence they have on their followers' attitudes, beliefs, and purchase intentions. Therefore, how the SMI engages with their followers should be able to predict how influential they could be for a brand.

Frequency

Experts recommend looking at the frequency of posts, their traffic, and the rate of return visitors (Hamann, n.d.). Primarily this is because (1) there is a direct correlation between how often a blogger posts and their traffic rate and rate of return visitors; and (2) it often takes multiple exposures to get a visitor to click and check out the partnered brand (Hamann, n.d.). As such, long-term partnerships are more beneficial than one-off exercises. The goal of influencer marketing is to build a relationship with consumers, through SMI. The amount or frequency of posts provides followers with an outlet where parasocial relationships may form and gives fans "strong feelings of 'being together' or 'being connected'" to a SMI (Kim & Song, 2016, p. 571). This feeling of togetherness and connectedness that followers may feel toward SMI typically extend to the brand as well. As such, it is no surprise that experts report that one-off exercises of influencer marketing are less effective compared with other strategic programs (Ranjan, n.d.). This means how often a SMI posts encourages a sense of togetherness, and when the SMI posts frequently about a brand, followers are more likely to extend that togetherness to the brand.

Organic and Authentic Content

Finally, the last important factor to consider when deciding to use influencer marketing is as influencer marketing has grown, brands that use traditional forms of packaged influencer marketing is not as effective as organic content created by the SMI. Organic content is conceptualized as "real people who already buy your products and services and create content about your brand—they're your genuine brand advocate" (DeGruttola, 2019, para. 14). Specifically, organic content is perceived by audiences as more influential than traditional forms of packaged influencer marketing. Cassidy (2017) states, "But as it turns out, most consumers aren't looking for picture-perfect ads or overly produced digital experiences. They want the authentic and trusted content that their friends, family, and peers are sharing on social media every day—organic inspiration and validation" (para. 22). Specifically, a 2017 consumer content report surveyed 2,000 adults in the United States, the United Kingdom, and Australia and concluded that consumers are more interested and positively responsive to authenticity, otherwise known as user-generated content (Stackla, 2017). Specifically, 90 percent of Millennials reported that brand authenticity is important and preferred organic promotions as opposed to traditional packaged influencer marketing (Cassidy, 2017). Surprisingly, celebrities and SMI were reported to have the least influence over people's purchasing decisions, with family members or friends having three times the influence over purchasing decisions compared to content from celebrities or influencers (Stackla, 2017). Therefore, user-generated organic content could serve as a "goldmine for marketers who are constantly struggling to break through the noise and reach people with content that resonates" (Stackla, 2017, p. 26).

Factors to Consider: Deciding to NOT Use Influencer Marketing

Despite the merits of companies collaborating with SMIs, sometimes the SMI route or even a specific influencer is not appropriate to employ. Further, while SMIs have become a positive pervasive tactic used in brand communication, as outlined above, it does not come without negative consequences. Social media guru, Rand Fishkin, suggests there are ten main problems plaguing influencer marketing that are not receiving the attention they should: (1) the practice is far too narrowly defined; (2) follower counts and keywords are a terrible way to select influencers; (3) measuring ROI is remarkably difficult; (4) likes, comments, impressions, and website visits are mediocre measures of impact; (5) variance of results is too high; (6) discovery of sources of influence is manual and difficult; (7) transparency, authenticity, and the integrity of influencers; (8) victim of platform algorithm changes; (9) fake followers, fake influencer, and fake numbers; and (10) over-abundance of some types of influencers and almost nothing anywhere else (Fishkin, 2018).

As such, experts have stated influencer marketing, in its current state, has peaked and is currently heading into a downward trend. Specifically, Casey Ferrell, vice president and head of U.S. Monitor, is quoted saying, "We are at peak influencer, and it's beginning to run its course" (as cited in DeGruttola, 2019, para. 3). In the following sections, we will explore some of the main factors that contribute to not using influencer marketing as a marketing tool as well as provide examples for each. Specifically, by curating information from experts, researchers, and Fishkin himself, the following sections will explore how influencer marketing is damaging to both the physical and mental well-being of society, encourages risky behavior, is not trustworthy or authentic in terms of the opacity of brand-influencer deals and the veracity of creators' large following, is over-saturated, ensues high-profile scandals, and is encircled by fraud.

Damaging to Society

According to a study conducted in 2018 across the United Kingdom, approximately 44 percent of individuals thought influencer marketing was damaging to society, and specifically damaging to those between the ages eighteen to twenty-four (Griggs, 2018). Due to the pervasive nature of influencer marketing and the idealization that goes along with it, influencer marketing presents damaging impacts, which arise due to the lack of critical evaluation by society in the types of ads created (Lin et al., 2019). Specifically, digital literacy is suggested to be the most valuable tool for lifelong learning and linked to the ability to critically evaluate content found on social media (Lynch, 2017). Due to the pervasive and influential nature of social media, technology, and online resources readily available to society, understanding digital authorship and representation are two important factors that make up digital literacy (Lynch, 2017). Both of these are important when creating, resharing, and evaluating content found on social media or technology spaces, without proper digital literacy individuals are susceptible to physical and mental harm.

SMIs are paid to sell an idealized image, including bodily perfection (Alexander, 2019). Being able to appropriately navigate digital representation, for what is authentic or not, is extremely important for the mental and physical health of consumers. One example that has recently came under criticism is skinny/detox teas—companies such as Flat Tummy Co, Skinny Mint, Slendertox, Teami Blends, and Bootea (Alexander, 2019). These products promise weight loss and use before and after pictures as a common digital marketing tool to influence purchase decisions (Tait, 2019). Additionally, these types of products have used many celebrities (e.g., Cardi B, Kylie Jenner, Kim Kardashian) to endorse the product on social media. Specifically, the health and wellness market in the United States is worth over $25 million, and the #teatox hashtag garners over 870,000 posts on Instagram (Alexander, 2019).

Detox teas are laxative-inducing teas that include a dangerous ingredient, senna. Senna is typically prescribed to those with irritable bowel syndrome; however, those with healthy bowels are warned not to take it without first speaking to a doctor because of its health-altering properties (Alexander, 2019). Specifically, Charlotte Kinder, a British Association for Nutrition and Lifestyle Medicine certified nutritional therapist, says, "when taken in excess or chronically, laxatives can damage the gut lining along with causing nutrient depletion, dehydration, and malabsorption. In some cases, anal blisters along with anemia or other nutrient-deficient disorders can also occur" (as cited in Alexander, 2019, para. 7).

Besides the physical ramifications caused by skinny teas, there are also mental side-effects. Specifically, skinny teas "can corroborate an already pervasive message that thin is king" (Alexander, 2019, para. 16). In an article by Tait (2019), one interviewee reported that they saw the skinny tea everywhere, and with her eating and dieting issues, seeing the tea pervasive on her social media feed harmed her mental well-being. Tait (2019) reported that the interviewee "began using the tea to binge and purge, calling it a 'reset button' that allowed her to 'poop out mistakes'" (para. 10).

The lack of transparency of SMIs and their real use of these products add to the reasons why individuals believe influencer marketing is harmful to society. Besides skinny teas and the perpetual skinny rhetoric pervasive on social media, other researchers have looked at how unhealthy food/junk food has been presented on social media to children and tweens. It was suggested that SMIs predominantly promote unhealthy drinks and foods to children, which could increase the risk of overweight, obesity, and noncommunicable diseases (Smit et al., 2019). The results of this longitudinal study suggested that "children's self-reported frequency of watching vlogs influenced consumption on unhealthy beverages two years later" (Smit et al., 2019, para. 1). These types of products and marketing tactics (influencer marketing) are harmful to society and do not take into consideration the physical and mental health of its consumers.

To combat conversations about SMIs' damaging effects on society, Instagram recently launched its "like" ban (Meisenzahl, 2019). Adam Mosseri, Instagram CEO, said that removing likes was "about creating a less pressurized environment where people feel comfortable expressing themselves" (as cited in Meisenzahl, 2019, para. 6). This is especially helpful, because "excessive social media use can be problematic, leading to sleep disruption, productivity loss, and interpersonal conflicts" (Leventhal, 2019, para. 2). Per conversations had with Adam Mosseri, anxiety and social pressures have become more prominent with the introduction of Instagram, especially with younger audiences, the change in showing "likes" could improve mental well-being, reduce anxiety, and reduce social comparisons (Leventhal, 2019). While this change could positively impact society's well-being, it does change how influencers will get paid for endorsements and remove the ability to use other influencers as reference points (Leventhal, 2019). Specifically, the like-ban changes how SMIs get paid because companies will be forced to look beyond the superficial metrics of the number of likes and comments used to report effectiveness and utilize more effective analytics and metric reporting such as video completion rates, videos viewed with/without sound, and other more sophisticated audience measurement practices (Droesch, 2019).

Overall, digital literacy plays an important role in reversing the damaging effects influencer marketing can have on society. Without the ability to critically analyze content shared on social media, or without proper education and training on being digitally literate, consumers will continue to reshare false information and be inspired to take on bad habits leading to poor psychological well-being (Lin et al., 2019). As such, SMIs and regulations around SMI endorsements should be made explicit and should be strictly enforced to limit the negative impacts influencer marketing has on society.

Encouraging Risky Behavior

Social media is a breeding ground for comparisons, specifically since SMIs are constantly trying to increase their followings, which results in more financial compensation. They employ risky behavior tactics to drive virality. In a recent study, researchers found that there is a correlation between excessive social media use and deficient value-based decision-making (Meshi et al., 2019). Specifically, creators, or influencers, are constantly comparing themselves to other SMIs and trying to have the trendiest viral content. This constant comparison leads them to create riskier and risker content, which leads to scandal and drives away advertisers.

For example, in 2018, Logan Paul, YouTube celebrity and SMI, posted a video of himself and others touring Japan's infamous "Suicide Forest," where they allegedly found the corpse of a suicide victim and laughed and joked with the body (PRWeek Staff, 2018). The ramifications from this incident were exponential—YouTube cut Logan Paul's advertising privileges and more than 750,000 people signed petitions calling for him to be banned from the platform (Cook, 2019). However, *Paul* was still one of the ten highest-paid YouTube SMIs in 2018, and *Forbes* estimated he earned approximately $14.5 million from influencer marketing in 2018 (Robehmed & Berg, 2018). Although Paul has deemed the suicide forest video one of his biggest regrets and has claimed he "didn't do it for the views" (Cook, 2019, para. 5), this scandal left him "relatively unscathed, with a higher income and more subscribers than ever" (para. 2) further perpetuating his risky posting behavior and perpetuating poor behavior within society.

Lack of Trust and Authenticity

Another factor for deciding not to use influencer marketing is the lack of trust or authenticity consumers feel toward SMIs. This is especially alarming since trust is a critical component to establishing credibility, which is needed to cultivate influence (DeGruttola, 2019). Specifically, in a study conducted in 2019 by media agency UM, they found only 8 percent of individuals trust the bulk of information shared on social media, and only 4 percent trust information when it comes from SMIs (Stewart, 2019). In this particular study, the researchers tracked more than 56,000 active Internet users across eighty-one counties and concluded that regulation needs to focus on the "opacity of brand-influencer deals and the veracity of creators' large followings" (Stewart, 2019, para. 6).

Opacity of Brand Iinfluencer Deals

The lack of transparent partnerships and the extent of the partnerships between SMIs and brands have led to the mistrust between followers and SMIs. Although the Advertising Standards Authority (ASA) does have rules and regulations in place around influencer marketing, most people are "not aware of the hashtags and language influencers must use to indicate their commercial relationship with a brand" (Griggs, 2018, para. 3). However, even though some SMIs do abide by the rules and regulations set in place by the ASA, there have been instances where "shady influencers" continue "to blur the lines—and get away with it" (Tait, 2019, para. 10). For example, Khloe Kardashian, American media personality, socialite, and model, posted a sly advertisement post on Instagram in 2017 about a sugary hair supplement, "This is more than just an #Ad because I truly love these delicious, soft, chewy vitamins" (Tait, 2018, para. 8). Although she did follow the guidelines set in place by the ASA by including #Ad, Khloe Kardashian was clever in the post, making the endorsement of the hair supplement more authentic by suggesting the post was not a traditional advertisement. While Khloe Kardashian was straightforward in her paid endorsement post, other SMIs have made efforts to evade or hide the #Ad. For example, Tait (2019) wrote:

> One famous British YouTuber has been known to place the word "ad" on the bottom right-hand corner of his YouTube thumbnails, conveniently behind YouTube's timestamps—while his girlfriend posts affiliated links to the products she uses in her videos without revealing that she's paid every time those links are clicked. (para. 12)

Veracity of Influencers' Large Followings

In terms of the veracity of creators' large following, recent discussions have been placed around fake followers used by SMIs to deceive brands and the public. Specifically, Procter & Gamble Co. "has been vigorously rooting out fraud and unverified data from its digital buys" (Neff, 2018, para. 1). Tressie Rose, Procter & Gamble Co. spokeswoman, stated, "there are a lot of companies out there offering services to combat this. Bot Fraud is an industry-wide issue and one we're continuing to actively work on" (as cited in Neff, 2018, para. 3). However, Procter & Gamble Co. are still one of the top brands using SMIs. Additionally, in a study conducted by Points North Group, it was reported that Procter & Gamble Co. was one of the top ten brands that are currently using paid SMIs who have a fake following (Neff, 2018). Peter Storck, co-founder of Points North Group, reports that one client he worked for, a large cosmetic brand, spent $600,000 on influencer impressions that weren't seen or were seen only by fake followers (Neff, 2018). In 2019, Roberto Cavazos, professor and economist from the University of Baltimore, states that fraudulent activity has cost advertisers $1.3 billion this year (as cited in Graham, 2019).

Market Oversaturation

Due to the pervasive, oversaturation, and inauthentic nature of influencer marketing, consumers are becoming more educated on influencer marketing and even turning away from it. In a consumer content report conducted in 2017 by Stackla, respondents reported that about 70 percent of the time they could tell that an image was created by the brand as opposed to the SMI (Cassidy, 2017). Specifically, researchers tested how well respondents could identify between images that were consumer-created as opposed to marketer-created. Results revealed that Millennials identified consumer-created content more accurately than Gen X or Boomers (Stackla, 2017). When individuals could identify that the content was not organic or authentic, 20 percent of respondents reported that they unfollowed a brand on social media because they felt their content was inauthentic (Cassidy, 2017). Therefore, not only can consumers identify brand-created content as opposed to consumer-created, they "punish brands that try to fake it" (Stackla, 2017, p. 26). For example, the 2017 Kendall Jenner and Pepsi partnership were accused of trivializing Black Lives Matter and resulted in media backlash and social media unfollowing of both Kendall Jenner and Pepsi (Victor, 2017).

High-Profile Scandals

In terms of inauthentic posts, establishing credibility, and increasing influence, multiple influencers have been "outed" for their inauthentic behavior (e.g., Marissa Fuchs, Elle Darby). These high-profile scandals further the mistrust in influencer marketing. The issue is not only the encouragement of inauthentic posts by brands but also SMIs encourage inauthentic posts when they seek out partnerships. Arron Shepherd, co-founder of influencer marketing agency GOAT, states that SMIs who seek out inauthentic endorsements are hurting themselves, and not the brand. "The people that will suffer the most will be the influencers, not the brands. Influencers have very specific audiences, who are sensitive to betrayal" (as cited in Hern, 2019, para. 8). As such, when SMIs have been outed for seeking free accommodations, free products, or free services for their endorsement, followers have shamed them. When SMIs are shamed the relationship between them and their followers is fractured, and the strength of an influencer is defined by the relationship they have with their audience (Hern, 2019).

For example, in 2019, Marissa Fuchs, a fashion influencer, shared a video of her boyfriend, Gabriel Grossman, professing his love and telling her that she is about to embark on an extraordinary adventure (Lorenz, 2019). The extraordinary adventure was a forty-eight-hour scavenger hunt that took Fuchs from New York City to Montauk to Miami and Paris, all the while collecting two diamond-and-gold necklaces, documenting every move on Instagram, and all leading up to an extravagant marriage proposal (Lorenz, 2019). The scavenger hunt went viral, everyone was so excited to see what would unfold, and from the first post, Fuchs gained an additional 20,000 followers (Lorenz, 2019).

> As fans waited eagerly for each new surprise, brand marketers couldn't believe it was all going to plan. Many knew exactly how the proposal would play out, hour by hour. They knew the couple's engagement hashtag. They knew what hotels Fuchs would be staying at, where she would eat, and when she'd post to her feed. They had seen it all before, in a pitch deck. (Lorenz, 2019, para. 5)

Later it was revealed that before the proposal scavenger hunt ever began, marketers at various brands and agencies had received a PDF outlining the future engagement in the context of a potential sponsorship, stating it would be "a one-of-a-kind proposal experience for a one-of-a-kind female ambitionist" (as cited in Lorenz, 2019, para. 6). In the partnership proposal, Fuchs included a full biography, a summary of metrics, and a detailed itinerary of how the proposal would proceed (Lorenz, 2019). While this partnership proposal was sent to multiple marketers and agencies, it is unclear which deals were sponsored due to the lack of #Ad included in the posts, even though businesses and products were tagged in the posts.

When the proposal was revealed to be a marketing stunt, media and follower backlash for Fuchs ensued. Kelsy Hodgkin, the head of strategy at Deutsch Los Angeles, an advertising agency, was reported to have viewed the business proposal and was unsurprised that the influencer couple would try to make money of a momentous life event (Lorenz, 2019). Specifically, she was quoted stating,

> influencer marketing is a free-for-all at the moment. Everyone is like, "How far can I push it? . . . this current state is unsustainable." The more influencers are fabricating scenarios for brands to be part of, the less influential they become. (as cited in Lorenz, 2019, para. 17)

Fraud

The final factor to consider when deciding to not use influencer marketing as a media tool is the amount of fraud that has encircled influencer marketing, which has contributed to the suggestion that influencer marketing is in a downward trend (DeGruttola, 2019). Some examples of fraud have been confounded in the examples illustrated above; however, the infamous 2017 Fyre Festival debacle is one example of SMI fraud that deserves to be mentioned. The Fyre Festival "promised a VIP experience on the island of Great Exuma in the Bahamas, turned into a nightmare situation as attendees were stranded with half-built huts to sleep in and cold cheese sandwiches to eat" (Hanbury, 2019, para. 4). When promoting the event multiple supermodels (e.g., Hailey Baldwin, Emily Ratajkowski, Bella Hadid), surfers, D.J.s, and even a few football players promoted it on social media under the guise that people would be able to party with them as well as other celebrities and be treated to a luxurious event. The majority of those who promoted the event were compensated, with Kendall Jenner, American socialite and model, receiving a reported $250,000 (Burrough, 2017). The social media promotion of the event is credited as one of the greatest social media campaigns ever seen (Burrough, 2017). However, none of the SMIs who promoted the event were even in attendance. Approximately 5,000 people showed up for the event, which included inadequate food, living accommodations, transportation, and even an inadequate headliner. Since this event, many celebrities and SMIs deny any knowledge or intention of going to the event. Two documentaries have been produced (i.e., Hulu and Netflix), and the creator of the Fyre Festival has been sentenced to six years in prison for fraud (Hanbury, 2019).

REJECTING A SMI

The term "SMI" was once considered one of the most enviable labels on social media, which came with status, popularity, and money (Bryant & Lothian-McLean, 2019). However, due to its damaging effects on society, encouragement of risky behavior, untrustworthy nature, oversaturation, high-profile scandals, and rampant reports of fraud, the word "influencer" has developed a negative connotation and social media stars are distancing themselves from the increasingly toxic SMI tag (Bryant & Lothian-McLean, 2019). Overall, SMIs have been making headlines for the wrong reasons: pushing products to young audiences including diet pills, pharmaceuticals, and tobacco; failing to declare sponsored content; purchasing followers, comments or likes, bombarding business with free requests; and even conducting fraud (Bryant & Lothian-McLean, 2019). For these reasons or others, a brand may decide that influencer marketing is not a lucrative business venture they would like to take part in.

In the traditional sense, brands seek out SMIs to offer their services in exchange for social media recognition. However, there are circumstances, like the Fuchs example outlined above, where SMIs reach out to businesses seeking free products or compensation for social media recognition (Dodgson, 2019). In some cases, when SMIs reach out to organizations with a partnership proposal and the organization does not see the potential for establishing a mutually beneficial relationship, the organization is then faced with the task to reject a collaboration idea presented to them by a SMI. This seems simple enough; however, rejecting SMIs has proven to be difficult.

For example, in 2019, one wedding photographer was called abusive after refusing to offer services to an Instagram influencer for free (Dodgson, 2019). Betrothed & Co, a small wedding photography business, was approached by an influencer's public relations representative and proposed to the company that the influencer could advertise the company to their 55,000 social media followers in exchange for free wedding photography services on their wedding day. Betrothed & Co declined the partnership and asked if there was a typo in the original e-mail because 55,000 followers "isn't a level of following which can command the free transfer of products worth between $5,000 and $8,000 total" (Dodgson, 2019, para. 9). The influencer's representative responded to the decline by calling Betrothed & Co "unprofessional" and saying their response was "appalling" (as cited in Dodgson, 2019, para. 12). Additionally, the representative signed the e-mail with a threat, saying if Betrothed & Co were to respond and "continue with this abuse" the representative would "name and shame" them (as cited in Dodgson, 2019, para. 15).

As evident in this collaboration proposal between Betrothed & Co and an unnamed SMI, rejecting an influencer is not a simple task. Jacquelyn from Scrunch (n.d.), offers five tips on how to politely handle and decline a collaboration offer: (1) always respond, (2) include your reasoning, (3) don't be rude, (4) send them details, and (5) do not be afraid to negotiate. However, if you are naturally sarcastic, feel snubbed by the SMI, or perceive the collaboration proposal to be entitled, a simple decline e-mail response may be hard to compose. In the case of #Bloggergate, Paul Stenson, hotel owner, provided a snarky decline of a collaboration proposal that was presented to him by SMI, Elle Darby. The collaboration proposal went very wrong, and eventually went viral resulting in controversy for both Stenson and Darby. The following section provides background information on #Bloggergate and presents primary research on the case with a theoretical discussion on why this particular case caused so much controversy and hatred directed at both Stenson and Darby.

CASE STUDY: #BLOGGERGATE

January 16, 2018, White Moose Café hotel owner Paul Stenson received an e-mail from a SMI requesting a free four-night accommodation in exchange for exposure on social media. His response was to post an image of this e-mail accompanied by a sassy rejection of the business proposal onto the hotel's Facebook page (White Moose Café, 2018). As part of this response, Stenson called out the influencer for not having "self-respect and dignity" and suggested that his following on social media was greater than hers (White Moose Café, 2018). Stenson (2018) added,

> If her lack of care about who she was writing to wasn't enough, the "me, me, me" style of writing that ensued suggested that not only was the addressee of the email non-existent, but there was a particularly strong chance that no other human being on planet earth existed, other than the emailer. (para. 3)

Stenson posted both Darby's e-mail and his remarks on the White Moose Café's Facebook page.

Although the hotel owner attempted to hide the influencer's identity, people on social media figured out that the influencer was Elle Darby and began to harass her. In response to the harassment, Elle Darby posted a seventeen-minute video on YouTube defending herself and her business (Darby, 2018). In this video, Darby made many claims, cried, and called out Stenson for being a bully. In the video, she also said she had observed that the majority of the "death threats" or criticisms she was receiving (e.g., that she was entitled) were from those who were over the age of thirty, and suggested that those over thirty do not understand how social media works and/or how social media influencing works, and that was why she was receiving so much backlash.

In response to the video and the backlash received from the blogging community, Stenson banned all bloggers from his business. He stated that the reason for the ban was because

> the sense of entitlement is just too strong in the blogging community and the nastiness, hissy fits, and general hate displayed after one of your members was not granted her request for a freebie is giving your whole industry a bad name. (White Moose Café, 2018, para. 2)

Due to the media frenzy, Stenson sent an invoice to Elle Darby for all the media coverage he had created for her by posting the initial e-mail and his response to social media (White Moose Café, 2018), stating that the amount of attention she received due to revealing herself in this situation could be translated into financial value, which was revealed in a fake press conference Stenson held (White Moose Café, 2018). Then on January 22, the White Moose Café created T-shirts with the logo, "I got exposed by White Moose," and began selling them on its website. Stenson emphasized that it was not he, but Darby who revealed her identity. In response to the invoice and the T-shirts, Darby created a second video on her YouTube blog, expressing her frustration about the situation and elaborated on her side of the story (Darby, 2018). Finally, on January 26, Stenson posted an opinion piece entitled "The Truth about #Bloggergate" on his personal blog and White Moose Café's Facebook page in which he expressed his side of the story and the motivations behind each of his actions in the case (Stenson, 2018).

The case created a media frenzy with almost 53 pieces of coverage in 11 countries secured for the White Moose Café, and almost 114 pieces of coverage in 20 countries secured for Elle Darby (McCann, 2018). This resulted in a potential reach of 120 million people for the White Moose Café and 450 million people for Elle Darby (McCann, 2018). To pay for this type of advertising, the White Moose Café would have had to spend almost $2 million and Darby would have had to spend almost $4.2 million (McCann, 2018).

Content Analysis: Social Media Mining #Bloggergate

To understand the full impact and valance of #Bloggergate, a content analysis was conducted by a research team on the social media posts made by the public on the case. Specifically, the content analysis examined social media posts from the public that used the hashtag, #Bloggergate, to fully understand why and in which ways people responded to the collaboration rejection on social media.

The full population for this study was all social media posts that discussed the situation between Elle Darby and the White Moose Café Owner Paul Stenson and used the #Bloggergate hashtag. Using a social media mining company to access social media data on the case, researchers collected $N = 1,001$ mentions. These mentions were collected from January 16 to February 28, 2018, for approximately a month and a half after the initial Facebook post made by the White Moose Café. These mentions originated from Facebook ($n = 62$), Twitter ($n = 453$), Instagram ($n = 91$), blogs ($n = 35$), news ($n = 63$), YouTube ($n = 146$), and the web ($n = 151$).

The overall estimated social media reach (potential audience size exposed to the messages) from these mentions was approximately 2,021,794. Specifically, the average number of followers for an author was around 14,991.67 ($SD = 52,251.44$), with the largest number of followers being 445,029 for one author. This suggests that the overall social media reach possible for these authors was an average of 2,115.45 ($SD = 6,057.96$), with a maximum social media reach of 44,502.9. Finally, the overall sentiment reported by the computer system ranged from negative (3.6 percent) to neutral (25.8 percent) to positive (9.3 percent).

However, to understand further what comprised of this reach and its valence, the research team individually coded the mentions. A random sample of the original population was conducted, and for the present study $n = 300$ mentions were examined, which was approximately 30 percent of the original population of mentions. Factors that makeup social identity theory and parasocial relationships were used as variables in the coding process to determine why and how users expressed sentiment toward or against Stenson and Darby.

Social Identity Theory

This case gives novel material for examining and understanding the role social identity plays in social media, particularly during a scandal, considering that the crisis created a feud between the White Moose Café and many other SMIs. Elle Darby's followers and fellow SMIs began bombarding the White Moose Café with false one-star ratings (Stenson, 2018), and it is particularly bad for a company when the one-star ratings come from other influencers, as their opinion influences others' perceptions. In this case, however, White Moose Café supporters began to leave five-star ratings and changed the distribution of the one-star reviews (6.6K) and five-star reviews (50K).

Considering #Bloggergate and the situation between Elle Darby and the White Moose Café, it can be suggested that identification with either Elle Darby (blogger, influencer, young, female) or the White Moose Café (small business owner, middle-aged, male) influenced actions taken by group members. Specifically, those who took action to express their opinion on the matter contributed to the overall identification with Darby or the White Moose, as those who gave one-star ratings to the White Moose Café had never visited the hotel but were bloggers/influencers themselves. This case impacted the self-concept of all bloggers, which in turn could explain why they united and formed the #Bloggergate campaign against the White Moose Café. This unification of bloggers harassing the hotel led owner Paul Stenson to ban all bloggers from his hotel. However, supporters of the White Moose Café also united when they came under attack from bloggers and took action to defend the hotel. The identification and group formation process that occurred, in this case, could help explain the divide between the two groups and the hostility that ensued.

Parasocial Relationships

Additionally, this case examined the relationship between SMIs and loyal followers during a scandal, yielding further insight into the role that parasocial relationships play with SMIs. Initially, the concept of parasocial relationships was used to primarily explain a phenomena in television audiences (Horton & Wohl, 1956). Recent studies, however, have applied the concept to other types of media, such as the Internet (Ballantine & Martin, 2004), and it has been recognized that the formation of parasocial relationships is not limited to characters in television shows, but may also occur with celebrities and Internet personalities (Ballantine & Yeung, 2015).

In the case of Elle Darby, her popularity arose from the content of her YouTube vlog. As noted, vlogs provide a platform where SMIs can share intimate pieces of their private and public lives, which can impact the relationship between SMIs and their followers. Due to the strength of the parasocial relationship that Elle Darby's vlog created among her fans, they were emboldened to come to her defense when she was publicly antagonized by the owner of the White Moose Café.

CONCLUSION

Influencer marketing is not an appropriate marketing tool for every brand. Many factors contribute to why a brand decides to use or not use influencer marketing as a tool to reach and influence its target audience. While influencer marketing has come under recent criticism, influencer marketing is still a pervasive part of society. Deciding to reject an influencer or collaboration idea is not easy, and special care and consideration should be taken when rejecting a partnership. The amount of power a SMI's following can have on a brand due to the strong social identity and parasocial relationships formed can bring down a brand faster than a SMI could build it up. As such, this chapter illustrated many examples of cases where SMIs and their followers brought negativity to a brand. Influencer marketing is a powerful tool that changes how brands create and form partnerships.

REFERENCES

Alexander, M. (2019, Sept. 5). The big fat problem with skinny tea: Detox culture and the brands who sell it. *Independent*. https://www.independent.co.uk/life-style/women/skinny-tea-detox-cleansing-instagram-kylie-jenner-laxative-a9080961.html

Ballantine, P. W., & Martin, B. A. (2005). Forming parasocial relationships in online communities. *Advances in Consumer Research*, *32*, 197–201.

Bryant, B., & Lothian-McLean, M. (2019, Feb. 23). How "influencer" became a dirty word. *BBC*. https://www.bbc.co.uk/bbcthree/article/61d019b6-fd08-4da5-aaf8-b28faf17e616

Burrough, B. (2017, June 29). Frye festival: Anatomy of a millennial marketing fiasco waiting to happen. *Vanity Fair.* https://www.vanityfair.com/news/2017/06/fyre-festival-billy-mcfarland-millennial-marketing-fiasco

Cassidy, P. (2017, Nov. 21). Survey finds consumers crave authenticity—And user-generated content delivers. *Social Media Today.* https://www.socialmediatoday.com/news/survey-finds-consumers-crave-authenticity-and-user-generated-content-deli/511360/

Cook, J. (2019, Jan. 4). 1 year after his infamous "suicide forest" video, Logan Paul is bigger than ever. *HuffPost.* https://www.huffpost.com/entry/logan-paul-1-year-suicide-forest_n_5c2e9b92e4b05c88b70798f5

Darby, E. (2018, Jan. 16). I was exposed (so embarrassing) [Video file]. https://www.youtube.com/watch?v=g8zElbN2_hg

DeGruttola, M. (2019, Nov. 17). Why the future of influencer marketing will be organic influencers. *Social Media Today.* https://www.socialmediatoday.com/news/why-the-future-of-influencer-marketing-will-be-organic influencers/567463/?fbclid=IwAR3O9UU_WLlH_uBbk7LxlCQn_2J2AY8BvbTh3RSBMlUsTBwf48x61LQ4igs

Dodgson, L. (2019, July 3) A wedding photographer was called "abusive" after refusing to offer services to an Instagram "influencer" for free. *Insider.* https://www.insider.com/wedding-photographer-called-abusive-unprofessional-refusing-influencer-freebie-request-2019-7

Droesch, B. (2019, Nov. 18). Hiding likes on Instagram could change influencer marketing for the better, marketers say. *eMarketer, inc.* https://www.emarketer.com/content/hiding-likes-on-instagram-could-change-influencer-marketing-for-the-better-marketers-say

Fishkin, R. (2018, Nov. 12). 10 problems plaguing influencer marketing. *SparkToro.* https://sparktoro.com/blog/10-problems-plaguing-influencer-marketing/

Freberg, K., Graham, K., McGaughey, K., & Freberg, L. A. (2011). Who are the social media influencers? A study of public perceptions of personality. *Public Relations Review, 37*(1), 90–92.

Graham, M. (2019, July 24). Fake followers in influencer marketing will cost brand & 1.3 billion this year, report says. *CNBC.* https://www.cnbc.com/2019/07/24/fake-followers-in-influencer-marketing-will-cost-1point3-billion-in-2019.html

Griggs, I. (2018, Feb. 15). Influencer marking damages public's perception of brands, survey finds. *PR Week.* https://www.prweek.com/article/1457215/influencer-marketing-damages-publics-perception-brands-survey-finds?fbclid=IwAR1p5nN1_6b56S2r7IjuKHe6PPArozaJVIrUBqLRiA6f1GhlI_5cQJiRLAg

Hamann, H. (n.d.). 5 tips for finding the right social influencers for your brand. *Convince & Convert.* https://www.convinceandconvert.com/digital-marketing/5-tips-for-finding-the-right-social-influencers-for-your-brand/

Hanbury, M. (2019, Jan. 19). These photos reveal why the 27-year-old organizer of the disastrous Frye Festival has been sentenced to 6 years in prison. *Business Insider.* https://www.businessinsider.com/fyre-festival-expectations-vs-reality-2017-4

Haplin, A. (2019, Oct. 14). 3 examples of influencer marketing gone wrong. *Hollywood Branded.* https://blog.hollywoodbranded.com/3-examples-of-influencer-marketing-gone-wrong

Hern, A. (2019, June 21). Instagram influencer stages "surprise" engagement weekend. *The Guardian.* https://www.theguardian.com/technology/2019/jun/21/instagram-influencer-staged-surprise-engagement-weekend

Horton, D., & Wohl, R. (1956). Mass communication and para-social interaction: Observations on intimacy at a distance. *Psychiatry, 19*(3), 215–229.

Jacquelyn. (n.d.). How to politely decline a collaboration [Blog post]. *Scrunch.* https://www.scrunch.com/blog/how-to-politely-decline-a-collaboration

Kim, J., & Song, H. (2016). Celebrity's self-disclosure on Twitter and parasocial relationships: A mediating role of social presence. *Computers in Human Behavior, 62,* 570–577.

Kirkpatrick, D. (2016, April 6). Influencer marketing spurs 11 times the ROI over traditional tactics: Study. https://www.marketingdive.com/news/influencer-marketing-spurs-11-times-the-roi-over-traditional-tactics-study/416911/

Leventhal, J. (2019, Nov. 25). How removing "likes" from Instagram could affect our mental health. *PBS.* https://www.pbs.org/newshour/science/how-removing-likes-from-instagram-could-affect-our-mental-health

Lin, M., Vijayalakshmi, A., & Laczniak, R. (2019). Toward an understanding of parental views and actions on social media influencers targeted at adolescents: The roles of parents' social media use and empowerment. *Frontiers in Psychology, 10*(2664), 1–16. doi: 10.3389/fpsyg.2019.02664.

Lorenz, T. (2019, June 20). Welcome to the era of branded engagements. *The Atlantic.* https://www.theatlantic.com/technology/archive/2019/06/was-viral-proposal-staged/592141/

Lynch, M. (2017, Dec. 30). Digital literacy is the most important lifelong learning tool. *The Tech Advocate.* https://www.thetechedvocate.org/digital-literacy-important-lifelong-learning-tool/

McCann, J. (2018, Jan. 19). Re: #bloggergate—Who benefited the most? [Blog post]. https://www.linkedin.com/pulse/bloggergate-who-benefited-most-james-mccann

Meisenzahl, M. (2019, Nov. 11). Here's what your Instagram posts will look like without "likes." *Business Insider.* https://www.businessinsider.com/instagram-removing-likes-what-it-will-look-like-2019-11

Meshi, D., Elizarova, A., Bender, A., & Verdejo-Garcia, A. (2019). Excessive social media users demonstrate impaired decision making in the Iowa gambling task. *Journal of Behavioral Addictions, 8*(1), 169–173. doi: 10.1556/2006.7.2018.138.

Morrison, K. (2015, April 3). Why influencer marketing is the new content king. *AdWeek.* http://www.adweek.com/digital/why-influencer-marketing-is-the-new-content-king-infographic/

Neale, D. (2016, June 7). Influencer marketing is a collaboration not a transaction. *Social Media Today.* https://www.socialmediatoday.com/marketing/influencer-marketing-collaboration-not-transaction

Neff, J. (2018, April 23). Study of influencer spenders finds big names, lots of fake followers. *AdAge.* https://adage.com/article/digital/study-influencer-spenders-finds-big-names-fake-followers/313223

PRWeek Staff (2018, Jan. 5). Your call: Will Logan Paul's misadventures force marketers to take a step back from influencers? *PRWeek.* https://www.prweek.com/ar

ticle/1453828/call-will-logan-pauls-misadventures-force-marketers-step-back-infl uencers#rolpCV8gVu0iKCVO.99%20

Ranjan, N. (n.d.). 7 mistakes that kill influencer relationships [Blog post]. https://me ntion.com/en/blog/influencer-relationships/

Robehmed, N., & Berg, M. (2018, Dec. 3). Highest-paid YouTube stars 2018: Markiplier, Jake Paul, PewDiePie and more. *Forbes*. https://www.forbes.com/sites /natalierobehmed/2018/12/03/highest-paid-youtube-stars-2018-markiplier-jake-p aul-pewdiepie-and-more/#71d07fb6909a

Ruiz-Mafe, C., Bigne-Alcañiz, E., Sanz-Blas, S., & Tronch, J. (2018). Does social climate influence positive eWOM? A study of heavy-users of online communities. *BRQ Business Research Quarterly, 21*(1), 26–38.

Sassine, R. (2017, April 6). What is the impact of social media influencers? [Blog post]. http://digital-me-up.com/2017/04/06/impact-social-media-influencers/

Smit, C., Buijs, L., Van Woudenberg, T. J., Bevelander, K., & Buijzen, M. (2019). The impact of social media influencers on children's dietary behaviors. *Frontiers in Psychology, 10*(TBD). doi: 10.3389/fpsyg.2019.02975.

Stackla. (2017). 2017 consumer content report: Influence in the digital age [Data Set]. https://stackla.com/wp-content/uploads/2018/05/Stackla-Data-Report-FINAL .compressed.pdf

Stenson, P. (2018, Jan. 26). The truth behind #Bloggergate. [Blog post]. https://pa ulvstenson.com/2018/01/26/the-truth-behind-bloggergate/

Stewart, R. (2019, May 9). Only 4% of people trust what influencers say online. *The Drum*. https://www.thedrum.com/news/2019/05/09/only-4-people-trust-what-influ encers-say-online

Tait, A. (2018, March 15). Can you really tell when you're being advertised to? *New Statesman America*. https://www.newstatesman.com/politics/media/2018/03/quiz -can-you-really-tell-when-you-re-being-advertised

Tait, A. (2019a, Jan. 25). Forcing social-media influencers to be clear about #ads? Good luck with that. *The Guardian*. https://www.theguardian.com/commentisfree /2019/jan/25/social-media-influencers-clear-ads-celebrities-authorities

Tait, A. (2019b, March 7). What happens when you get scammed by an influencer. *Vice*. https://www.vice.com/en_us/article/8xym9x/instagram-influencer-scams-flat -tummy-tea-fyre-fest

Victor, D. (2017, April 5). Pepsi pulls ad accused of trivializing black lives matter. *New York Times*. https://www.nytimes.com/2017/04/05/business/kendall-jenner-p epsi-ad.html

Weinswig, D. (2016, Oct. 5). Influencers are the new brands. *Forbes*. https://forbes. com/sites/deborahweinswig/2016/10/05/influencers-are-the-new-brands/#3ac7c0 267e6d

White Moose Café. Timeline [Facebook page]. https://www.facebook.com/ WhiteMooseCafe/

Woods, S. (2016). #Sponsored: The emergence of influencer marketing. (Honor's thesis). University of Tennessee, Knoxville. http://trace.tennessee.edu/utk_chan honoproj/1976

Chapter 8

Framing the Impact of Pseudo-Influencers via Communication Ethics

Jenna M. Lo Castro

Within today's sociopolitical milieu, it has become increasingly more difficult to discern the credibility and veracity of information. In the midst of unstable narratives, deceptive information generates "skepticism that [denies] the possibility of *knowledge*" (Bok, 1978/1999, p. 21). The emergence of a posttruth era in the United States reflects a society that has grown increasingly suspicious and skeptical toward the exorbitant amount of unverified and unreliable information emitted by both media sources and the Internet alike. Likewise, it illustrates advances in the power of influencer marketing and its ability to impact and unfortunately, hijack the consumer decision-making process. Posing as credible resources of information, individuals are flocking to social media platforms touting products and services with the intention of garnering large followings, solidifying corporate partnerships, and exposing consumers to particular brands including their very own. Now more than ever, consumers, brands, and the influencer industry are being confronted with a new wave of deceptive promotional schemes. These are schemes that are ultimately affecting purchasing decisions, brand image, and reputation, along with the credibility of the influencer industry.

The use of social media influencers (SMIs) to tout brands and products is now one of the fastest growing segments in the marketing industry and is leading the crusade in reshaping the way agencies handle both media and creative executions (Neff, 2019). SMIs are also used to manage consumer relationships, which has given birth to a myriad of ethical concerns and has brought forth the challenge of institutionalizing ethical standards in influencer marketing practices. This is a major issue for an industry that is projected to spend upward of $15 billion on influencer marketing by 2022 (Mediakix, 2019). Traditionally, companies utilizing SMIs to promote their brand have sought out influencers who post quality content such as photos, videos, and blogs while maintaining large social media followings (see Maheshwari, 2018). Brands hire SMIs as a conduit for marketing to key audiences and are seen as a valuable brand resource for pushing product promotion (Schwemmer & Ziewiecki, 2018).

However, a new trend has emerged in which individuals who are not paid or sponsored by brands are posting content. This content appears to be posted by legitimate sponsored SMIs, but is a ruse. Not only does this impact followers but also creates a major problem for brands that are unaware of these pseudo–social media influencers' (pseudo-SMIs) behaviors. Because of this alarmingly growing trend, ethics is a vital consideration in gauging the impact that pseudo-SMIs are having on the industry as well as helping to regulate future influencer marketing endeavors. The panacea for such challenges is considering the impact of lying and deception, and grounds social media influencer behavior in three ethical theories: virtue ethics, deontology (duty ethics), and discourse ethics. Within this chapter, these ethical universals will provide a framework for understanding how fraudulent SMI behavior raises several stakeholder concerns, specifically, its impact on consumer decision-making and purchase intentions, brand image, and the influencer industry.

SMIS, BRAND COMMUNICATION, AND ETHICS

For social media platforms, such as Instagram and YouTube, posts exhibiting sponsored content are under suspicion—more than a third of female users believe that a SMI is less credible when they are featuring content that is sponsored (PR Newswire, 2018). As such, marketers are now advocating for authentic brands and real consumer relationships as the antidote to a postmodern paradigm "where authority in general is rejected and skepticism becomes the defining cultural characteristic" (Sim, 2000, p. 104). Similar to the tenets of religious ideology, political affiliation, or education, brands serve as intangible commodities that impact attitudes, beliefs, and behaviors and elicit opportunities for meaning-making in the twenty-first century. As Arvidsson (2005) notes:

> Brands work as platforms for action that enable the production of a particular immaterial use-value: an experience, a shared emotion, a sense of community. This way, brands work as a kind of ubiquitous means of production that are inserted with the socialized production process that consumer engage in. (p. 248)

The value that brands possess ultimately highlights the possible impact it can have on consumers if it is represented by the right people through the appropriate channels of communication.

In the United States, building and retaining a brand is wholly dependent on cultivating a genuine relationship with consumers, one that depends "on the accumulation of memories, emotions, personal narratives, and expectations" (Banet-Weiser, 2012, p. 9). Traditional advertising tactics embracing a "push" attitude struggle to create these types of relationships and remain inauspicious as consumers look for ways to cultivate real-time meaningful relationships with brands. However, while the solution to this challenge has recently presented itself in the form of SMI, it also introduces yet another conundrum that serves as a larger threat.

Issues surrounding the rapidly growing SMI industry have recently seen an uptick due to the simultaneous growth of pseudo-SMIs. Their proliferation persists primarily as a result of their ability to inculcate themselves into their followers' social media feeds and ultimately, their followers' lives by cultivating what appears to be transactional relationships. Individuals rely on word of mouth (WOM) information issued forth by SMIs because of their expertise, knowledge, or interest in a product, and as Kozinets et al. (2010) explain, WOM is inherently unique in that "it depends on this transformation from persuasion oriented, market-generated, sales objective-oriented 'hype' to relevant, useful, communally desirable social information that builds individual reputations and group relationships" (p. 83). This is what functions as the chassis for relational communication.

Electronic WOM, or eWOM, functions in the same manner. Thurau et al. (2004) define eWOM as "any positive or negative statement made by potential, actual, or former customers about a product or company, which is made available to a multitude of people and institutions via the Internet" (p. 39). While eWOM serves to educate particular publics, it also facilitates and maintains brand communities of individuals who ascribe to common interests and/or share similar values (McWilliam, 2000). In this sense, following SMIs contribute to an individual's social capital, and ultimately, the presentation of their self-identity to the world. eWOM remains practical to marketers because followers of SMIs oftentimes feel a relational closeness or affinity toward the influencer and as such, are more likely to find the influencer both credible and invested in the best interests of their followers.

While brands spent $2.1 billion on influencer-sponsored posts on the social media platform Instagram in 2017, 11 percent of the engagement with those posts was executed by fraudulent or fake accounts (Captiv8, 2018). This means that while brands are investing in real influencers, they may be inadvertently engaging with fake followers. Brands must not only be concerned with how SMIs are impacting their image and reputation, but they must also be vigilant toward the SMIs' followers. Additionally, it has been estimated that more than 90 percent of the social media endorsements that SMIs and celebrities post is not compliant with Federal Trade Commission (FTC) guidelines (Mediakix, n.d.).

The notion of "influencer" is hardly a new term. Influencers can be traced back to the medieval period when individuals believed astrological phenomena emanated "invisible fluid" that could ultimately influence human behavior (Zimmer, 2016). The contemporary understanding of the moniker has seen its share of unique iterations and has found explosive growth with its application to social media. SMIs, as part of a subset of native advertising, are seen as "a new type of independent third-party endorser who shape audience attitudes through blogs, tweets, and the use of other social media" (Freberg et al., 2011, p. 90). Generally speaking, native advertising is published content that is indistinguishable from content such as reviews, news, feature articles, and matches the style of surrounding content (Federal Trade Commission, 2015b, p. 2). Recent research (Lorenz, 2018) reveals that individuals who strive for influencer status are fabricating their relationship with brands through inaccurate content and are fixated on the size of the following leading them to buy followers through third-party companies (Confessore et al., 2018). In the United States, this is a prevalent trend—findings show that American social media users privilege larger followings and networks of people and will connect with "remote or loose contacts" to do so (Chu & Choi, 2011, p. 275).

SMIs and Deceptive Practices

As social media usage continues to grow, the SMI industry likewise continues to gain steam at exponential rates. Research indicates several key trends that have emerged. On Instagram alone, it was reported that in mid-2018, the platform reached one billion monthly active users and that ninety-four million photos and videos were posted each day (Influencer Marketing Hub, 2019). The high volume of users has been able to generate a tremendous amount of earned media. In 2018, campaigns averaged an earned media value of $5.20 per dollar spent on influencer marketing (Influencer Marketing Hub, 2019). This means that social media users who are interested in content that they identify with on a personal level are also interested in developing relationships with brands and individuals that they see as authentic and real. The problem emerging out of this transaction, though, is consumer engagement with SMIs who are not formally endorsed or sponsored by the brands they are promoting in their posts and videos. The desire to have a large following, be seen by a particular brand, and recruited to be a legitimate influencer, or to be seen as someone who has expertise on a particular topic such as fashion, travel, or makeup, has generated a significant influx of pseudo-SMIs. These pseudo-SMIs are individuals who have no affiliation with a brand, but postpromotional content about a brand on their social media pages that looks like it is sponsored content.

Oftentimes, pseudo-SMIs will tag a brand and use relevant hashtags to drive up reach and the likelihood that a user will see the post and start following their content. In reality, pseudo-SMIs have no legitimate relationship with a brand. While these individuals do not explicitly lie to their followers, they do alter and edit the content they are posting in order to elicit engagement. This approach is different from user-generated content since pseudo-SMI rhetoric frequently includes characteristics such as including a particular call to action, using language that mirrors or echoes a brand's personality and tone, or using language that tries to generate a conversation (Walker, 2017). Oftentimes, these pseudo-SMIs often go one step further by "buying" followers (bots) and likes from third-party companies (Confessore et al., 2018). Aside from buying followers, pseudo-SMIs will also deceive users by buying "bot comments" in which comments are posted on an individual's post to make it appears as though they have a high level of engagement. It has been reported that on Twitter alone, there are several types of bots that can be bought and employed: schedule bots (posts messages based on the time), watcher bots (posts based on other post activity and then tweets content when that has changed), and amplification bots (follow, retweet and like tweets sent by clients who have bought their services) (Confessore et al., 2018).

Another way of deceiving followers is the use of "pods" whereby would be influencers trade likes and comments with other influencers. The reciprocal nature of the transaction allows both influencers to expand their number of followers with little cost. The process of gaining followers is even easier overseas; in downtown Moscow, individuals are able to purchase 100 Instagram likes on a post for just \$.89 at shopping center kiosks (Matsakis, 2017). These deceptive behaviors result in the creation of a user feed, whether it be on Instagram, Twitter, Facebook, Pinterest, so forth, where it becomes difficult for the user to discern the difference between legitimate influencer content and its fake counterparts. While academic work has been done on what constitutes an influencer (Freberg et al., 2011; Casaló et al., 2019), there remains a paucity of scholarship on the ethics pertaining to pseudo-SMIs. Industry practitioners are working to educate clients on how to spot these accounts and the effects they can have both on their brands and consumers. Additionally, this next section offers an overview of how the FTC works to regulate this content.

REGULATION EFFORTS

In December 2015, the FTC aggressively addressed sponsored content on social media and the Internet in order to combat dishonest practices and place the onus of responsibility on those companies and individuals associated with violating the rules by creating *Native Advertising: A Guide for Businesses.* The guidelines address the question of what constitutes deceptive forms of native advertising, alongside situational examples to help advertisers recognize potentially deceptive content. Lastly, the FTC offers a rulebook for how sponsored content should be ethically communicated. The rulebook focuses on the three key areas of proximity and placement, prominence, and clarity as well as explained that the terms "ad," "Advertisement," "Paid Advertisement," "Sponsored Advertising Content" are more desirable than terms such as "Promoted" or "Promoted Stories" because the latter can be vague. The FTC also encourages the discontinued use of other rhetoric such as "Presented by [X]," "Brought to You by [X]," "Promoted by [X]," or "Sponsored by [X]" to mean that a sponsoring advertiser funded or "underwrote" but did not create or influence the content (Federal Trade Commission, 2015a).

In addition, the FTC released an enforcement policy statement that addresses deceptive advertising that is directly produced not just by advertisers, but generally anyone. This policy argues that there exists an imperative to disclose advertising information to consumers because "knowing the source of an advertisement or promotional message typically affects the weight or credibility consumers give it. Such knowledge also may influence whether and to what extent consumers choose to interact with content containing a promotional message" (Federal Trade Commission, 2015b, par 2). In an effort to combat the somewhat esoteric language of its first document, the FTC released another document deemed more "influencer friendly" in November 2019. This document, released in conjunction with short "how to" videos directed specifically toward influencers, highlights best practices for disclosing sponsorships and brand relationships to their followers.

Further, the FTC has started to crack down on advertisers and SMIs that violate the standards set forth in these policies. Particularly, the FTC has honed in on SMIs who fail to disclose that the content of their post is not just sponsored content, but that they are being compensated by a brand for their post. In recent years, the FTC has brought lawsuits against companies such as Lord & Taylor, Warner Bros. Studio, and D.J. Khaled. In the case of the clothing retailer, Lord & Taylor, the company was accused of paying SMIs to post photos of themselves wearing a particular dress. But the SMIs failed to communicate that they were paid to post these photos and endorse the brand (Federal Trade Commission, 2016a). In the case of Warner Bros. Studio, the FTC sued and won when it was confirmed that the company's SMIs were paid to post gameplay videos on YouTube of the video game, *Middle Earth: Shadow of Mordor*, but failed to disclose that they were paid endorsements. According to the complaint, Warner Bros. told influencers to promote the video game as well as avoid any criticism they may have about it (Federal Trade Commission, 2016b).

While the FTC continues to target advertisers and companies who do not follow protocol, little has been done by the FTC to enforce the rules specifically on pseudo-SMIs. Though the FTC has sanctioned stiff guidelines on how sponsored SMIs should be posting and the mandatory language that must be included, these guidelines do little to address the myriad of individuals who are feigning sponsorship and posting identical content as well. While it may be implied that pseudo-SMIs are likewise violating the FTC's policies because the content of their posts is deceptive and has the capability of persuading subscribers, language in the FTC guidelines fail to reflect specific language that highlights how this too, is unethical. Typically, FTC regulation is aimed at ensuring that individuals posting content are including the appropriate rhetoric to inform its audiences about the type of content they are viewing. But how do we regulate individuals who are being "transparent" as a means to deceive their audiences? Additionally, regulation has become more difficult and will continue to increase in difficulty as social media grows in complexity with subgroups of influencers such as microinfluencers and nanoinfluencers since their smaller followings makes them more niche-specific and as a result, more convincing (Goodwin, 2018).

Challenges in Pseudo-SMI Regulation

Challenges with regulation remain routine since, while it is difficult to estimate the number of influencers on social media, it is projected that in 2019, there will have been roughly 4.4 million Instagram posts using easily recognizable hashtags to denote advertising or promotion (Influencer Marketing Hub, 2019). These numbers illustrate the prodigious task of trying to find and reduce the number of pseudo-SMIs. Additionally, it highlights the challenge of ensuring a clear delineation between real influencer content and user-generated content. As a result, a handful of companies have resorted to personally cracking down on pseudo-SMIs that may threaten to harm their brand. In 2018, the international consumer goods company Unilever announced that it would not "work with influencers who buy followers and said its brand would never buy followers on their own" (Pearl, 2018). And in May 2019, Facebook announced that the company disabled more than two billion fraudulent accounts in its first quarter (Wagner, 2019).

Regardless of how much or how little companies and governments are working to regulate and censor the proliferation of pseudo-SMIs and fraudulent behaviors associated with them, there remains reverberations that ultimately affect both brands and followers. These effects yield both tangible and nontangible challenges that cannot always be reconciled by a brand. Cavazos

(2019) estimates that fake influencer marketing will cost advertisers $1.3 billion in 2019 and that number is projected to grow to $1.5 billion by 2020 if nothing is done to thwart the deceptive tactics. More so, Cavazos (2019) notes that pseudo-SMIs will also continue to engender suspicious followers who are wary of both influencers' intentions and posted content, as well as organizations who have become more conscious of safeguarding their brands by creating and implementing guidelines for paid influencers. Additionally, Cavazos (2019) maintains that pseudo-SMIs devalue and "water down" the nature of the platform, particularly when platforms are having to constantly delete considerable amounts of fake accounts daily.

This should come as no surprise since the public has seen the evolution of social media sites shift from a focus on networking and connecting to a large emphasis on advertising and promotional initiatives. While the growth of SMIs continues to spur debate about authenticity and transparency and has elicited some regulation by the federal government, confronting and understanding the long-term effects on users as well as the ethical issues affecting stakeholders, brands, and the influencer industry may help to rectify currently existing issues and help to anticipate future threatening ones.

ETHICAL ISSUES SURROUNDING PSEUDO-SMIS

As far back as antiquity, philosophers and scholars recognized the inherent connectivity between moral action and the "good life." For the ancient philosopher Aristotle (1925/1998), lying was considered "mean and culpable" and that an individual who felt compelled to lie had a "worse character" (p. 101). SMIs who communicate through social media play a particularly vital role in deciding what and how they communicate information to their followers. Since these individuals function as brand ambassadors, their ability to persuade and impact key publics entails a tremendous amount of responsibility. Followers look to these individuals for guidance and seek information that they believe will be of benefit to them. In this sense, SMIs command an extreme amount of authority.

Sissela Bok, in an Aristotelian voice, is concerned with end goals or the *telos* of human behavior. In particular, Bok is interested in the *telos* for those who voluntarily lie or practice acts of deception. While certain types of lies such as white lies can be beneficial and in a utilitarian sense serve some practical need (Bok, 1999/1978), other lies consequently remain groundless and thus detrimental to both the self and others. In the case of creating and communicating deceptive content on social media platforms, this act functions as a detriment to multiple stakeholders, including the SMI since deception reifies itself in the exploitation of associating oneself with a brand in order to generate a larger following or to get a brand's attention. The pseudo-SMI essentially brandishes the essence of what it means to be an influencer and embodies what it means to "sell out." In addition, pseudo-SMIs peddling false content have a far-reaching impact that surpasses the unethical act of posting deceptive content; it also effects stakeholders, brands, and the influencer industry.

Followers Concerns

Pseudo-SMIs not only sabotage followers by influencing their decisions, but they can also compromise followers' ability to exercise the decision-making process since oftentimes pseudo-SMIs function as peripheral shortcuts. Individuals process posted social media content with less cognitive scrutiny than they would if the content were coming from a more traditional advertising vehicle, not only because the content takes the shape of native advertising but also because of the connectedness that the follower feels with the SMI in the first place. In this sense, pseudo-SMIs not only deceive the individual by lying about their affiliation, but they likewise do a disservice to the individual by taking away the individual's agency to make choices that are founded on legitimate information.

Bok (1978/1999) argues that deception can "initiate actions a person would otherwise never have chosen, so it can prevent action by obscuring the necessity of choice" (p. 20). Pseudo-SMIs' inauthenticity has the ability to persuade followers to purchase products and follow other pseudo-SMIs. Additionally, a slippery slope presents the possibility of developing when followers encourage their own friends to engage with pseudo-SMIs. The deviant nature of fake influencers is then able to propagate itself all over social media, blurring the lines of real content and sophistic content. Likewise, brands face similar issues with individuals who are posing as legitimate brand ambassadors.

Brand Concerns

While prima facie, free promotion or earned media for a brand, appears advantageous to a company, pseudo-SMIs can, in fact, do more harm than good. A major challenge for brands is identifying those SMIs who may be a good fit for the brand and also those who might pose risk for the brand. This of course is no easy task since there are roughly 3.5 billion people online and social media platforms are used by one out of three people in the world (Ortiz-Ospina, 2019). Moderating what SMIs post as well as verifying the legitimacy of content is difficult. Pseudo-SMIs whose personal brand contrasts with the brand or products they promote through social media content run the risk of tarnishing the emotional, mental, or even physical associations that consumer creates with a brand in their mind. Moreso, pseudo-SMIs have the ability to present a product/service that is not concordant with the brand's voice. What ensues is damage to both the reputation and image of a brand that is caused with an unaffiliated pseudo-SMI. Oftentimes, this is difficult to ameliorate and has the ability to produce damaging consequences.

Cresci et al. (2015) notes that an account that has a lot of followers, but follows very few accounts itself, shows that the followers might be fake, thus decreasing the legitimacy of the account. An account that associates itself with a particular brand or product runs the risk of devaluing those products and services, unbeknownst to the company. This is backed by research conducted by De Veirman et al. (2017) that shows that the number of followers a SMI has ultimately impacted a consumer's perception of the brand or product being presented. Their works show that when a SMI with a high number of followers promotes a product, the product's uniqueness and consumer's attitude toward the brand are lower compared to when it is endorsed by a legitimate influencer with a moderate number of followers (p. 813). A brand's inability to control and moderate the content of pseudo-SMIs places them at risk of being exposed to negative consumer feedback as well as a tarnished image and reputation that proves difficult to ameliorate. As Lorenz (2018) noted, sometimes brands are hesitant to reach out to pseudo-SMIs for fear that there might be some type of social media backlash that has the ability to ultimately damage the brand's reputation worse than if the brand said nothing at all.

Influencer Industry Concerns

Aside from the detrimental impact that pseudo-SMIs have on both followers and brands, this impact has the ability to produce a long-lasting ripple effect that has implications for the influencer industry. On the one hand, pseudo-SMIs are slowly eroding the credibility of real SMI content and diminishing the value of trust as a social good. Because WOM has the powerful ability to alter "commercial information into cultural stories relevant to the members of particular communities" (Kozinets et al., 2010, p. 86), pseudo-SMIs are able to use that power to exploit their followers and bastardize the content that other SMIs are touting as part of their particular narrative. Knowledge of this will only increase consumer skepticism toward influencer content as well as the brand and as Cain (2011) points out, directly impacts the degree of credibility the individual possesses.

Ultimately, this has the power to impact marketer decision-making and budget expenditures. While the market is currently seeing explosive growth in the amount of money brands are willing to spend on their influencer marketing initiatives (as mentioned previously in this chapter), the rise of pseudo-SMIs will certainly play a role in the future.

ETHICAL IMPLICATIONS

The proliferation of pseudo-SMIs raises normative questions within the context of key ethical theories. Engaging in ethical communication demands an attentiveness to an historical moment defined by posttruth and fake news. Examining the fraudulent and deceptive behaviors of pseudo-SMIs in conversation with an ethical backdrop helps to amplify the issues at hand and may offer direction for how those impacted by pseudo-SMIs may address such ensuing challenges.

First, from a deontological (or "duty") perspective that focuses on action, one is led to consider whose responsibility it "ought" to be to ensure that truthful content is being communicated by SMIs. This circles back to Bok's (1999/1978) contention that being truthful is an individual's duty. Does the dissemination of content by fraught SMIs promote a social good for society? Understanding the function and impact of what it means to be a SMI illuminates the obligatory nature of engaging in transparent and authentic behaviors. The aim of influencing should not be merely for financial gain or social notoriety, but instead to serve public desirable and valid content. Rather than see followers as a means to a personal gain, followers should be viewed as part of the goal. While the FTC has stepped in and is trying to regulate the industry, the vastness of the Internet makes this a dubious task and should place the onus on SMIs.

Second, from a virtue ethics framework (an additional approach to normative ethics), we are invited to consider how character impacts ethical communication and decision-making. Aristotle (1925/1998) argues that virtuous behavior involves choice which constitutes who we are as human beings. By engaging in virtuous behavior, individuals are able to reach *eudaimonia* or "happiness." Virtues such as courage, truthfulness, justice, shame, and magnanimity all encourage deliberation and making choices functions as a means and implies having a telos or end. In other words, we deliberate in order to reach an end. Choice, according to Aristotle, is what also makes us human beings because it implies rationality. From this perspective, we can consider whether or not SMIs who exhibit these traits allow us to categorize the SMI industry as producing a meaningful social good. In other words, brands must ask themselves whether or not influencer marketing, aside from generating financial gain and brand awareness, is cultivating meaningful communities of followers.

From a discourse ethics standpoint, how might we be able to develop a moral point of view from which normative discourse can be impartially judged? The major intent within this framework is reciprocity and consensus within discourse. By reaching consensus, words can be deemed as communal and meaningful. Habermas (1981) contends that individual behavior is influenced by social norms and that those norms must first be agreed upon by individuals through the act of choice in order to be validated. Because language in this sense can be transformative, it embodies an intrinsic ethical element. In the case of pseudo-SMIs, discourse between all effected stakeholders regarding SMI content should be considered. It is important to consider who needs to be included within that discourse and how can brands improve their communication practices with real and pseudo-influencers in order to increase the likelihood that truthful, authentic content is being created and disseminated on social media platforms.

Considering these perspectives, the next step to determine whether or not it is possible to create a more ethically sound SMI industry in which followers' interests and needs rise to the top, rather than profitability and exposure. Normative ethics, while not a silver bullet to combating the current issue of deceptive SMIs, advances the importance of addressing the situation beyond federal regulation and reframes the issue on a micro level that concerns itself with the roots of the problem—the pseudo-SMIs.

DIRECTIONS FOR THE FUTURE

According to a study by Vosoughi et al. (2018), false information spreads more quickly and reaches more individuals on social media that truthful information. More specifically, according to the researchers, it takes the truth roughly six times as long as falsehoods to reach 1,500 people (Vosoughi et al., 2018). What this means is that the propagation of false information is able to be shared more frequently and thus able to travel further on the Internet and across social media platforms. This is a startling piece of evidence, particularly when considered in the context of social media where information runs rampant and eWOM remains influential in determining consumer decision-making and purchasing habits.

While the FTC continues to regulate the SMI industry by enforcing rules and regulations as well as rely on consumers and consumer protection organizations for information (Campbell & Grimm, 2019), pseudo-SMIs will continue to generate deceptive content that will inevitably be mistaken as authentic. Questions circulating around the legitimacy of these pseudo-SMIs and whether their promotion of particular products and services lend itself to something constructive and beneficial to their followers is secondary to the form of their content.

Cain (2011) argues that the purpose of the expression in most advertising (to promote goods and services) is legitimately subject to regulation. However, in citing Anonymous (2005), Cain (2011) explains that "the mechanism of expression (the speech, whether it is expressed in words, logos, or a combination) is protected under the First Amendment" (p. 231). Considering this, pseudo-SMIs present an even more nuanced dilemma for regulation since the expression of content, while appearing authentic, is ultimately flawed alongside their mechanism of expression. The current historical moment reminds us that discerning what is true from what is false will continue to be a formidable ongoing task, especially as the use of influencer marketing continues to grow in popularity and marketers look toward other advertising avenues that feel less intrusive and more organic for the consumer.

Brands that consider a SMI's credibility and dedication to providing a service and whose focus is on creating a dialogue with their followers will help to strengthen the validity of the SMI industry. Providing ethical and authentic voices for their consumers is a powerful step that brands can take in combating the proliferation of pseudo-SMIs. Additionally, working toward creating a discourse that not only educates SMIs on appropriate posting practices but also communicates the ethical and moral implications of providing such services at the very least, helps to illuminate the inherent connection between the function of SMIs and communication ethics.

REFERENCES

Anonymous. (2005). Making sense of hybrid speech: A model for commercial speech and expressive conduct. *Harvard Law Review, 118*(June), 2836–2857.

Aristotle. (1925/1998). *The Nicomachean ethics.* Oxford University Press.

Arvidsson, A. (2005). Brands: A critical perspective. *Journal of Consumer Culture, 5*(235), 235–258. doi: 10.1177/1469540505053093.

Banet-Weiser, S. (2012). *Authentic™: The politics of ambivalence in a brand culture.* New York University Press.

Bok, S. (1978/1999). *Lying: Moral choice in public and private life.* Vintage Books.

Cain, R. (2011). Embedded advertising on television: Disclosure, deception, and free speech rights. *Journal of Public Policy and Marketing, 30*(2), 226–238.

Campbell, C., & Grimm, P. (2019). The challenges native advertising poses: Exploring potential federal trade commission responses and identifying research needs. *Journal of Public Policy & Marketing, 38*(1), 110–123. doi: 10.1177/0743915618818576.

Captiv8. (2018). #Nofilter: How to uncover the fakes. https://cdn2.hubspot.net/hubfs /4274052/%23NoFilterHow%20to%20Uncover%20the%20Fakes_Captiv8%20Re port_Final.pdf?utm_campaign=fraud%20report&utm_source=hs_automation&ut m_medium=email&utm_content=68486655&_hsenc=p2ANqtz-_7XKDQzzX

kihFUpC7-NvH3osbFYzdDXSq2SnBR3_8rLuQ5cEUJ1MVHIM48mi-ybW
RZnNP0kgnZCq7OeJzNwmcyzxCjZA&_hsmi=68486655

Casalo, L., Flavian, C., & Ibáñez-Sánchez, S. (2018). Influencers on Instagram: Antecedents and consequences of opinion leadership. *Journal of Business Research.* doi: 10.1016/j.jbusres.2018.07.005.

Cavazos, R. (2019). The economic cost of bad actors on the internet: Fake influencer marketing in 2019. *Cheq.* https://www.cheq.ai/influencers

Chu, S., & Choi, S. (2011). Electronic word-of-mouth in social networking sites: A cross-cultural study of the United States and China. *Journal of Global Marketing, 24,* 263–281. doi: 10.1080/08911762.2011.592461.

Confessore, N., Dance, B., Harris, R., & Hansen, M. (2018, January 27). The follower factory. *The New York Times.* https://www.nytimes.com/interactive/2018/01/27/tec hnology/social-media-bots.html

Cresci, S., Di Pietro, R., Petrocchi, M., Spognardi, A., & Tesconi, M. (2015). Fame for sale: Efficient detection of fake Twitter followers. *Decision Support Systems, 80,* 56–71. doi: 10.1016/j.dss.2015.09.003.

De Veirman, M., Cauberghe, V., & Hudders, L. (2017). Marketing through Instagram influencers: The impact of number of followers and product divergence on brand attitude. *International Journal of Advertising, 36*(5), 798–828. doi: 10.1080/02650487.2017.1348035.

Federal Trade Commission. (2015a, December). Native advertising: A guide for busi-nesses. https://www.ftc.gov/tips-advice/business-center/guidance/native-advert ising-guide-businesses

Federal Trade Commission (2015b, December). Commission enforcement policy statement on deceptively formatted advertisements. https://www.ftc.gov/publi c-statements/2015/12/commission-enforcement-policy-statement-deceptively -formatted

Federal Trade Commission. (2016a, March 15). Lord & Taylor settles FTC charges it deceived consumers through paid article in an online fashion magazine and paid Instagram posts by 50 "fashion influencers." [Press release]. https://www.ftc.gov/ news-events/press-releases/2016/03/lord-taylor-settles-ftc-charges-it-deceived-c onsumers-through

Federal Trade Commission. (2016b, July 11). Warner Bros. settles FTC charges it failed to adequately disclose it paid online influencers to post gameplay videos. [Press release]. https://www.ftc.gov/news-events/press-releases/2016/07/warner -bros-settles-ftc-charges-it-failed-adequately-disclose-it

Federal Trade Commission. (2017, November). Disclosures 101 for social media. https://www.ftc.gov/tips-advice/business-center/guidance/disclosures-101-social-media-influencers

Freberg, K., Graham, K., McGaughey, K., & Freberg, L. (2011). Who are social media influencers? A study of public perceptions. *Public Relations Review, 37,* 90–92. doi: 10.1016/j.pubrev.2010.11.001.

Godwin, R. (2018, November 14). The rise of the nano-influencer: How brands are turning to common people. *The Guardian.* https://www.theguardian.com/comment isfree/2018/nov/14/rise-nano-influencer-brands-celebrities-youtube-instagram

Habermas, J. (1981). *The theory of communicative action, vol. 1: Reason and the rationalization of society.* Beacon Press.

Hennig-Thurau, T., Gwinner, K.P, Walsh, G., & Gremler. D. D. (2004). Electronic word-of-mouth via consumer opinion platforms: What motivates consumers to articulate themselves on the internet? *Journal of Interactive Marketing, 18*(1), 38–52. doi: 10.1002/dir.10073.

Influencer Marketing Hub. (2019). Influencer marketing report 2019. https://influen cermarketinghub.com/influencer-marketing-2019-benchmark-report/

Kozinets, R., de Valck, K., Wojnicki, A., & Wilner, S. (2010). Networked narratives: Understanding word-of-mouth marketing in online communities. *Journal of Marketing, 74,* 71–89.

Lorenz, T. (2018, December 18). Rising Instagram starts are posting fake sponsored content. *The Atlantic.* https://www.theatlantic.com/technology/archive/2018/12/ influencers-are-faking-brand-deals/578401/

Maheshwari, S. (2018, November 12). The newest influencers don't need big numbers. *The New York Times. Gale General OneFile.* https://link.gale.com/apps/doc/ A561863539/ITOF?u=pit59917&sid=ITOF&xid=d071b2b3

Matsakis, L. (2016, June 6). This Russian vending machine will sell you fake Instagram likes. *Vice.* https://www.vice.com/en_us/article/xw8yv3/russian-vendi ng-machine-fake-instagram-likes

McWilliam, G. (2000). Building stronger brands through online communities. *Sloan Management Review, 41*(Spring), 43–54.

Mediakix. (2019). Influencer marketing 2019 industry benchmarks. https://mediaki x.com/influencer-marketing-resources/influencer-marketing-industry-statistics-su rvey-benchmarks/

Mediakix. (n.d.). 93% of top celebrity social media endorsements violate FTC guidelines. https://mediakix.com/wp-content/uploads/2017/05/Celebrity-Social-Media -Endorsements-FTC-Violations-Instagram2.jpg

Neff, J. (2019, January 21). How to succeed with influencers: Influencer marketing is becoming a bigger piece of the toolbox. *Advertising Age, 90*(2), 19.

Ortiz-Ospina, E. (2019, September 18). The rise of social media. https://ourworldinda ta.org/rise-of-social-media

Pearl, D. (2018, June 18). Unilever to crack down on influencers who buy fake followers and use bots. *AdWeek.* https://www.adweek.com/brand-marketing/unilever -to-crack-down-on-influencers-who-buy-fake-followers-and-use-bots/

PR Newswire. (2018, April 27). *New research reveals inauthentic influencer content on the rise as consumer skepticism grows.* http://link.galegroup.com/apps/ doc/A536428961/BIC?u=pit59917&sid=BIC&xid=8b67b493. Accessed 30 July 2019.

Schwemmer, C., & Ziewiecki, S. (2018). Social media sellout: The increasing role of product promotion on YouTube. *Social Media & Society,* 1–20. doi: 10.1177/2056305118786720.

Sim, S. (2000). *Post-marxism: An intellectual history.* Routledge.

Vosoughi, S., Roy, D., & Sinan, A. (2018, March). The spread of true and false news online. *Science, 359*(6380), 1146–1151. doi: 10.1126/science.aap9559.

Vranica, S. (2018, June 17). Unilever demands influencer marketing business clean up its act. *The Wall Street Journal.* https://www.wsj.com/articles/unilever-demands-influencer-marketing-business-clean-up-its-act-1529272861

Wagner, K. (2019). Facebook removes a record 2.2 billion fake accounts. *Bloomberg.* https://www.bloomberg.com/news/articles/2019-05-23/facebook-removed-2-2-billion-fake-accounts-in-first-quarter

Walker, T. (2017). Why influencer generated content is the new UGC. https://www.aspireiq.com/blog/why-influencer-generated-content-is-the-new-ugc. Accessed 11 February 2020.

Zimmer, B. (2016). The growing influencer of "influencer." *The Wall Street Journal.* https://www.wsj.com/articles/the-growing-influence-of-influencer-1461874150

Chapter 9

Playing by the Rules

Legal Restrictions Surrounding Brand-Influencer Relationships

Courtney A. Barclay and Kearston L. Wesner

More than 90 percent of consumers report trusting social media influencers more than traditional brand messages or even celebrity endorsements (Weinswig, 2016). Although Millennials report a declining level of trust in influencers, it is still the first place many millennials and postmillennials turn when deciding what brands and looks to shop (Crowdfire, 2018). With this level of trust, transparency is important for consumers to understand the context of a post. In fact, advertising laws in the United States require that any significant relationship between an endorser and a brand be clearly disclosed. Despite this requirement, social influencers at all levels, including high-profile celebrities, have been criticized for posting deceptive messages. They either fail to reveal the brand relationship or bury the #paid #advertising tags so far down a post that the average consumer never sees it.

The level of influence that social media influencers are wielding, as well as the increased use of SponCon—paid endorsement messages—in brand communication strategy, has drawn the attention of not only advertising ethicists but also lawmakers. Congress has repeatedly and extensively interviewed social network executives about data practices and user behavior (Owens, 2019). The Federal Trade Commission (FTC) has monitored the adequacy of disclosure statements and material claims, sending nearly 100 letters in 2017 to influencers and brands to inform them that existing endorsement disclosures apply to social influencer messages, specifically noting that disclosure should be included conspicuously in promotional posts (FTC News Release, 2017). In 2019, the FTC released a brochure with tips for social media influencers on the best ways to make those disclosures (FTC, 2019b).

It's not only brand-sponsored messages that have drawn criticism. Influencers, or aspiring influencers, have started faking sponsored ads to increase their own legitimacy (Lorenz, 2018). These fake SponCon messages mislead the poster's followers, as well as potential brand partners. And while some brands might be happy for the free publicity, there could be brand image issues with the post or the behavior of a poster. Brands have few legal remedies to address this behavior.

The rise of SponCon, and faked SponCon, has raised substantial legal questions that the FTC has struggled to answer. One reason for this is that the sheer volume of social media posts has severely limited enforcement. However, there is increasing demand from consumer watch groups and lawmakers for effective regulation. Likewise, brands are becoming more vigilant, monitoring for SponCon cons. It is increasingly important for social influencers, and brands, to understand the legal landscape of endorsement-based messages.

This chapter examines the current structure for regulating social influencer advertising and messaging, as well as the legal recourse available to brands that are misappropriated by want-to-be influencers.

PROTECTING CONSUMERS FROM DECEPTIVE ADVERTISING

Commercial speech has long been more heavily regulated than political or social speech in the United States. This lower status afforded to commercial speech, articulated in the Supreme Court decision in *Central Hudson Gas & Electric Corp. v. Public Service Commission* (1980), has paved the way for regulation of even truthful speech in order to protect consumers from harmful messages.

The FTC is the federal government agency primarily charged with protecting consumers (FTC Act, §§41 *et seq.*). Congress first charged the FTC with this duty in 1914 within the larger social context of mistrust of large companies and unprecedented integration. Since then, the FTC has investigated and remediated a variety of "unfair methods of competition" with growing authority (FTC Act, §45; Fair, 2014). The enforcement authority of the FTC includes investigative powers, including the power to subpoena individuals to appear before the FTC, and enforcement actions including specific actions, such as corrective advertising, and civil penalties, such as consumer refunds or government fines (FTC, 2019c).

In 1983, the agency clarified its investigatory practice used to actively protect consumers from false or misleading advertising, including any brand endorsements from celebrities, experts, or "average" consumers (FTC, 1983).

In this Policy Statement, the FTC announced the three-part standard it would use in evaluating whether a brand had engaged in deceptive advertising. The agency deems messages to be false or misleading when three conditions are met: (1) there is a misrepresentation or omission likely to mislead a consumer, (2) the consumer would be *reasonably* misled, and (3) the misrepresentation or omission is material (FTC, 1983). These elements are used to review advertisements on case-by-case basis.

Likely to Mislead

When evaluating whether an advertiser has been deceptive, the FTC traditionally reviews written and oral communications (FTC, 1983). The context of the entire publication is used to determine whether the meaning of the advertisement is explicitly false or implies falsehood. Implied falsehood can be shown when necessary information has been omitted. The agency has found that omission of payment or inducement for endorsements constitutes a representation that is likely mislead consumers.

Reasonable Consumer

In evaluating whether a statement is likely to mislead, the FTC uses the perspective of a "reasonable consumer" (FTC, 1983). The standard asks whether a reasonable member of the target audience would interpret the message in a way that is deceptive. The target audience can be the general public, or a special public, like children. When the message is targeted to a special public, the FTC limits the scope of the inquiry to the reasonable consumer who is part of the target audience. For example, if a company markets a toy to children, the Commission will ask how the message would affect an ordinary child.

Material Fact

The final element of review is whether the statement is material—that is, whether the message at issue is likely to affect a consumer's choice (FTC, 1983). The Commission asks, is this information important to consumers? Some types of information are generally presumed material: cost, warranties, durability, and performance. Other types of information may be deemed material if it is proven by price differentiation, market research, testimony, or other evidence.

When these three elements are present, the message is considered deceptive and is subject to FTC action. To guide companies in how to avoid deceptive messaging, the FTC requires necessary disclosures and substantiation of brand's claims. These requirements have consistently, if not always effectively, been applied to online communications, as well as traditional advertising in print, radio, and television (FTC, 2000). However, significant developments in online communication has challenged the implementation of these standards, and in 2020, the FTC voted to publish a notice seeking public comment on the need to revise endorsement guidelines in light of the importance of influencer marketing in the digital economy (FTC, 2020a).

DEVELOPING ENDORSEMENT GUIDELINES

Federal enforcement actions against false endorsements can be traced to the 1930s when the U.S. Supreme Court upheld a cease-and-desist order for deceptive practices issued by the FTC against Standard Education Society (Washburn, 1981, p. 711). The FTC found that endorsements for the company's encyclopedias included exaggerated statements or outdated reviews from previous issues. The Supreme Court ruled that the FTC had more than sufficient evidence to support its finding of deception. Since then, the FTC has aggressively sought to regulate false and misleading endorsements in a variety of industries and media. The FTC first outlined regulation of endorsement statements in the 1970s when it proposed *Guides Concerning the Use of Endorsements and Testimonials in Advertising* (Washburn, 1981, p. 718). In the ensuing years, the FTC codified these guides, defining an endorsement as an

> advertising message (including verbal statements, demonstrations, or depictions of the name, signature, likeness or other identifying personal characteristics of an individual or the name or seal of an organization) which message consumers are likely to believe reflects the opinions, beliefs, findings, or experience of a party other than the sponsoring advertiser. (FTC, 1980, §255.0)

The guides make clear that the statement does not have to explicitly state the message is a personal opinion or experience to be considered an endorsement. All endorsement messages must adhere to three main requirements. First, any endorsement must be clearly and conspicuously disclosed. Second, if the endorsement includes information on the endorser's experience with using a product or service, the message must represent honest opinions and accurately reflect actual usage. Third, any endorsement statements must meet the same substantiation and qualification standards as messages directly from the advertiser—that is any statement made by an endorsing personality or expert must not be deceptive or misleading.

In 2000, the FTC released *Dot Com Disclosures*—a booklet for advertisers—to clarify that these endorsement rules applied not only in traditional advertising but also in online communications (FTC, 2000). Compliance with and enforcement of the disclosure and qualification requirements proved problematic for online communications, especially as more advertising messages moved to space-restricted formats on social media. The FTC continued to refine its guidance through new guidelines, as well as investigations, in three key areas: defining an endorsement, including necessary qualifications or message disclosures, and adequately disclosing a material connection.

Defining Endorsements

The FTC has consistently ruled that a specific medium does not impact the definition of an endorsement. An endorsement exists if there is any material connection between the advertiser and the person promoting a product or service. This includes not only direct payments but also free products, ownership stakes, commissions, or any other inducements. When this standard is met, requirements for disclosure are triggered.

Early guidance documents focused on traditional media, but in *Dot Com Disclosures*, the FTC specified that endorsements included online advertisements as well. In 2009, the FTC officially revised its rules, specifying that the definition of an endorsement is medium-neutral. The *2009 Revised Guides* state that disclosure requirements would be triggered by online endorsements, testimonials, and any other word-of-mouth campaigns—digital or otherwise. To illustrate when user-generated content would constitute an endorsement, the agency described a consumer of dog food who posts an online review sharing positive results of changing to the product in three scenarios:

1) the consumer tries the new food without any compensation or connection with the dog food manufacturer;
2) the consumer tries the new dog food after receiving a coupon for a free trial generated by the retail store; and
3) the consumer receives a free trial bag as part of her participation in a network marketing program.

In the first two scenarios, the FTC finds that a post reviewing the product would not constitute an endorsement. However, because in the third scenario, she is induced through a systematic program, her post would be considered an endorsement (FTC, 2009). This type of statement would require a disclosure of that connection.

The FTC has investigated compliance of these rules and through its findings, clarified the application to social media. Some of the applications seem obvious. For example, in a settlement with Lord & Taylor, the FTC found deceptive the absence of any disclosure statement in the postings of fifty fashion bloggers who promoted a dress in the retailer's new fashion line (*FTC v. Lord & Taylor*, 2016). The retailer had paid the bloggers and provided them with a free dress to feature in their posts. In return, bloggers would post positive messages on Instagram about the dress, tagging the Lord & Taylor account and using a brand-approved hashtag. Despite preapproving and even editing the posts to ensure compliance with these requirements, Lord & Taylor failed to require or add in any disclosure language. The bloggers' social media followers were not made aware of the inducements Lord & Taylor provided to gain these mentions. The final settlement against this clear violation of the Endorsement Guidelines prohibits Lord & Taylor from "misrepresenting that paid ads are from an independent source or that an endorser is an independent or ordinary consumer. In addition, the company must ensure that its endorsers clearly disclose when they have been compensated in exchange for their endorsements" (FTC v. Lord & Taylor, 2016).

Other brand relationships do not constitute an endorsement as obviously as the Lord & Taylor example. In 2014, the FTC investigated a social media contest conducted by shoe and clothing brand Cole Haan (Engle, 2014). The contest, focused on Pinterest, encouraged individuals to pin shoe images paired with "places to wander." The winner of the contest would be awarded $1,000. The FTC noted that viewers of contest entry posts would not necessarily know that the posts were being made only in response to the contest incentives. Because this was the first time the FTC had addressed online contests, there was no enforcement action taken against Cole Haan. However, the investigation did clarify that contest entries would be considered a material connection and that advertisers using this messaging strategy must educate participants on disclosure requirements and monitor users' posts for compliance.

In response to social media campaigns like those used by Lord & Taylor and Cole Haan, the FTC again refined its guidance. In *Disclosures 101 for Social Media Influencers*, the FTC spoke directly to influencers about understanding when a disclosure is necessary (FTC, 2019b). Notably, the brochure instructs influencers, "Don't assume your followers already know about your brand relationships" and "make disclosures even if you think your evaluations are unbiased" (FTC, 2019b, p. 3). The brochure also classifies an endorsement as containing the following: compensated likes, tags, pins, or other methods of showing public support on social platforms. This inclusion expanded the understanding of what triggered endorsement disclosure requirements.

Disclosing Material Connections

Once disclosure requirements have been triggered by an endorsement, the FTC requires that the material relationship between the advertising company and the endorser be disclosed to avoid consumer confusion or deception. Before the introduction of blogs and social media, these disclosure statements were primarily the obligation of the advertisers—the sponsoring company and the advertising agency. They were integrated into the design of a print ad, or the script of a TV or radio advertisement. Therefore, the Endorsement Guides focused on requirements for those types of messages (FTC, 1975, 1990). Nontraditional media message, like 140-character tweets, presented new challenges for the forms these disclosures would take.

The FTC first addressed the challenges of digital disclosures in its May 2000 booklet, *Dot Com Disclosures*, in which the agency declared that "the same consumer protection laws that apply to commercial activities in other media apply online" (FTC, 2000, p. 1). Disclosures online, as well as in traditional media, should be designed with consideration for consumer experience, evaluating the placement, proximity, prominence, clarity, and complexity of the disclosure. Although *Dot Com Disclosures* mandated these considerations be platform neutral, the FTC failed to consider the forthcoming development of user-generated content and space-restricted content native to social media networks.

The examples in *Dot Com Disclosures* concentrated on Internet content, but still assumed the traditional advertising operations in which the advertiser creates, publishes, and controls the message. The context was largely websites—considering hyperlinks, scrolling, click-through pages, and pop-up windows. The example most comparable to social media posts discussed was banner ads. Like social media posts, these ads are space-limited. The agency encouraged advertisers to creatively include disclosures in the ad itself, rather than relegating it to the linked webpage.

Despite the hint of a proximity requirement in space-limited online messages, *Dot Com Disclosures* still focused on advertiser-generated content. In the years following the 2000 guidance, bloggers began endorsing products through independently operated websites; e-commerce sites provided review feedback opportunities; and social media platforms provided new, more accessible outlets in which users controlled their own statements and offered product endorsements, including compensated messages.

In response to these developments, the FTC offered revised guidance in 2009—the first since 1980. In addition to clarifying that disclosure requirements apply to bloggers, online discussion boards, and word-of-mouth campaigns, the FTC directed that the relationship needs to be "clearly and conspicuously" disclosed (FTC, 2009). However, the *Revised Guides* still did not provide adequate guidance on *how* to meet the "clear and conspicuous" standard (Feinman, 2011). Concerns were raised that advertisers were embedding disclosures so that they were not conspicuous to end users and user-generated content rarely included adequate disclosures.

In a 2013 guidance document, the FTC provided more specific information on how disclosures should be made online to adequately inform consumers. In the 2013 *.com Disclosures* guidance document, the agency enumerated a variety of factors that advertisers should consider when making disclosures including the nature of the advertisement, the disclosures required, the specific medium, and the perspective of the consumer (.com Disclosures, 2013). The FTC emphasized that the disclosure should be physically connected to the statement, not consigned to the user's profile page or a linked website. In one example, a disclosure made on a celebrity's social media profile is not sufficient when the celebrity makes an endorsement post. The FTC reasoned that users may not visit the profile, but rather the post will likely be seen on its own (Byrne, 2015).

Rather the FTC suggested that disclosures be made in the post itself, using clear language. Paid endorsements should begin with the word "ad." The guidance points out that this only takes up four characters and clearly communicates the nature of the post to consumers (FTC, 2013). Abbreviations that may not be known to consumers are not sufficient substitutes. In one example, the letters "FS" followed an endorsement statement. Although meant to indicate "free sample," the FTC deemed this not adequate to alert consumers to the relationship between the endorser and the advertiser. Similarly, in a 2015 publication, *The FTC's Endorsement Guides: What People Are Asking,* the agency stated that the phrase "affiliate link" would also potentially be misunderstood or overlooked by consumers. Again, the agency urged explicit disclosure with statements such as "I receive commissions on sales" or "Company X gave me [name of product]" (FTC, 2015).

Even with this guidance, brands and influencers continued to deemphasize disclosures. For example, Warner Bros. settled an enforcement action with the FTC for failing to require and facilitate adequate disclosure (FTC, 2016). In a campaign promoting a video game based on The Hobbit, Warner Bros. hired online influencers to develop gameplay videos. The influencers were told to include disclosure statements in the video description boxes, which appear below the video and often require users to click an expansion for the text to fully display. Some of the influencers also only disclosed the early access to the game, failing to include the payments they received.

In 2019, the FTC investigated endorsements made by a company's employees (FTC, 2019a). According to the FTC complaint, the CEO of Sunday Riley, a cosmetics firm, instructed employees to post positive reviews of their products on a national retailer's website using fake customer accounts (In re Sunday Riley, 2019). The employees never disclosed their affiliation with Sunday Riley. Employees were provided with detailed instructions, including how to mask their IP address to hide the corporate affiliation of the posters. Management instructed employees to "Leave a review—make sure to NOT compare the product to other products, to not use foul language, and to be very enthusiastic without looking like a plant. Always leave 5 stars" (In re Sunday Riley [Complaint], 2019, p. *2).

The FTC settled with Sunday Riley, prohibiting any future misleading endorsements and requiring specific recordkeeping of all advertisements and customer reviews. Two FTC commissioners argued this action did not go far enough to deter this kind of fake endorsement practice (In re Sunday Riley [Statement], 2019):

- Fake reviews distort our markets by rewarding bad actors and harming honest companies. The problem is growing, and the FTC should attack it.
- Regulators around the world are concerned about fake review fraud. But by proposing a no-money, no-fault order for an unambiguous violation of law, this action does little to address the epidemic of fake reviews online.
- Going forward, the FTC should seek monetary consequences for fake review fraud, even if the exact level of ill-gotten gains is difficult to measure. The agency should also comprehensively analyze the problem of fake reviews, including whether or not e-commerce firms have the right incentives to police their platforms.

In the 2019 *Disclosures 101 for Social Media Influencers*, the FTC provided even more direct instructions for how to disclose brand relationships. The mandate: "Make sure people will see and understand the disclosure" (FTC, 2019b). In addition to reiterating the proximity requirement, the agency addressed issues like photo and video content. For photos, especially for Instagram Stories or Snapchat posts, the disclosures should be added to the photo itself. This is easy to do with native app editing or production apps that help influencers prepare story content. Disclosures related to video content should not be exclusive to the captions, but incorporated into the video, ideally using both audio and video as it will be more conspicuous to users. The guidance also addressed live stream content, directing influencers to repeat the disclosure periodically through the stream so that viewers that join at any time will be informed about the nature of the endorsement.

In 2020, the FTC settled a $15.2 million judgment against Teami, a company selling tea products and skincare products (FTC, 2020b). The complaint alleged that Teami failed to enforce its own social media policy, resulting in hundreds of social media posts that failed to adequately disclose influencer-brand relationships (FTC, 2020c, p. 13). In addition to a settlement with Teami, the FTC sent warning letters to individual influencers requiring a written response and strategy for future endorsement posts:

Individual influencers who fail to make adequate disclosures about their connections to marketers are subject to legal enforcement action by the FTC. Please provide a written response to this letter by March 30, 2020, describing what actions you are or will be taking to ensure that your social media posts endorsing brands and businesses with which you have a material connection clearly and conspicuously disclose your relationships.

(FTC, 2020d)

Moreover, the guidance emphasized the need to use simple, clear language that is commonly understood by consumers. Disclosures that use words like "'advertisement,' 'ad,' and 'sponsored'" are less likely to lead to consumer confusion than using vague terms or hashtags, such as #spon, "thanks," and "collab." These terms are well-known indicators within the influencer community, but the average consumer won't necessarily understand the industry shortcuts.

Ensuring Truthful Statements

Statements, whether part of an endorsement or not, must not be misleading or deceptive. For social media influencers, this requirement applies to any paid endorsements. The information included in blogs, social posts, photos, videos, infographics, or the like, must represent truthful information and opinions. In its 2020 complaint against Teami, the FTC complaint alleged that, in addition to failing to disclose their brand relationships, some influencers made unsubstantiated claims about weight loss, metabolism, headache relief, and mental clarity (FTC, 2020c, pp. 16–17).

Sometimes, truthful statements require qualification to avoid consumer confusion. For example, if an "actual customer" of a weight loss product provides a paid endorsement including the number of pounds they lost, the company is responsible for providing qualifying information about the average weight loss results. These qualification statements—often related to pricing, warranties, return policies, or product performance—also must meet the clear and conspicuous standard.

In its *.com Disclosures* guidance document, the FTC specifies that, like material connection disclosures, qualifying information should be incorporated into the core of the message (FTC, 2013). Using voiceovers for video, superimposed text for photos, and consistent typefaces for written messages are all recommended to ensure compliance. Advertising messages should not use hyperlinks to communicate integral information. When hyperlinks are used to provide supplementary information, they should be adjacent to the related claims or qualifications; they should not be isolated or deemphasized by proximity.

Brands engaging influencers as part of their strategic communication efforts, must ensure that their contracted influencers comply with the *Guidelines Concerning the Use of Endorsements and Testimonials in Advertising* (FTC, 2009). Any statement constituting an endorsement must be accompanied by a disclosure statement describing the relationship between the brand and the influencer. This statement, and any necessary qualifications to the claim or claims being made, must be prominently placed and simply written to ensure consumers see and understand the disclosures and qualifications.

CONTROLLING THE SPONCON CONS

It is not only brands who benefit from endorsement partnerships—an influencer's social and financial worth depends on their online audience. By entering into partnerships with brands, influencers can gain clout, which boosts their online following and their profits. Successful influencers can realize a significant windfall from these partnerships. Influencers with a sizeable following (one million or more followers) can charge upward of $100,000 per post. Even nanoinfluencers, who may have as few as 1,000 followers, can make $30,000 to $60,000 annually for their sponsored posts (Lieber, 2018). The lure of a huge payday has motivated some influencers to aggressively seek lucrative partnerships, even buying fake followers to make their accounts seem more desirable.

The potential for monetary gains and celebrity-like status also has motivated some less scrupulous influencers to fake brand partnerships and falsify sponsored posts to boost their perceived market value. While it may seem counterintuitive for influencers to fake sponsored posts, as they are not actually getting paid, merely having a #SponCon hashtag indicates that an influencer has credibility and appeal. Clout may not have a specific dollar value, but having clout may enable influencers to command lucrative sponsorships:

> Many people associate a branded content tag with a high level of influence—so high, that some companies are willing to pay up to six-figures for it. So, if an influencer's page contains sponsored content, or what looks like sponsored content, others will assume this influencer is "worth" following. And the more followers one person has, the more likely he/she will get actual paid content offers. (Espinoza, 2018)

Brands may be more willing to work with influencers who demonstrate that they have value in the market. Sponsored posts are indicative of social value and function as a "verification badge" (Lorenz, 2018). This is powerful pressure for an influencer who seeks validation to invent a sponsored relationship.

This scenario raises a critical question: SponCon cons seem awfully misleading, but are they illegal? The answer is complicated. A SponCon con itself does not violate any laws. The FTC requires that influencers disclose paid advertisements, but the FTC has not yet proposed any specific rules barring unpaid influencers from making their posts look like paid advertisements.

From a brand perspective, this reality is concerning. A fake SponCon post may be relatively benign, conferring credibility upon the influencer who fabricates a relationship but safeguards, or even improves, the perception of the brand. Even in this best-case scenario, though, it is troubling that an influencer can use fake #SponCon posts to position themselves as a brand ambassador without permission. FTC guidelines are aimed at creating transparency, but fake SponCon posts are rooted in deception. Consumers cannot reasonably be expected to view these influencers' posts and understand the actual nature of the relationship between the influencer and the brand. The structure of these posts gives rise to the perception that the influencer is a vetted endorser. Valid disclosures would enable consumers "to accurately evaluate and give appropriate weight to an influencer's endorsement" (Bladow, 2018, p. 1132).

Additionally, many of these posts could conceivably be quite damaging to a brand. There are myriad plausible scenarios in which the brand suffers significant damage by virtue of a rogue influencer's unsanctioned posts. For example, an influencer could taint the brand by using objectionable or offensive language. Perhaps the situation is as simple as the brand preferring not to be associated with a specific influencer. In these and similar situations, a faux #SponCon post could give rise to actionable claims, particularly for false advertising and trademark dilution. Because the issue is relatively novel, however, there is a lack of case law directly on point. However, there is precedent suggesting that brands could do the following: initiate an FTC investigation for deceptive advertising or bring a civil action against the influencer for false advertising or false endorsement.

FTC Investigation for Deceptive Advertising

Section 5 of the FTC Act empowers the FTC to regulate endorsements and protect consumers from deceptive advertising (FTC Act, 2012, §45(a)(2)). The FTC defines a forbidden deceptive practice as "a representation, omission or practice that is likely to mislead the consumer acting reasonably in the circumstances, to the consumer's detriment" (Miller, 1983, p. 2). The endorsement need only deceive a "significant minority" of the audience in order to be actionable (In re Telebrands Corp., 2005, p. *8).

The FTC Guides, which provide parameters for the legal use of endorsements in advertising, are broad and flexible. The FTC has, thus far, focused on ensuring that influencers clearly and conspicuously disclose when they are being paid to endorse a brand (FTC, 2009). The FTC has yet to address the specific issue of influencers falsely suggesting a paid relationship.

Despite this lack of targeted guidance, the FTC Guides arguably encompass fake SponCon. The FTC's disclosure requirements are centered on the perspective of the reasonable consumer. An influencer is required to disclose material connections to the brand so a reasonable consumer can make informed purchasing decisions. When an influencer falsely suggests a paid relationship, a consumer may be misled. The consumer may imbue the influencer with unearned authority derived from the perceived backing of the brand. The consumer may rely on the influencer's fabricated authority to purchase other products the influencer endorses. The consumer might also decline to purchase a product based on its falsified relationship with certain influencers. According to the FTC's Policy Statement on Deception, consumers suffer actionable injury when they would have made different purchasing decisions absent the deception (Miller, 1983, p. 6).

Aggrieved brands can request that the FTC investigate whether the influencer has engaged in deceptive practices. Depending on the outcome of the investigation, the FTC can pursue a variety of options, from closing the investigation to seeking a consent order to filing a formal complaint (ABA Section of Antitrust Law, 2014, p. 195). Typically, the FTC brings action against brands and advertisers, but there is nothing precluding it from pursuing actions against influencers. In fact, since 2017, the FTC has opened investigations and several complaints against influencers, individually as respondents, who have failed to adequately disclose their material connections to various brands (Bladow, 2018, pp. 1146–1150). Although in most of the investigations, the FTC ultimately focused enforcements' efforts on the brands rather than the influencers, these demonstrate the FTC's actions to pursue action against individual influencers. This, coupled with the agency's broad guidelines for deceptive advertising, suggest that brands may successfully pursue FTC actions against SponCon cons. Should the FTC pursue this kind of individual action, the deceptive influencer could potentially face mandatory corrective messaging in future posts, injunctions against implied brand relationships, or monetary damages.

Civil Lawsuits for False Advertising

Brands may be able to file civil lawsuits against influencers for deceptive advertising. These brands could realize recourse under both federal and state law. The federal Lanham Act prohibits making false or deceptive representations regarding another's goods and services. In addition to authorizing FTC actions, this law creates a right of action for brands to directly seek a remedy in the federal courts. Typically, these actions are aimed at individuals or companies that malign a brand via false advertising. However, a broad reading of the Lanham Act would encompass an action against SponCon cons. The Lanham Act would require the brand to show that

1) the influencer made a false statement of fact about the product;
2) the statement deceived or tended to deceive a substantial segment of the audience;
3) the deception was likely to influence the audience's purchasing decisions;
4) the influencer caused the statement to enter interstate commerce; and
5) the brand was injured (15 U.S.C.A. §1125(a)).

Although there is no precedent directly on point, these elements are arguably met in the context of a SponCon con. The influencer's post deceives the audience into thinking a reciprocal relationship exists between the influencer and the brand. The post functions as the brand's tacit approval of the influencer. It is inherently deceptive and prone to influencing the audience's purchasing decisions.

In addition to pursuing federal civil actions for false and deceptive advertising, brands may file false and deceptive advertising claims in all fifty states. These actions vary from state to state. For example, the language in California's deceptive advertising laws closely mirrors the federal language and guidance that the FTC has developed. Under California law, an advertisement is misleading if it is likely to deceive the public. A lawsuit can be maintained even if no consumer has actually been misled. The plaintiff need only demonstrate that there is "a likelihood of confounding an appreciable number of *reasonably prudent purchasers* exercising ordinary care" (Baron, 2019, §60:10). Aggrieved parties can bring action under California's False Advertising Law and/or California's Unfair Competition Law (2019).

As a second example, New York's laws employ more general language, prohibiting false advertising "in the conduct of any business, trade or commerce or in the furnishing of any service" (Consumer Protection from Deceptive Acts and Practices, §350). False advertising is defined to include any advertisements that are "misleading in a material respect" (Consumer Protection from Deceptive Acts and Practices, §350-a(1)). The laws explain that an advertisement can be misleading based on both the representations made and the failure to reveal necessary material facts. The law also enables consumers to bring action when they are damaged by deceptive acts and practices (Consumer Protection from Deceptive Acts and Practices, §349). However, this cause of action is reserved for consumers, not competitors.

Trademark Claims

The Lanham Act also prohibits deceptive practices that cause confusion regarding sponsorship or endorsement of a product. Typically, these cases arise in the context of trademark or trade dress that causes consumer confusion. "Trademark law encourages owners to provide a consistent level of quality in their products, to ensure consumer confidence and repeat purchases" (Katyal & Grinyald, 2018, p. 1145). The Lanham Act defines a trademark as any:

> word, name, symbol or device or combination thereof, used by a person or company, in order to differentiate his/her or its products, including a unique product, from the goods or merchandise of another, and to identify the source of those goods, even if that source is unknown. (Lanham Act, §1127)

Trademarks enable a consumer to make purchasing decisions with confidence. They give the consumer critical information about the origin and quality of the goods so that the consumer can decide whether to buy those products and inform the consumer that a particular producer will benefit financially from the products' sale (Qualitex v. Jacobson Products Co., Inc., 1995). To function effectively, companies are granted limited exclusivity in their trademarks. When a brand's trademark is used to falsely suggest endorsement, it creates consumer confusion and damages the brand.

False endorsement actions have also been allowed when the use involves one's "persona, likeness, or other uniquely distinguishing characteristic to cause such confusion" (*Brown v. Electronic Arts*, Inc., 2013, p. 1239). These actions typically involve public figures whose images or identifying characteristics are used without permission to imply that they endorse a product (Parks v. LaFace Records, 2003).

While the FTC has not directly addressed the issue of influencers falsely suggesting a paid relationship with existing brands, it has demanded transparency in social media advertising. In October 2019, the FTC issued orders requiring two companies to cease their deceptive online marketing practices. The first company, Devumi, sold fake social media followers to individuals and organizations who sought to artificially boost their online presence. The court order settling this case prohibits the named respondents from engaging this kind of influence peddling, as well as enjoins any misrepresentations about any entity's social media influence. The owner of Devumi was additionally assessed a $2.5 million judgment.

The second order regarding deceptive social marketing was against Sunday Riley Skincare, a company whose executives directed employees to assume false online identities and post fake reviews of their products on a major retailer's website. The FTC recognized that the online deception exhibited by both companies "harms shoppers, as well as firms that play fair and square" (FTC, 2019a). In the settlement order, contained similar prohibitions on misrepresentations of influence level as were included in the Devumi settlement. Additionally, the order requires that any connection between an endorser and Sunday Riley be "clearly and conspicuously" disclosed (FTC, 2019a). Further, the order mandates Sunday Riley Skincare conduct employee and influencer partner education on the responsibilities and requirements of disclosure.

Furthermore, there is direct precedent indicating that companies may suffer actionable damage when their brands are used to suggest affiliation. For example, Dallas Cowboys Cheerleaders, Inc., a subsidiary of the Dallas Cowboys Football Club, successfully sued an adult movie company depicting an actor engaging in sexual activities while dressed as a Dallas Cowboys cheerleader. The court held that a reasonable consumer might believe that the Dallas Cowboys organization approved or sponsored the use of its trademark in the movie (Dallas Cowboys Cheerleaders, Inc. v. Pussycat Cinema, Ltd., 1979, p. 204).

A brand's trademark may be used without permission if it qualifies as nominative fair use. To qualify, the user must show three things: the brand's product is not readily identifiable without the trademark, the use is limited to that "reasonably necessary," and the use does not imply sponsorship or endorsement by the brand (New Kids on the Block v. News America Publishing, Inc., 1992, p. 308). Fake SponCon posts fail this third factor because they hinge on deception.

RECOMMENDATIONS FOR ENGAGING IN SPONCON

In 2009, the FTC clarified that not only is it the responsibility of the brand but also the influencer to ensure the consumer is made aware of any material relationships (FTC, 2009). Brands and influencers should exercise caution when entering into an endorsement agreement; policies should facilitate compliance with the *Guidelines Concerning the Use of Endorsements and Testimonials in Advertising*, as well as any state laws related to deceptive advertising. Brands and social media users should also be aware of the growing tactic of some disreputable posters to fake these endorsement relationships in an effort to quickly gain unwarranted social currency. The following are recommendations to help the brand protect their reputations and the influencers maintain their credibility.

Brands incorporating sponsored content as part of their communication strategy should research potential influencer partners, use written policies for managing influencer relationships, and closely monitor influencer communications for brand reputation and legal issues.

- *Research potential influencer partners.* An influencer with a verified account has been vetted and, therefore, is likely to be trustworthy, but this badge is only doled out to celebrities, large brands, and major influencers. Other investigative tools should be applied for smaller influencers to make sure they are trustworthy. If an influencer's followers are mostly bots or inactive users, this might indicate that the influencer has purchased followers. Other account characteristics that should raise red flags are unstable account growth or a sudden unexplained large spike in followers, inactivity on other social media platforms, low follower engagement, or suspicious follower engagement including numerous generic comments or a questionably high number of likes or comments. Brands should also consider the percentage of sponsored posts an influencer makes. If the percentage is too high, the influencer's engagement rate may suffer.
- *Share written policies with influencers.* Brands should work closely with influencers to foster a relationship built on trust. Brands also should actively educate influencers on relevant FTC regulations, specifically regarding disclosure requirements. The influencer and brand should develop clear guidelines for the content and tone of the influencer's posts to ensure that the brand's needs are met. Brands with written policies can encourage consistent compliance among all contracted influencers.
- *Monitor influencers' posts for compliance with brand style and legal requirements.* Brands should routinely monitor posts made by influencer partners to ensure that they are truthful, authentic, effective, and in compliance with disclosure requirements. Brands should analyze audience engagement, including comments, likes, and shares, to ensure that brand goals are being met and that influencer messages are being interpreted as intended.

Influencers who partner with brands for endorsement contracts should familiarize themselves with FTC guidelines. In making disclosures, influencers should use simple, easy to understand language; they should include disclosures adjacent to important claims; and they should foster authentic audience engagement.

- *Use simple language for disclosures.* Influencers should use simple language to indicate when they are making a sponsored post. FTC guidelines state that the language must be "clearly and conspicuously disclosed." An easy way to comply with FTC requirements is to use language directly thanking the brand for sponsoring the post or providing the free product. The language should be prominent and placed proximate to the main content. Most social media users will stop reading a caption or post after three lines; disclosures must be likely to be seen, so they should appear in the first three lines. The FTC suggests starting a sponsored post with the word "ad" for optimum clarity.

- *Don't hide behind hashtags and links.* Influencers must clearly and conspicuously disclose when they are being paid by a brand to endorse a product. Hasthtags, such as #ad or #sponsored, may be used in addition to, but not in place of, the disclosures. However, more obscure hashtag references, such as #sponcon, should not be used as the average consumer won't understand the meaning of such industry-specific terms.

- *Build an organic following aligning with the targeted brands.* Instead of faking an endorsement relationship or buying fake followers, influencers should earn trust and credibility by developing an organically engaged following. Influencers who ultimately want to work with a brand should create content, especially quality visual content, that resonates with the audience of that brand. This content should be posted on a consistent schedule to build and sustain follower engagement. Influencers should engage directly with followers to sustain momentum. Brands are more inclined to work with influencers who share the same aesthetic and have the same core following.

REFERENCES

American Bar Association, Antitrust Section. (2014). *FTC Practice and Procedure Manual* (2nd ed.). Chicago: ABA Book Publishing.

Baron, E., & LaMothe, L. (2019). *California Civil Practice: Business Litigation.* Bancroft Whitney. https://store.legal.thomsonreuters.com/law-products/Practice-Materials/Business-Litigation-California-Civil-Practice/p/100028388

Bladow, L. (2018). Worth the click: Why greater FTC endorsement is needed to curtail deceptive practices in influencer marketing. *William and Mary Law Review*, 59(1123).

Brown v. Electronic Arts, Inc., 724 F.3d 1235 (9th Cir. 2013).

Byrne, S. (2015). The age of the human billboard: Endorsement disclosures in new millennia media marketing. *Journal of Business & Technology Law*, 10(393).

California False Advertising Law, Cal. Bus. & Prof. Code §17500 *et seq.* (West 2019).

California Unfair Competition Law, Cal. Bus. & Prof. Code §17200 *et seq.* (West 2019)

Central Hudson Gas & Elec. Corp. v. Public Serv. Comm'n, 447 U.S. 557, 564. (1980).

Consumer Protection from Deceptive Acts and Practices, N.Y. Gen. Bus. §§349-350-F-1. (2019).

Crowdfire. (2018, Aug. 29). How your brand can overcome millennials' dwindling trust in influencers. *Crowdfire*. Retrieved from https://blog.crowdfireapp.com/how

-your-brand-can-overcome-millennials-dwindling-trust-in-influencers-95983ded7
825.

Dallas Cowboys Cheerleaders, Inc. v. Pussycat Cinema, Ltd., 604 F.2d 200. (2d Cir. 1979).

Engle, M. (2010, Apr. 20). Closing letter to Kenneth A. Plevan, counsel for AnnTaylor Stores Corp., No. 102-3147. Retrieved from https://www.ftc.gov/sites/ default/files/documents/closing_letters/anntaylor-stores-corporation/100420anntay lorclosingletter.pdf.

Engle, M. (2014, Mar. 20). Closing letter to Christie Grymes Thompson, counsel for Cole Haan, Inc., No. 142-3041. Retrieved from https://www.ftc.gov/system/files/ documents/closing_letters/cole-haan-inc./140320colehaanclosingletter.pdf.

Espinoza, J. (2018, Dec. 18). How up-and-coming influencers are using fake ads to gain clout. *Complex.* Retrieved from https://www.complex.com/life/2018/12/rising -instagram-influencers-accused-of-posting-fake-sponosred-content.

Fair, L. (2014, Dec. 4). *FTC Milestones: Weighing in on Weight Loss Cases.* Retrieved from https://www.ftc.gov/news-events/blogs/competition-matters/2014 /12/ftc-milestones-weighing-weight-loss-cases.

Federal Trade Commission. (1975). *Guides Concerning the Use of Endorsements and Testimonials in Advertising.* 40 Fed. Reg. 22.

Federal Trade Commission. (1980). *Guides Concerning the Use of Endorsements and Testimonials in Advertising.* 16 C.F.R. §255.

Federal Trade Commission. (1983). *FTC Policy Statement on Deception.* Retrieved from https://www.ftc.gov/system/files/documents/public_statements/410531/83 1014deceptionstmt.pdf.

Federal Trade Commission. (2000). *Dot Com Disclosures: Information About Online Advertising.* Retrieved from https://www.ftc.gov/sites/default/files/attachments/press -releases/ftc-staff-issues-guidelines-internet-advertising/0005dotcomstaffreport.pdf.

Federal Trade Commission. (2009). *Guidelines Concerning the Use of Endorsements and Testimonials in Advertising.* 16 C.F.R. §255. Retrieved from https://www .ftc.gov/sites/default/files/documents/federal_register_notices/guides-concerning -use-endorsements-and-testimonials-advertising-16-cfr-part-255/091015guidescon cerningtestimonials.pdf.

Federal Trade Commission. (2013). *.com Disclosures: How to Mke Effective Disclosures in Digital Advertising.* Retrieved from https://www.ftc.gov/sites/defa ult/files/attachments/press-releases/ftc-staff-revises-online-advertising-disclosure- guidelines/130312dotcomdisclosures.pdf.

Federal Trade Commission. (2015). *The FTC's Endorsement Guides: What People Are Asking.* Retrieved from https://www.ftc.gov/tips-advice/business-center/gu idance/ftcs-endorsement-guides-what-people-are-asking.

Federal Trade Commission. (2016, July 11). *Warner Bros. Settles FTC Charges It Failed to Adequately Disclose It Paid Online Influencers to Post Gameplay Videos* [Press release]. Retrieved from https://www.ftc.gov/news-events/press-releases /2016/07/warner-bros-settles-ftc-charges-it-failed-adequately-disclose-it.

Federal Trade Commission. (2017, Apr. 19). *FTC Staff Reminds Influencers and Brands to Clearly Disclose Relationship.* Retrieved from https://www.ftc.gov/

news-events/press-releases/2017/04/ftc-staff-reminds-influencers-brands-clearly-disclose.

Federal Trade Commission. (2019a). *Devumi, Owner and CEO Settle FTC Charges They Sold Fake Indicators of Social Media Influence; Cosmetics Firm Sunday Riley, CEO Settle FTC Charges That Employees Posted Fake Online Reviews at CEO's Direction* [Press release]. Retrieved from https://www.ftc.gov/news-event s/press-releases/2019/10/devumi-owner-ceo-settle-ftc-charges-they-sold-fake-indicators.

Federal Trade Commission. (2019b). *Disclosures 101 for Social Media Influencers.* Retrieved from https://www.ftc.gov/system/files/documents/plain-language/1001a -influencer-guide-508_1.pdf.

Federal Trade Commission. (2019c). *A Brief Overview of the Federal Trade Commission's Investigative, Law Enforcement, and Rulemaking Authority.* Retrieved from https://www.ftc.gov/about-ftc/what-we-do/enforcement-authority.

Federal Trade Commission. (2020a). *FTC Seeks Public Comment on its Endorsement Guides* [Press Release]. Retrieved from https://www.ftc.gov/news-events/press-re leases/2020/02/ftc-seeks-public-comment-its-endorsement-guides.

Federal Trade Commission. (2020d). *Warning to Prominently Disclose Paid Endorsements* [Letters to Adrienne Eliza Houghton, et al.]. Retrieved from https:// www.ftc.gov/system/files/documents/cases/1823174teamiwarningletters.pdf.

Federal Trade Commission Act, 15 U.S.C. §41 *et seq.* (2019).

Federal Trade Commission v. Lord and Taylor, No. C-4576. (F.T.C. 2016).

Federal Trade Commission v. Teami, No. 8:20-cv-00518. (F.T.C. 2020b). Retrieved from https://www.ftc.gov/system/files/documents/cases/stipulated_order.pdf.

Federal Trade Commission v. Teami, No. 8:20-cv-00518 [Complaint]. (F.T.C. 2020c). Retrieved from https://www.ftc.gov/system/files/documents/cases/compla int_4.pdf.

Feinman, L. (2011). Celebrity endorsements in non-traditional advertising: How the FTC regulations fail to keep up with the Kardashians. *Fordham Intellectual Property Media & Entertainment Law Journal*, 22(97).

In re Sunday Riley Skincare, F.T.C. [Statement of Commissioner Rohit Chopra Joined by Commissioner Rebecca Kelly Slaughter], 2019 WL 5587319. (2019, Oct. 21).

In re Sunday Riley Skincare, LLC, F.T.C. [Complaint], 2019 WL 5419394. (2019, Oct. 21).

In re Telebrands Corp., 140 F.T.C. 278, 2005 WL 62410108. (2005, Sept. 19).

Katyal, S., & Grinvald, L. (2018). Platform law and brand enterprise. *Berkeley Tech Law Journal*, 32(1135).

Lanham Act, 15 U.S.C. §1051 *et seq.*

Lieber, C. (2018, Nov. 28). How and why do influencers make so much money? The head of an influencer agency explains. *Vox.* Retrieved from https://www.vox.com/ the-goods/2018/11/28/18116875/influencer-marketing-social-media-engagement-instagram-youtube.

Lorenz, T. (2018, Dec. 18). Rising Instagram stars are posting fake sponsored content. *The Atlantic*. Retrieved from https://www.theatlantic.com/technology/archive/201 8/12/influencers-are-faking-brand-deals/578401/.

Miller, J. (1983, Oct. 14). Letter from James C. Miller III, Chairman, Fed. Trade Comm'n, to John D. Dingell, Chairman, Comm. on Energy & Commerce, U.S. House of Representatives. Retrieved from https://www.ftc.gov/system/files/do cuments/public_statements/410531/831014deceptionstmt.pdf.

New Kids on the Block v. News America Pub., Inc., 971 F.2d 302 (9th Cir. 1992).

Owens, S. (2019, Jan. 17). Is it time to regulate social media influencers? *New York Magazine*. Retrieved from http://nymag.com/intelligencer/2019/01/is-it-time-to-re gulate-social-media-influencers.html.

Parks v. LaFace Records, 329 F.3d 437 (6th Cir. 2003).

Qualitex v. Jacobson Products Co., Inc., 514 U.S. 159. (1995).

Washburn, W. F. (1981, Apr. 15). FTC regulation of endorsements in advertising: In the consumer's behalf? *Pepperdine Law Review*, 8(697).

Weinswig, D. (2016, Oct. 15). Influencers are the new brands. *Forbes*. Retrieved from https://www.forbes.com/sites/deborahweinswig/2016/10/05/influencers-are -the-new-brands/#10f9a7b67919.

Index

About the Editor and Contributors

ABOUT THE EDITOR

Brandi Watkins, PhD (The University of Alabama), is an associate professor in the School of Communication and Digital Media at Virginia Tech where she teaches courses in social media and public relations. Her research examines the role of social media in brand communication and as a way to build, enhance, and maintain organization-public relationships. She is the author of the book *Sports Teams, Fans, and Twitter: The Influence of Social Media on Relationships and Branding*. Her work has been published in *Public Relations Review*, *Journal of Brand Management*, and *International Journal of Sport Communication*.

ABOUT THE CONTRIBUTORS

Alisa Agozzino, PhD, APR, is an associate professor of public relations at Ohio Northern University. As the PR program head, she has taught over sixteen different classes within the major and developed a social media minor at ONU. She has received numerous awards for teaching, including the international Pearson Award for Innovation in Teaching with Technology. Dr. Agozzino's current research agenda examines how social media or digital platforms impacts different industries. Her work has been published in over twenty academic and trade publications.

Courtney A. Barclay, PhD, JD (University of Florida), is an associate professor in the Department of Communication at Jacksonville University, where she teaches courses in communications law, social media, and public relations.

Dr. Barclay's research focuses on the intersection of First Amendment protections and the regulation of emerging media, such as behavioral targeting practices, online political speech, and chatbot-consumer interactions.

Kelli S. Burns, PhD (The University of Florida), is an associate professor in the Zimmerman School of Advertising and Mass Communications at the University of South Florida where she teaches public relations and social media courses. Her research interests include social media influencers, social media activism, and the intersection of social media and popular culture. She is the author of two books on the topic of social media: *Social Media: A Reference Handbook* (ABC-CLIO, 2017) and *Celeb 2.0: How Social Media Foster Our Fascination with Popular Culture* (Praeger, 2009).

Lisa Harrison, a doctoral candidate (Queensland University of Technology), owns and manages Social Media Mastery, a digital creative and marketing agency. Her research examines personal influence gained using a social media platform identity leading to the nuanced profession of microinfluencers, as a way of establishing best practice for the purpose of communication pedagogy.

Terri N. Hernandez, PhD (Texas Tech University), is an assistant professor in the Department of Communication at Mississippi State University where she teaches public relations courses. Her research examines intergroup relations, consumer behavior, and social and digital media as an intersection to organization-public relationships and branding.

Alexa Landsberger graduated with a Bachelor of Arts from Davidson College (2019) with a major in Communication Studies and minor in Economics. In her honor's thesis, she investigated how macro and micro social media influencers accumulate fame and social capital through brand communication. She currently works in the client services department at The Mx Group, a marketing agency based in the Chicagoland area, where she helps facilitate marketing initiatives and strategies for a diverse clientele base.

Jenna M. Lo Castro, PhD (Duquesne University), is an assistant professor in the School of Communication at Point Park University where she teaches advertising and public relations courses. Her research areas include communication ethics, philosophy of communication, integrated marketing communication, and branding.

Regina Luttrell, PhD, is an assistant professor of public relations and social media plus serves as director of the graduate program in public relations at S.I. Newhouse School of Public Communications at Syracuse University.

Regina researches, publishes and discusses public relations, social media for strategic communication, Gen Z and the Millennial generation, and the intersection of social media within society. She is a Tow Center Fellow and the author of multiple books including *Social Media: How to Engage, Share, and Connect* and *The Millennial Mindset: Unraveling Fact from Fiction.*

Ronda Mariani, PhD, is an associate professor of marketing at the Bloomsburg University of Pennsylvania. After spending several years in industry working in graphic design and advertising, she went on to open her own Multimedia Design Studio, where she had the opportunity to work with a variety of clients developing and implementing strategic integrated marketing campaigns for both traditional and digital delivery. Dr. Mariani has been teaching in Higher Education for about fourteen years and enjoys bridging the gap between academia and industry for her students. Her research interests are in digital advertising/marketing, the customer's journey process and behaviors, and consumerism within social platforms.

Amanda R. Martinez, PhD (Texas A&M University), is associate professor in Communication Studies and Sociology at Davidson College where she teaches media effects, gendered communication, and theory and research courses. She studies media effects and health communication with a focus on underrepresented populations, identity, intersectionality, race-based media stereotyping, humorous communication in entertainment contexts, and intergroup communication dynamics. Her publications appear in several peer reviewed journals, including *Mass Communication & Society, The Howard Journal of Communications, Southern Communication Journal,* and *Women's Studies in Communication,* as well as edited books.

Kylie Torres, MA, is an instructor at Kennesaw State University where she teaches communication courses in theory and speech communication. She is passionate about all things related to theme parks, fandoms, intercultural communication, and LGBTQ+ issues.

Adrienne A. Wallace, PhD, is an assistant professor in the School of Communications at Grand Valley State University where she teaches technology and campaigns courses in the advertising and public relations major program. She is a Michigan Political Leadership Program (Michigan State University) Fellow with research interests in how digital media intersects with public affairs, political movements, and public relations pedagogy.

Kearston L. Wesner, JD (Cornell Law School) and PhD (University of Florida), is an assistant professor in the Department of Media Studies at

Quinnipiac University, where she teaches courses in communications law and policy, celebrity culture, and media industries and trends. Her research focuses primarily on First Amendment and privacy issues in the context of new technologies.

Lightning Source UK Ltd.
Milton Keynes UK
UKHW021255140223
416998UK00009B/265